How to Select Undervalued Stocks

BY ROBERT N. PEISNER

How to Select Rapid Growth Stocks

How to Select Undervalued Stocks

ROBERT AND DARRYL PEISNER

E. P. DUTTON & CO., INC. | NEW YORK | 1973

Published simultaneously in Canada by
Clarke, Irwin & Company Limited, Toronto and Vancouver

SBN: 0–525–12943–X
Library of Congress Catalog Card Number: 74–158587

Contents

Figures

Tables

The following firms and organizations were kind enough to furnish the authors with data and illustrations, and a debt of gratitude is acknowledged to them:

Dow Jones & Company, Inc.
Standard & Poor's Corporation
R. W. Mansfield Company
New York Stock Exchange, Inc.
Federal Reserve System
U.S. News & World Report, Inc.
F. W. Stephens Company

The opinions contained herein are solely the personal opinions of Robert and Darryl Peisner and do not necessarily reflect the opinion of their past or present affiliations or any of the firms or organizations kind enough to furnish data and illustrations.

The 1971 editions of the Tide Table, which gives information on the time and height of tides, phases of the moon, and sunrise and sunset contains the following legend: "Information contained herein is based upon sources deemed to be reliable and is believed to be correct but it is not guaranteed." The U.S. Coast Guard won't even predict the tides, sunrises and sunsets without hedging.

So shall it be with this book and the stock market.

How to Select Undervalued Stocks

1

You and Your Investment Goals

Can You Become a Millionaire?

Why not? Others have become millionaires. It is often asked today what your chances are to accrue a million dollars by the time you are ready to retire. The authors believe that, if you are young, with money that you can invest shrewdly, and if you can avoid drawing from your investments as they build, and if you take advantage of the astounding power of compounded growth—then it is within the realm of reason that you may acquire a million dollars before you reach sixty-five. You might even achieve it earlier.

Understanding the Power of Compound Growth

So that you can see what potential wealth awaits you at the end of your personal investment road, look at Figure 1. It illustrates graphically the possible riches that compounded growth makes available to you using an original investment of $10,000 as an example. The accumulation for ten-, twenty-, and thirty-year periods is plotted according to different growth rates—0 percent to 25 percent—*compounded annually*.

Two important assumptions underlie the dollar amounts shown in this figure. The first is that all of your dividends and capital gains are reinvested. The second is that you possess other money sources to pay the income taxes on the dividends and capital gains and do not draw on your investment.

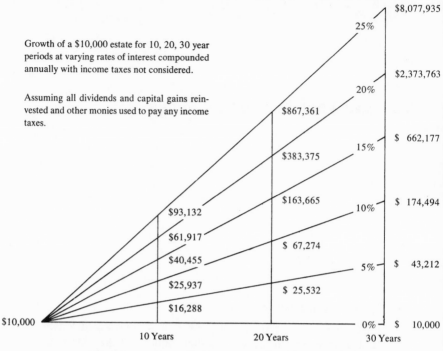

Growth of a $10,000 estate for 10, 20, 30 year periods at varying rates of interest compounded annually with income taxes not considered.

Assuming all dividends and capital gains reinvested and other monies used to pay any income taxes.

25% — $8,077,935

20% — $2,373,763

$867,361

15% — $ 662,177

$383,375

$163,665

10% — $ 174,494

$93,132

$61,917

$ 67,274

$40,455

5% — $ 43,212

$25,937

$ 25,532

$16,288

0% — $ 10,000

$10,000

10 Years   20 Years   30 Years

FIGURE 1: THE POWER OF COMPOUNDED GROWTH.

Be Honest with Yourself

Before you spend one dollar for any investments it is important to understand thoroughly your investment goals. You are probably aware that others tend to judge you by your external "picture"— the place where you live, the clothes you wear, the friends you have, the pastimes you enjoy, your reactions to events. But only you—if you are sincerely honest with yourself—possess the best knowledge of what makes you feel most comfortable when it comes to money and investments. Others, within your business and social sphere of influence, who outwardly appear conservative to you in the management of their lives, property and investments, may be at ease with themselves using part of their money in wildly speculative ventures—perhaps thousands of shares of penny stocks in undeveloped gold mines, for example. They may enjoy the thought that spectacular riches could be theirs overnight, and— in their secret thoughts—they are happy to risk their money in search of their Golden Fleece.

You, on the other hand, may feel repelled by such ventures, which you may consider rash. You may decide that it's the height of folly to subject yourself to tormented, sleepless nights if you believed that it was imminently possible a good portion of your investment capital could be wiped out overnight.

Two Important Questions

Before you decide to invest your money in the stock market (or anywhere else), there are two questions you must ask of yourself and answer honestly.

Is it surplus money that you will be investing? "Surplus" money is money you will not normally need during the next six months or more for your usual living purposes. If you are contemplating any kind of use for that money in the next few months—to pay taxes, life insurance, medical bills, or to send your children to college—there is just one answer: *Don't* invest it. Put it in the bank.

What kind of investment gives you the greatest sense of security and comfort? Asked another way—*Is a feeling of complete security about your money important to your well-being?* If you are honest with yourself, perhaps the only way you can avoid day-to-day worry about your invested surplus money is to place it in a savings account that returns about 5 percent annually and provides you with the insured certainty that the principal amount will never diminish. Perhaps you feel most comfortable owning real estate. Or perhaps it makes good sense to you to have your surplus funds invested in carefully selected stocks that will provide you, after some astute research, with both potential capital gains and attractive dividends income.

Objective of This Book

In Robert Peisner's previous book, *How to Select Rapid Growth Stocks* (New York: E. P. Dutton & Co., Inc., 1966) three general objectives of investment were presented:
1. Investing for income.
2. Investing for the preservation of capital (high safety factor).
3. Investing for potential capital gains (profit).
The six investment tools outlined in that book were designed to apply primarily to the higher rewards and higher risks of potentially large capital gains.

It is important to note that the investment tools in *this* book are designed to select stocks that have each of the above-mentioned objectives. The authors believe that such stocks—considered undervalued—should provide you with:

- a large, well-protected yield (satisfying the income requirements of item 1),
- a minimum downside risk (meeting the high safety-factor needs of item 2 to a degree),
- and a potential for capital gains (for fulfillment of item 3).

In the chapters to follow you will be shown how to select stocks that give you the possibility of meeting the above criteria.

The Potential Results of Compounded Growth

Let's illustrate the money-growth results you can achieve from the various types of investments you choose.

For example, if you really feel comfortable only with a federally insured savings-and-loan account that returns about 5 percent, Figure 1 informs you that a $10,000 investment would grow to a value of about $16,288 in ten years, to $26,532 in twenty years and to $43,212 in thirty years. This satisfies investment objectives 1 (income) and 2 (preservation of capital). However, it is important to realize that you are denying yourself the opportunity of meeting objective 3, *profit from potential capital gains.*

Moving up the chart in Figure 1, as another example, if you feel you possess both the knowledge to handle and the time to "deal in" second trust real-estate deeds, you could possibly put your finger on approximately the 10 percent compounded-growth line. You can now "see" about $25,937 in ten years and up to $174,494 after thirty years.

Money-Growth Rates Above Ten Percent Usually Are Difficult to Achieve

If you want to move above the 10 percent line, you enter another area. Here is where considerable astuteness is required to make your capital grow aggressively at the rates and to the amounts indicated in Figure 1. Certainly the amounts shown are worthy goals if you know that you possess the drive and temperament. If—and it's a big if—if you could achieve a steady 25 percent annual compounded-growth rate, Figure 1 shows that your original $10,000 investment would make you nearly a millionaire after twenty years—and eight times a millionaire within thirty years!

The purpose of this book and the investment tools it outlines is to guide you in selecting investments so that you are "shooting for" at least the 15 percent compounded-growth line and, ideally, at or above the 20 percent line. These are attractive goals to be reckoned with, as you shall see.

The Results of a 15 Percent Compounded-Growth Rate

Two money-growth techniques to consider using to build toward the goal of becoming a millionaire are shown in detail in Figure 2. One is for you to invest a lump sum of $20,000 and let it grow by reinvesting the annual income from dividends and capital gains. The second is to invest continually the same sum of money each year—illustrated as $2,400 in Figure 2—until the overall amount,

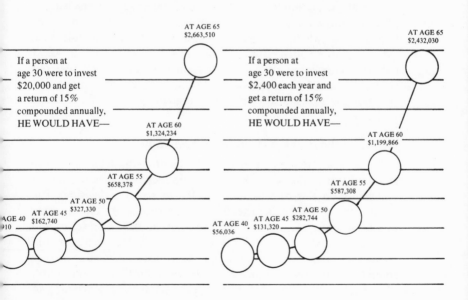

Assuming all dividends and capital gains reinvested and other monies used to pay any income taxes.

FIGURE 2: TWO VARIATIONS OF A 15 PERCENT COMPOUNDED GROWTH RATE.

including the reinvested dividends and capital gains, totals over a million dollars.

In addition to the two assumptions mentioned earlier, a third assumption—and a very important one—applies, namely, that you are able to secure a return on your investments equivalent to an average of *15 percent compounded annually* over a long period of time, which would double your money every *five* years.

As a point of reference, over the past twenty years (to 1969) the combined annual return from both dividends and capital appreciation on the Standard & Poor's Industrial Stock Average of 425 stocks amounted to a little over 14 percent per year.

No one, of course, can foretell with certainty that individual stocks or the stock market will continue to equal the performance of the past, which additionally had the benefit of being a period of generally rising stock prices.

Yet the authors believe that opportunities currently exist and should continue to exist. Hence, if you possess the key ingredients of the financial resources to get started on a regular investment program, the willingness and temperament to risk your money, the time and knowledge to devote to analyzing various investments, the discipline to stick to your plan and the good fortune to select astutely, on average, the "right" investments year in and year out regardless of the stock market's performance, then it is likely that you can accrue upwards of a million dollars by the time you reach your early sixties.

Books on the Stock Market Are Often Vague

In the authors' opinion, the key problem of most books on the stock market is that they deal in generalities and require difficult judgments on the part of the investor to reach a decision. The authors make it a point to read all of the new books on the stock market so as to uncover new pertinent data to help themselves and their clients. Unfortunately the authors have consistently found themselves unable to develop the investment judgments and/or compile the necessary information suggested in the various books. The sought-after data often proved excessively time-consuming to acquire, frequently led to no specific answer, had their roots in rumor and hearsay and, most important, failed to achieve investment satisfaction and gave only haphazard results.

This Book Aims to be Specific

It will be the objective of this book to be specific. You will be shown exactly what to look for. The sources of investment information will be clearly spelled out, so that you will know precisely where to look to find the specific data you need. These sources have been selected because they are internationally available. The authors believe your investment satisfaction will be increased by astute use of the stock-selection technique explained in the following chapters.

2

You, Your Emotions and the Stock Market

It is one of the ironies of the stock market that usually a stock appears to be most attractive as a potential buy when investors are gripped helplessly by the panic of falling prices. On the other hand, the choicest selling opportunities for profits frequently present themselves when investors are most elated by rising prices and the financial gains seem boundless.

The aim of this book is twofold:

First, to help you select companies whose stocks appear to be undervalued, high-quality securities and, thus, potentially ripe for an attractive rise in price. This, in the authors' opinion, is reasonably easy.

Second, the authors hope to make you more aware of your own stock-market emotions. When you understand your emotions, you stand a better chance of acting courageously and astutely at the opportune times.

The Importance of Knowing Your Stock-Market Emotions

The importance of having an insight into your own stock-market emotions has rarely received the attention it merits. Most financial writers tend to view the stock market with the dispassion of a surgeon. There are scholarly articles and books by the dozen on subjects such as how to analyze a balance sheet, how to analyze earnings, how to analyze chart patterns, *How to Select Rapid Growth Stocks* (written by Robert Peisner), etc. But this knowledge is useless unless you have an understanding of your emotions.

Knowing your emotions can be compared to walking through a room full of furniture. In the dark you can bump into every blessed item and bruise yourself. With the lights on you can steer a safer course. When you know your stock-market emotions, your defenses are up. The opportunities are clearly evident, because you have a better "sense of feel" of when to buy and sell.

The Act of Buying or Selling Tends to Be Emotional

The act of buying and selling a stock—while on the surface appearing logical and physical—is basically emotional. You instruct your broker to buy or to sell; he executes your order. But in the crucial moments before you ordered your broker to buy or to sell you had to make a decision about the future of that stock. *And the future is unknown.* So you are beset by all the fears connected with the unknown. A normal person making a decision about the future is usually plagued by nagging doubts. Will the stock go up or down? Is now a good time to act? Both the beauty and the curse of the stock market are its inherent liquidity, so that you usually know rather quickly the accuracy of your decision. You can't fool yourself. The price of the stock you select is published daily.

The Major Barrier to Stock-Market Success

It is fairly well established that the stock market tends to move up and down in broad cycles. A good deal of this movement tends to be emotional. How you, as an investor, react to these emotional gyrations frequently determines your success.

Over the twelve years that the authors have been associated with the stock market, they have formed the general opinion that the majority of stock buyers must surmount a major hurdle before they can hope to be successful. By successful is meant having good judgment of *when* to buy or sell and—more important—possessing the *courage* to act. The single most important barrier to the average investor's success is his *lack of knowledge* of his own *emotional* responses to the rise and fall of stock prices. Let the authors state loudly and clearly at this point that they are not psychologists. However, after being closely associated with the general public through three major rising (bull) markets and three major falling (bear) markets, they have formed some general opinions.

The Emotional Cycle

During the 1960's many types of stocks and industries, at different times, were the favorite "playthings" of investors, traders, brokers and portfolio managers. Surprising to many—including "astute" professionals—a common emotional pattern tended to repeat itself throughout the 1960's. This pattern—like a movie being replayed over and over—was an *emotional* cycle of *fear* being overcome by *confidence,* which in turn usually gave way to *greed,* which set the stage for the return of *fear,* and the repeat of the cycle.

During the 1960's, if your reactions were at all typical, your emotional response to the stock market's cycles was generally as follows: *fear* most often affected your decisions at market bottoms, usually after a severe drop in stock prices. Your *confidence* in companies, in their managements, in their reports and in the opinions of investment advisors and government leaders was then also usually at a low point. However, the sell-off in stock prices ended—as all sell-offs to date have ended—and the majority of stocks began to rise, some rapidly, some slowly. As a swimmer tests the chill of the ocean with his toe and edges forward into the water, so you began to regain *confidence* and bought equities, first a little, and then more. Soon the painful memory of rapidly falling stocks was the faintest of echoes. Your *confidence* overcame your *fear* because the charging bull of the stock market now appeared to reign supreme. Stock prices tended to move upward aggressively.

Some stocks became "hot." Their prices jumped dramatically— seemingly from day to day. Your *confidence,* inflated like a balloon about to burst, frequently at this point gave way to *greed.* "Put me in the next hot one," you ordered your broker. In your rational, quiet moments you know your broker doesn't have clairvoyant powers, does not receive messages about the stock market from "outer space," and can only hope to have an educated guess as to which stocks or industries might be "hot" next week or next month.

Ultimately most stock prices were bid up to such high levels that even the most foolhardy began to have second thoughts about the prices being quoted. And so stock prices tended to retreat, first slowly, almost imperceptibly, then with increasing speed. And then the bear stomped onto the center of the financial stage. Your *greed* gave way to *fear,* and that terrifying emotion then appeared fully to dominate your decisions. Stock prices were smashed by heavy waves of selling. Few stocks were spared. Only a bare handful managed to maintain their lofty price levels. You became fearful that you would be wiped out, that you would never recoup, that your life savings were evaporating before your eyes.

The emotional cycle usually comes full circle, ready to repeat itself. At the bottom of the bear market, your *confidence* is at a low ebb, and you begin the same cycle over again.

Some General Opinions

1. The human nature of investors tends to be constant in that it frequently repeats itself with each market cycle.

2. Each phase of the stock market (up or down) tends to evoke a particular emotion or mood in the investor, which is unique to that phase of the stock market. By being aware of that emotional phase of the stock market, you can be better aware of buying or selling opportunities.

3. The average stock buyer tends to buy and sell in tune with the market's prevailing emotional mood. You may say that prices "Sure are low now. This is a great time to buy," or "Prices just can't keep on going up forever. I ought to sell and nail down some profit." Unfortunately you too often do not act as you speak.

4. Professionals in the stock market—portfolio managers, mutual-fund managers, brokers and analysts—are not immune to being swept up by the market's prevailing emotion and carried helplessly along in its mainstream. These professionals may possess an incredible amount of knowledge concerning stocks and economics, yet they may find it difficult to fully control their emotions.

5. A well-equipped investor has a "sense of feel" for the market's current mood, and—more important—is both aware and in control of his own emotional responses to the market's gyrations and is able to act with decisiveness.

6. Unfortunately such well-equipped investors, even among supposedly "astute" professionals, tend to be a rare breed.

Investment Strategy of This Book

The investment strategy explained in this book is intended to give you some emotional and investment tools so that you may have the courage and conviction to *buy* when those around you are selling and fear appears dominant. We shall show you a reasonably easy selection technique by which you can buy stocks when prices are low (and may go lower), and yet be in a strategic position for attractive capital gains. The intent is also to give you other emotional and investment tools so that you can make a decision to *sell* (hopefully at a profit) when those around you are buying and confidence and greed appear to be supreme. In short, the aim is to show you how to *buy low* and *sell high*.

Briefly Identifying Undervalued Securities

While it is important to have an understanding of the emotional cycle of the stock market, it is also important to know the characteristics that tend to identify clearly what the authors believe constitutes an "undervalued" security. You'll find that such a security tends to possess the following investment characteristics.

1. The company is large and well entrenched. These companies are often known as "blue-chips" or "baby blue-chips."
2. The company's stock is down in price as compared to the past few months or years. You want to *buy low* so as to *sell high*.
3. The company is paying out to its stockholders a large, well-protected cash dividend.
4. The company has on its horizon the attractive possibility of an increase in sales and earnings.

The essential characteristic of an undervalued stock—and its attractiveness to you as an investor—is that it should be giving an investor a large, well-protected cash dividend while he waits for a potential rise in that stock that may give him a capital gain of 20 to 40 percent or more.

3

Understanding Your Emotional Cycle in the Stock Market

Examples of the Emotional Cycle

It should prove quite enlightening to take a stroll down stock market's memory lane. To illustrate best the continuing emotional cycle of *fear, confidence* and *greed* in action, we shall follow the action of the stock market from the autumn of 1958 to mid-1971, the most recent thirteen years. If you are an old hand in the market and are chagrined at your continued lack of success, you may recollect that you experienced at various times some of the emotions described in this chapter.

Chart of the Dow-Jones Industrial Average

Figure 3 is a thirteen-year chart of the "stock market." Specifically, it is a weekly chart of the Dow-Jones Industrial Average. Each line on the chart represents the high, low and close of the average for each week. The numbers at the peaks and valleys on the chart note the highest or lowest values reached.

The Dow-Jones Industrial Average

The Dow-Jones Industrial Average is the oldest and most popular barometer of the stock market. The average is the property of Dow-Jones & Company, Inc., which also publish *The Wall Street Journal*. Dow-Jones calculates and maintains the average, and the New York Stock Exchange has no control over it. Thirty

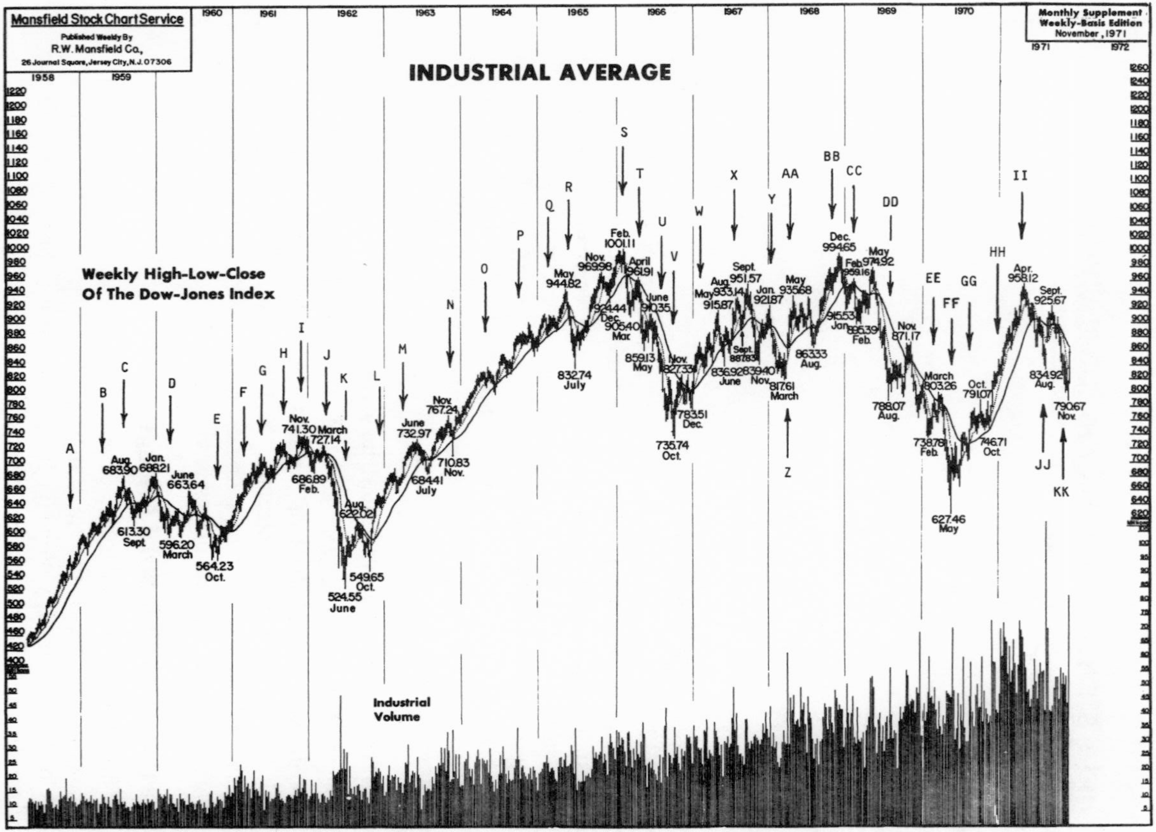

FIGURE 3: LONG-TERM CHART OF DOW-JONES INDUSTRIAL AVERAGE (1958–1971).

stocks (see Table A, below) make up the average. These thirty stocks are selected by and, from time to time, are changed by Dow-Jones. Here is the 1971 list:

TABLE A

Stocks in the Dow-Jones Industrial Average (1971)

STOCK	TICKER SYMBOL	STOCK	TICKER SYMBOL
Allied Chemical	ACD	International Nickel	N
Aluminum Company	AA	International Paper	IP
American Can	AC	Johns Manville	JM
American Tel. & Tel.	T	Owens-Illinois	OI
American Brands	AMB	Proctor & Gamble	PG
Anaconda	A	Sears	S
Bethlehem Steel	BS	Std. Oil of California	SD
Chrysler	C	Std. Oil of New Jersey	J
Du Pont	DD	Swift	SWX
Eastman Kodak	EK	Texaco	TX
General Electric	GE	Union Carbide	UK
General Foods	GF	United Aircraft	UA
General Motors	GM	U. S. Steel	X
Goodyear	GT	Westinghouse	WX
International Harvester	HR	Woolworth	Z

In the investment world the Dow-Jones Average is often thought of as mirroring the action of the "blue-chips." Currently there appear to be no outright "glamour" stocks among the thirty in the average. A point of interest is that these thirty stocks usually account for 7 percent to 9 percent of the volume traded daily on the New York Stock Exchange. For example, on Wednesday, August 26, 1970, 1,583 stocks were traded on the New York Stock Exchange. The volume of shares traded was 15.9 million. The volume of the thirty Dow-Jones stocks accounted for 1.2 million shares, or roughly 7.5 percent of the total. This is generally in line with historical trends.

It is important to note that the majority of the stocks in the Dow-Jones Average are among the largest in the United States and the world. General Motors is the world's largest automobile manufacturer. U.S. Steel is one of the world's largest producers of steel. Du Pont is the world's largest in the field of chemicals. Sears ranks as the world's largest retail chain.

Stock Trends and Emotions

In Figure 3 there are a number of points noted with the letters A, B, C, etc. These refer to general periods when a dominant mood or emotion tended to be felt by the majority of stock buyers. Articles describing these periods were published in major newspapers such as *The Wall Street Journal, The New York Times, The Los Angeles Times,* etc. By reading the "heart" of these articles you can gain an insight into the emotional tone and temper of the times.

Intent of Market Analysis

Let us analyze the Dow-Jones Average. The analysis has the intent of showing that when investors were dominated by fear, the prices of stock tended to be at low levels and thus more attractive for purchase. Yet the historical records indicate that most investors remained frozen on the sidelines. On the other hand, when confidence and greed appeared on the scene, stock prices had already had a major rise. Investors then seemed more prone to enter the market more aggressively. Unfortunately a number of the stocks had already risen significantly. The analysis starts at point A in Figure 3.

Point A—November 1958   The market is at Dow-Jones 560 and has been rising aggressively for seven months. *The Wall Street Journal* reports that (1) small investors grow rapidly in number and push stock prices to new highs, and (2) boom boosts earnings of brokers and salesmen, and increases employment and overtime on Wall Street.

Mood: strong confidence.

The information given here under each point is set up in a special way, to help you make your own decision about the emotional tone of the market. The lead-off is a comment about the current level of the market as measured by the Dow-Jones Industrial Average. Then come succinct items from major financial newspapers. Last is the authors' opinion about the emotional mood of that market period, as they experienced it, being very much aware of their own emotions, the emotions of associates and, most important, the emotions of clients. As you read the capsule versions of each point in stock-market history, you may sometimes have a different interpretation of the *then* prevailing emotional mood. That is good. It shows that you are coming to your own conclusions. Your success in the stock market will depend, in a large part, on having the courage of your convictions.

Point B—April 1959 The market touched Dow-Jones 630 after a thirteen-month steady rise. *The Wall Street Journal* reports that (1) Keith Funston, President of the New York Stock Exchange, cautioned against "gullibility and greed," citing inexperienced investors buying highly speculative stocks, and (2) the New York Stock Exchange, the Securities and Exchange Commission and leading brokers increase efforts to stem widespread speculation in lower-priced stocks.
    Mood: greed.

Point C—August 1959 The market reaches Dow-Jones 680 after an eighteen-month steady rise. *The Wall Street Journal* reports that (1) an anonymous Mrs. "E," a banker's wife, makes a hobby of speculating in stocks with her savings, buys shares at a rapid pace, sells them when they have risen five points, has made a 20 percent profit since entering market in May 1958; and that (2) institutional investors reduce holdings of common stocks slightly, buy more bonds, weed out overpriced issues, accumulate larger reserves of cash for investment when the market trend becomes clearer.
    Mood: intense greed.

Point D—February and March 1960 The market is at Dow-Jones 600, down eighty points (around 12 percent) from the highs reached earlier, in January. *The Wall Street Journal* reports that (1) few shareholders seem deeply worried about sharp market decline and most predict an upturn after "correction," (2) Wall Street brokerage firms push expansion plans despite decline in volume and stock prices, and (3) "We do not anticipate a major decline in stock prices," said C. M. Werly, chairman of the Putnam Fund.
    Mood: beginning of fear.

Point E—October and November 1960 The market has declined for nine months to Dow-Jones 565, a drop of 20 percent. *The Wall Street Journal* reports that (1) decline in odd-lot business indicates smaller stock buyers cutting purchases; mutual-fund sales drop, (2) more investors appear hesitant about buying stock—worried about further market decline, (3) investment companies turn increasingly to foreign securities and put money in short-term securities, reacting to uncertainty about the direction of domestic stock and bond markets, and the state of national economy, (4) Wall Street brokerage firms expected to cut Christmas bonuses for employees, citing poor business.

Mood: fear.

Point F—February 1961 The stock market is trading at Dow-Jones 650, up approximately 15 percent from its October 1960 low of 565. *The Wall Street Journal* reports that trading volume grows as some mutual funds and pension trusts increase buying.

Mood: beginning of confidence.

Point G—April and May 1961 The Dow-Jones Industrial Average closes above 700 for the first time, having risen 25 percent in the past six months. *The Wall Street Journal* reports that (1) heavy stock trading clogged brokers' phones; some investors have complaints about delays, (2) many investors are seen bypassing "blue-chip" companies, bidding up lesser-known shares, (3) Keith Funston, President of the New York Stock Exchange, cautions against stock speculation, terming as "thoughtless" the current preoccupation with low-priced shares and issues, and (4) some bankers and others get favored allotments of "hot" new stock issues and many turn short, quick profits.

Mood: confidence changing to greed.

Point H—August 1961 The stock market is at Dow-Jones 720, the highest ever to that time. *The Wall Street Journal* reports the Securities and Exchange Commission says that speculation by small investors pushes "put and call" trading to new highs.

Mood: greed.

Point I—November and December 1961 The stock market is hovering around the Dow-Jones 730 level, up 4 percent in the last seven months. *The Wall Street Journal* reports that (1) investors prefer common stocks but see risk in current high price level, (2) dividend yields on stocks near the lows of the 1930's as market rises to another new high, and (3) brokerage firms participating in "hot" new issues get queries from the S.E.C. for stock market study.

Mood: greed.

Point J—March and April 1962 The stock market has recovered to the Dow-Jones 725 range after having dropped in February to 686. *The Wall Street Journal* reports that, (1) despite January's drop in stock prices, many analysts believe prices will go higher, citing heavy government spending and good business, (2) new stock issues lose a good deal of their luster, with half selling at or below the originally offered price, and (3) the price drop reflects investor doubts on business upturn and future profits.

Mood: beginnings of fear.

Point K—May and June 1962 The Dow-Jones Average has dropped to 525, a decline of 27 percent in three months. *The Wall Street Journal* reports that (1) many individual investors sit on sidelines as stocks fall to sixteen-month low, (2) many small investors bet on further stock market drop and step up short sales, (3) brokerage firms drop employees, tighten reins on expenses in the wake of the volume drop, and (4) lower stock prices spur many institutions to start buying again, though some still prefer bonds.

Mood: fear bordering on panic.

Point L—November and December 1962 The market has risen to the Dow-Jones 650 level, up 24 percent from the June 1962 low. *The Wall Street Journal* reports that (1) the bulk of stock buying comes from traders and some institutional investors, (2) some brokers state smaller investors warm up again to stock investments, and (3) brokerage firms hold off rehiring laid-off workers despite stock market upturn.

Mood: ending of fear.

Point M—April 1963   The market is over Dow-Jones 700 again, about the same level as 1961. *The Wall Street Journal* reports that (1) the stock market nears a record; prices of "speculative" issues trail established shares; small investors are not so active, and (2) over-the-counter issues still trade sluggishly; price recovery lags; a number of salesmen and firms fall.

Mood: ending of fear.

Point N—October and November 1963   The market is at Dow-Jones 760, the highest ever. *The Wall Street Journal* reports that (1) President Kennedy laments that the public seems to identify him with slumping stock markets, but not with rising ones, (2) individual investors return to the market, but very slowly and cautiously, (3) lofty stock prices cause institutions to become more conservative, (4) President Kennedy is assassinated, prices plunge in panic selling, trading is suspended on all stock exchanges, and (5) the Dow Average advances a record 32.03 points on first day of trading after President Kennedy's death, volume is the highest in eighteen months.

Mood: cautious confidence changing swiftly to aggressive confidence.

Point O—March and April 1964   The market is at Dow-Jones 820, up 56 percent from the June 1962 lows, and has now risen steadily for twenty-two months. *The Wall Street Journal* reports that (1) good stock salesmen get more job offers as brokerage competition rises, and that brokers say (2) small investors begin to buy more shares than they are selling.

Mood: confidence.

Point P—August and September 1964   The market is at Dow-Jones 875, having risen steadily throughout 1964. *The Wall Street Journal* reports that (1) customer complaints to the New York Stock Exchange increase as heavy trading slows delivery of stock certificates, and (2) advisory services ride high again as public returns to stock buying; some private advisory services triple circulation.

Mood: confidence turning toward greed.

Point Q—March 1965   The market is at Dow-Jones 900 after a twenty-nine month rise. *The Wall Street Journal* reports that buying by the "public" once more gives a lift to low-priced stocks, but brokers say speculation is less intense than before 1962's sharp break.
   Mood: greed.

Point R—May and June 1965   The market has reached Dow-Jones 940. *The Wall Street Journal* reports that (1) Federal Reserve Board Chairman Martin warns of stock market boom-bust peril and finds similarities between the current speculative mood and the stock market of the late 1920's, and (2) institutional investors are playing a major role in the sharp stock price slump, many cut buying, some sell because they feel shares are "overpriced."
   Mood: greed shifting toward fear.

Point S—January and February 1966   The market is near Dow-Jones 1000. *The Wall Street Journal* reports that (1) a big surge of women into the stock market helps volume hit highs, (2) Keith Funston, President of the New York Stock Exchange, states that the Big Board is concerned about recent rises in market speculation and asks member firms what they are doing to curb speculation, and (3) institutions trade stock more often to catch short-term swings.
   Mood: greed.

Point T—April 1966   The market is at Dow-Jones 960, down 4 percent from its February high. *The Wall Street Journal* reports that (1) E. D. Etherington, President of the American Stock Exchange, cautions against a high degree of speculation, and (2) a "hot issue" rerun: many new, unseasoned stocks soar above offering prices similar to 1961–62; some double in first days.
   Mood: intense greed.

Point U—July and August 1966   The Dow falls to 770, down 23 percent in six months. *The Wall Street Journal* reports that (1) investors' buying of mutual fund shares fell off; a six month's decline is blamed, and (2) brokers strive to get customers off the sidelines, back into the market.

Mood: beginnings of fear.

Point V—October 1966 The market has slid to Dow-Jones 736, down 26 percent in eight months. *The Wall Street Journal* reports that (1) portfolio pilots of big investment trusts eye stocks more hopefully, and (2) most "new issues" are postponed because of market conditions as investors are wary.

Mood: public fear and institutional confidence.

Point W—January and February 1967 The market has rebounded to Dow-Jones 871, up 18 percent from October 1966 lows. *The Wall Street Journal* reports that there is a return of the bulls and many brokers and some investors expect rising prices.

Mood: beginnings of confidence.

Point X—July and August 1967 The market has reached Dow-Jones 930, up 26 percent from the October 1966 low ten months ago. *The Wall Street Journal* reports that (1) the American Stock Exchange warns against speculation and asks members to tighten policy, (2) both the New York and American stock exchanges cut trading time from five and a half hours to four hours to reduce back-office backlog from heavy trading, and (3) "Why Trading Soars": institutional investors hoping for fast gains keep the market boiling; individuals are also active.

Mood: beginnings of greed.

Point Y—January 1968 The market has rallied to Dow-Jones 920, after having been as low as 840 in November 1967. *The Wall Street Journal* reports that telephone facilities in the Wall Street area are inundated by record trading volume.

Mood: greed.

Point Z—March and Early April 1968 The market is at Dow-Jones 820, down 15 percent in the last seven months. *The Wall Street Journal* reports that President Johnson's "I will not run" speech brings heavy stock buying by institutions, but the small investor is cautious and remains on the sidelines.

Mood: fear.

Point AA—Late April and May 1968 The market has rallied quickly to Dow-Jones 930, up 13 percent in six weeks from its March 1968 low. *The Wall Street Journal* reports that (1) mutual fund actions in the market now parallel the public's, ending the tradition of bucking trends; public buying is sparked by Vietnam peace hopes, (2) phone lines are choked in Wall Street because of heavy trading; some say they wait an hour for a dial tone, and (3) Wall Street veterans say, "Hot issue fever is hotter and worse than 1961–62."
Mood: confidence turning toward greed.

Point BB—November and December 1968 The market has reached Dow-Jones 990, up 34 percent in an erratic rise in 26 months from the October 1966 lows. *The Wall Street Journal* reports that (1) investors are surprisingly unemotional about the international money crisis, and (2) many brokerage firms spurn small accounts and small investors to reduce costs; customers are angered.
Mood: intense greed.

Point CC—January Through March 1969 The market is hovering in the low 900's. *The Wall Street Journal* reports that (1) an increasing number of new stock issues are sputtering in their market debut, (2) the deepening price slump batters bonds and high yields don't pull buyers, and (3) "Stockbroker Blues": slowdown in trading affects their earnings.
Mood: end of greed.

Point DD—June Through August 1969 The market has dropped to Dow-Jones 790, a decline of 20 percent in eight months. *The Wall Street Journal* reports that (1) brokerage firms, beset by rising costs and sagging business, cut branches and staff, (2) "Faltering Funds": investors' ardor for mutual fund shares is cooled by the stock drop, (3) "Hedge Fund Heebi-Jeebies": stock market dip a short-seller's dream? "More like a nightmare," say professionals, who are guessing wrong, and (4) "Sitting Tight": small investors watch the market plunge with "philosophical" mood, nobody panics, few sell off their stocks.
Mood: beginning of fear.

Point EE—February 1970 The market is around Dow-Jones 740, down 25 percent in fourteen months. *The Wall Street Journal* reports that depressed stock prices are upsetting plans of a lot of Americans; some postpone retirement, others put off purchase of houses and cars.

Mood: fear.

Point FF—April and May 1970 The market has slid to Dow-Jones 630, down 36 percent in nineteen months. *The Wall Street Journal* reports that (1) mutual funds are hit by redemptions, sales drop as stocks fall and nervous investors bail out as losses mount, (2) many small investors stay on the sidelines as their losses mount; they neither buy nor sell, just hope for turn-around, (3) the stock market plunge brings salary slashes and layoffs on Wall Street; brokerage officials take cuts in pay and some brokers quit the business, (4) small investors stay bearish, so analysts foresee market upturn, and (5) bond prices take a battering from the shock waves of the Cambodian invasion; U.S. Treasury's $3.5 billion refunding is imperiled; there are few buyers for U.S. government securities as bankers sit tight.

Mood: fear bordering on panic.

Point GG—July and August 1970 The market has moved up sharply to Dow-Jones 730, up 16 percent in eight weeks. *The Wall Street Journal* reports that security analysts struggle to find jobs as brokerage firms retrench and merge.

The Los Angeles Times report that (1) the big boys—the active mutual funds and managers of large pools of private money say they are either selling into the rally, or, at best, are none too eager to buy, and (2) Robert Peisner advises selected buying, calling the current mood of pessimism the normal birthplace of major rallies.

Mood: fear trending toward confidence.

Point HH—December 1970 The Dow has risen briskly to the 820 area, up 30 percent in eight months. *The Wall Street Journal* reports about Happy Days: many on Wall Street expect stock market to continue to climb; easing of fiscal, monetary restraints is big factor; large institutions jump in.

Mood: confidence.

Point II—March Through May 1971   The Dow has gone above 950, an increase of 50 percent from the lows of twelve months earlier. *The Wall Street Journal* reports: (1) stocks surge ahead: industrials close over 900 for the first time in twenty-one months; trading brisk, (2) no one is sure why, but investors flock to a not-so-hot issue; small guys buy Penn Central as the big guys bail out; is it "greater fool theory"? and (3) Onward and Upward: Experts now say it is just a matter of time till Dow index hits 1000.

The Los Angeles Times reports that brokers, public are riding rebound of stock market: The customer's man has clients again as small investors take plunge.

Mood: beginning of greed.

Point JJ—August 1971   The market has declined to the Dow-Jones 830 area, down 12 percent from the April highs three and a half months earlier. *The Wall Street Journal* reports that (1) President Nixon imposes wage, price controls and import surcharge, and (2) ebullient investors send stocks soaring in record daily climb; crowds jam brokers' offices; tape watchers praise Nixon, scramble to purchase stocks.

Mood: strong confidence and beginnings of greed.

Point KK—November 1971   The market has retreated sharply to the Dow-Jones 790 area, down over 13 percent from the September high of 920 just eleven weeks ago. *The Wall Street Journal* reports that (1) analysts and businessmen fret over unknowns of Phase 2 of Nixon's wage, price controls; Europeans warn of worldwide depression if 10 percent import tax not removed and monetary problems not resolved, (2) stock salesmen in many smaller cities find it a difficult time to do business, and (3) people are just sitting on their hands. Nobody wants to be the first in starting to buy.

The Los Angeles Times reports that most money managers are cautious and uncertain. Some are apathetic.

The New York Times reports that a famous economist predicts stock market decline to Dow-Jones 500.

Mood: beginning of fear.

You Can't Trust Your Emotions

The dominant theme that seems to emerge from this quick glance back into recent history is that you can't trust your own emotions. Another way you may think of it is that your own emotions are often your own worst enemy insofar as gaining stock market profits is concerned. Notice how consistently the worst times to buy generally took place when investors were on a "buying binge." It seemed that they couldn't buy stocks fast enough. Phone lines were jammed. There were enormous paper-work jams. Yet customers kept coming to buy stocks like waves assaulting a beach. It seemed like Christmas, New Year's and the Fourth of July all rolled into one.

On the other hand, the best times to buy actually tended to occur when fear and panic prevailed. Unfortunately the ability to buy stocks when prices have been falling requires a steadfastness, a resolve and a certain knowledge that most people appear sadly to lack. They feel more comfortable following the crowd.

In the future, when you read the daily paper and come upon the symptoms of greed such as a hot new-issue market, low-price speculative stocks moving up aggressively, record trading volume—pause and think; perhaps it is time to sell.

On the other hand, when you read of the symptoms of fear such as brokerage firms closing branch offices because of low trading volume, most investors sitting on the sidelines, mutual funds complaining of low sales—pause and think; perhaps it is time to buy.

And if you decide to buy, you'll find in the next chapters some suggestions, guidelines and ideas on how to judge the country's economic climate and how to select companies that appear to be undervalued, high-quality securities and thus potentially ripe for an attractive rise in price.

Good luck.

4

You, Your Investments
and the Federal Reserve Board

Winter—and you know the land shivers beneath blankets of mingled snow, slush and mud under lead-gray clouds.

Summer—and the land blossoms with fields of flowers, greenery and leaf-heavy trees kissed by warm, blue skies.

In January ten-foot snowdrifts chill Maine and tourists toast in the sun on white Miami beaches. The seasons blend gradually into one another on a fixed astronomical time schedule that cannot be altered or restrained.

The discomforts of winter may be compared to bear markets and your distress at watching the prices of your stocks decline; the pleasures of summer, to bull markets and your happiness at seeing your participating stocks rally. And that's just about where any similarities abruptly end. Summer comes on June 21, give or take a day if you are a purist. But on what day (give or take a week or a month or a year) does the next bull market begin? No computer has as yet clicked out any specific time schedule for the start of bull markets, when an investor can look forward to rising stock prices, or when bear markets begin so that he can astutely cash in his profits and stand aside as stock prices fall.

Many books have been written, computers programmed and reprogrammed, and untold millions of man-hours expended trying to find the answers to two questions:

1. When will the next bull market start?
2. When will it end?

Here is a suggested answer:

1. *Bull markets tend to begin when the Federal Reserve System loosens credit and spurs spending.*

2. *Bull markets tend to end, and bear markets to begin, when the Federal Reserve System restricts the supply of credit to inhibit spending.*

A great amount of economic research done in the last fifteen years seems to support these answers. Before touching on the high points of this research, the Federal Reserve System—which controls the supply of money and the availability of credit in the United States—should be briefly explained.

The Federal Reserve System

The Federal Reserve System is a United States government agency. One of its purposes is to control the activities of the nation's commercial banks. Commercial banks perform three basic functions:

1. They provide the bulk of the nation's money supply in the form of checking accounts.

2. They extend credit by making loans to individuals and businesses, or by buying IOUs (notes and bonds) issued by individuals, businesses and government agencies.

3. They "house" the savings of individuals and business and pay interest on these savings.

Since the Federal Reserve System controls the majority of the nation's commercial banks, in essence, the Federal Reserve System acts as *the central bank* for the United States of America.

The "Fed," as the Federal Reserve System is familiarly called by bankers, was created in 1913 by Congress. Earlier, in 1895 and 1907, the United States had suffered through two agonizing money crises that triggered depressions. In searching for a remedy Congress ascertained that the establishment of a central national bank, patterned after those existing in European countries, might avoid or mitigate such economic catastrophies in the future.

The Fed, through its existing legal control over most of the nation's commercial banks, now possesses the power to manipulate the quantity of money and credit available to the public and to business. Thus, the Fed is strategically well placed to influence economic conditions in the United States. More specifically, it has the legal and financial muscle to dampen economic boom periods, to precipitate a recession, to end a recession and to rekindle the next boom. Publicity is usually shunned by the Fed, which, dealing with billions of dollars, prefers to work in secrecy.

What authority states that the Federal Reserve System shall have this weighty influence, which directly and indirectly affects almost every facet of American business and touches the life of practically every person in the United States? The authority is the United States Congress through its passage of the 1913 Federal Reserve Act and its approval of subsequent amendments to the Act.

Congress has given the Federal Reserve System a *mandate* to watch over the economic growth and stability of the United States. The Federal Reserve's purpose is to *counterbalance* inflationary or deflationary pressures so as to prevent such pressures from getting out of hand and injuring the United States' financial health.

The study of the Federal Reserve System and the interpretation of its past actions and future policies have been, and continue to be, a favorite of candidates for doctoral degrees in economics in major universities. This book will not delve into any subtle economic theories. Instead, the purpose of this chapter is to alert the investor to those powers and actions of the Federal Reserve System, which tend to have a direct bearing on the market value of your stocks and bonds.

Congress Made the Federal Reserve System Independent

At the start it is important to realize that the 1913 Federal Reserve Act made the Federal Reserve System virtually immune from direct political influence. There is no appeal to a higher authority for relief from Federal Reserve decisions. An important example of the Fed's independence of day-to-day politics was clearly demonstrated in December 1965, when the Federal Reserve Board raised the discount rate from 4 percent to 4½ percent. This action was directly contrary to President Johnson's policies. In reporting the story, the opening paragraph of *The Wall Street Journal* article read:

The Federal Reserve Board, directly defying the Johnson Administration, raised the discount rate to 4½ % from 4% to head off inflationary pressures.

President Johnson immediately issued a public statement:

The Federal Reserve Board is an independent agency. Its decision was an independent decision. I regret, as do most Americans, any action that raises the cost of credit, particularly for homes, schools, hospitals and factories.

Congressman Patman, Chairman of the House Banking Committee, voiced greater outrage:

The latest action can only be characterized as arrogant, and a complete betrayal of the will of the people.

General Setup of the Federal Reserve System

Economics historians generally believe that the unique structure of the Federal Reserve System resulted from the tug of war of political compromise of the 1913 era. Twelve Federal Reserve districts were originally established throughout the country, and such is the format today. A regional Federal Reserve Bank is headquartered in a major city within each of the twelve districts:

District 1: Federal Reserve Bank of Boston
District 2: Federal Reserve Bank of New York
District 3: Federal Reserve Bank of Philadelphia
District 4: Federal Reserve Bank of Cleveland
District 5: Federal Reserve Bank of Richmond
District 6: Federal Reserve Bank of Atlanta
District 7: Federal Reserve Bank of Chicago
District 8: Federal Reserve Bank of St. Louis
District 9: Federal Reserve Bank of Minneapolis
District 10: Federal Reserve Bank of Kansas City
District 11: Federal Reserve Bank of Dallas
District 12: Federal Reserve Bank of San Francisco

In 1913 the dominant political philosophy seemed to be that each district Federal Reserve Bank would be particularly attuned to the banking needs of its specific region to help it in a financial emergency. A money crisis in the East could possibly be dampened to have less effect in the West or in the South. Technically each Federal Reserve Bank is privately owned by the member banks in its district. The services performed by each regional Federal Reserve Bank for its member banks such as lending money at the discount rate to the member banks and the yield on its enormous portfolio of government bonds, etc., produces the income that keeps the Federal Reserve System financially independent.

Currently there are over 15,000 banks in the United States. Less than half that number actually belong to the Federal Reserve System. National commercial banks are legally required to be members. It is optional for state banks. However, the banks that do currently belong hold over 80 percent of America's money deposits.

Real Power of the Federal Reserve System is Vested in Its Board of Governors

As an investor you should be aware of the particular method that Congress employed to put the Federal Reserve System *outside* of the direct political control of individual Presidents of the United States and political parties.

The Federal Reserve Board of Governors, located in Washington, D.C., has seven members and is directly charged with supervising the Federal Reserve system. Each member of the Board of Governors is appointed for a fourteen-year term. Like a justice of the Supreme Court, a Board governor is appointed by the President of the United States with the advice and consent of the Senate. Nominating one or perhaps two Board governors is the total extent of the direct influence that any President has over the makeup of the Board. So that one President could not unduly control the Board, the 1913 Congress deliberately staggered the terms of their office, with one expiring every two years.

Powers of the Board of Governors

The seven-member Board of Governors possesses broad policy-making powers over the twelve Federal Reserve Banks, and *thus* over the national banks, and *thus* over the economy of the United States, and *thus* over you and American business. The Board's powers include:

- The power to vary the reserve requirements of deposits of all member banks, thereby influencing their lending capacity.
- The power to vary the liquidity of the assets of the member banks, which similarly influences their lending capacity.
- The power to vary the maximum interest rates that member banks can pay on the monies that the public has on deposit.
- The power to approve the discount interest rate set by the boards of directors of the regional Federal Reserve Banks to their member banks.
- The power to control the amount of coin and currency put into public circulation through each regional Federal Reserve Bank.
- The power to vary the margin requirements for the credit purchases by the public of stocks and convertible bonds traded on the national stock exchanges and in the over-the-counter market.
- The power to approve the appointment of the president and first vice-president of each regional Federal Reserve Bank.
- The power to exercise general supervision over each Federal Reserve Bank.
- The power to act as fiscal agent for the U.S. Treasury in issuing and redeeming Treasury securities, nationally and internationally.

The Federal Reserve System is Financially Independent

Additionally, and perhaps equally important, the Fed is financially independent. Congress does not vote any funds to operate the Federal Reserve System. The government's money watchdog, the General Accounting Office, does not audit the Fed. The Fed's income, to pay its salaries and bills, comes solely from its internal earnings.

Flow of Federal Reserve Influence

Figure 4 is a chart, entitled "Flow of Federal Reserve Influence," from the book *Federal Reserve System—Purposes and Functions.* The book was first published in 1939 by the Board of Governors of the Federal Reserve System as an information guide, and over a million copies are in print. The chart shows clearly that the Federal Reserve authorities—namely, the Board of Governors—regulates the *volume of member bank reserves,* which *largely determines* production, employment and prices.

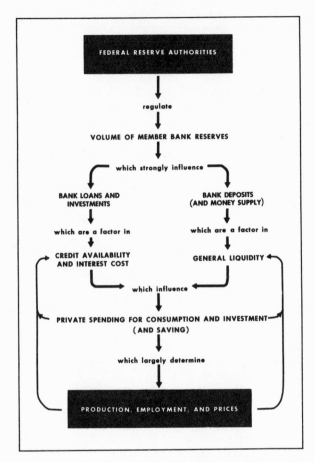

FIGURE 4: FLOW OF FEDERAL RESERVE INFLUENCE.

The essence of the power of the Federal Reserve Board is summed up in this little jingle:

> If the banks have *more* to lend,
> You have *more* to spend.

Or turned around:

> If the banks have *less* to lend,
> You have *less* to spend.

How the Fed Influences Production, Employment and Prices

First Example: The Trend of Starting a Boom: The generalized description below of the basic mechanics of how the Fed influences business conditions—particularly stock prices—is purposely over-simplified. Let us assume the country is suffering through a recession and, with it, high unemployment and low stock prices. Here's generally how a business recovery gets under way. *Easier money* is usually the key to ending these negative economic conditions and starting a boom. "Easier money" is another way of saying that more money is made available to the public for circulation so as to increase spending.

The Fed puts money into the banks. The Fed also lowers interest rates. Practically all the banks in the country are now able to make more loans. The businessman can borrow to build inventory. Contractors can borrow to build more apartment houses, homes and office buildings. People can borrow to buy real estate, cars, refrigerators and other items. Sales start to rise. Manufacturers increase production. More people are hired. Payrolls increase. This recovery process has an attractive built-in ability to feed on itself. More people on the payroll usually means more money in circulation, which means more sales, which in turn means more production—and the boom keeps rolling.

A psychological ingredient in the early stages of a recovery is the principle that many manufacturers tend to hesitate in hiring more workers until they feel secure that sales and production are truly rising. So there frequently is a time lag in unemployment reduction, even though business is picking up. The existing employees are asked to work harder, longer and more efficiently. In the jargon of economists this economic principle is called *increased productivity.*

From the point of view of an investor, the usual sequence witnessed as a recession ends and a boom starts is this:

1. The Fed starts to loosen money.
2. Sensitive interest rates such as the yield on 91-day Treasury bills should begin to trend downward.
3. The stock market tends to end its downward or sideward

movement and starts to rally in anticipation of the beneficial economic effects of easier money and lower interest rates.

4. The economic indicators termed "leading" bottom out and start an upward movement.

5. Business conditions, as measured by industrial production, start to improve as the nation's factories increase their output.

6. Employment starts to rise as employers begin to rehire because conditions are improving and sales are rising.

As an investor you should understand the principle that easier money should tend to help stock prices rise due to two positive implications:

1. More money in circulation implies that companies' sales and profits may rise and that their dividends may be increased, thus making the companies' stocks more attractive as investments.

2. More money in circulation implies that investors have more funds to buy stocks.

Second Example: The Trend of Starting a Recession: Here's how the Fed generally tends to engineer a business slowdown or a *recession.* Let us assume the country is enjoying economic boom conditions (which the Fed believes to be unsustainable) and, with it, usually full employment, inflation and high stock prices. Tightened money and restrictive credit have been the weapons used by the Fed in the past to end booms. Tight money is another way of saying less money is made available to the public for circulation, thereby inhibiting spending.

The Fed takes money out of the banks. Most banks in the country are forced to reduce their loans. The businessman borrows less and is forced to reduce his inventory. The contractor borrows less and can build fewer apartment houses, homes and office buildings. People borrow less and can buy less real estate and fewer cars, refrigerators, and so on. Sales trend downward and manufacturers' inventories rise. Manufacturers reduce production due to higher inventories and lower sales. Fewer people are hired and some are laid off. Payrolls shrink. This deteriorating process feeds on itself. Fewer people on the payroll usually means less money in circulation, which means fewer sales, which in turn means more production cutbacks and more layoffs and still lower payrolls. This cycle, if permitted to run its course unchecked, has, in the past, been known to terminate in economic depressions. A characteristic of the early stages of a business downturn is the reluctance of employers to lay off highly skilled workers, because they feel that the slowdown may be temporary in nature. So there often occurs a time lag as employment stays high even though business conditions are worsening.

The sequence the investor will witness as the momentum of the boom grinds to a halt and a business slowdown begins is this:

1. The Fed starts to tighten money

2. Free-market, short-term interest rates, such as the yield of 91-day Treasury bills or commercial paper, would tend to rise. (For example, in the economic climate of the 1970's the interest yield on short-term 30-day commercial paper rising into the 6 to 7 percent range, above the 5 to 6 percent yield the Fed permits to be available at banks, could be construed by many as a sign of tight money.)

3. The stock market encounters difficulty in rising and begins to retreat, perhaps in anticipation of the negative effects that tighter money and higher interest rates would have on the profits and dividends of companies.

4. The "leading" economic indicators tend to top out and begin a downward drift.

5. Business conditions, as measured by industrial production, actually begin to deteriorate as production is reduced in the nation's factories.

6. Unemployment starts to climb as business conditions worsen.

From an investor's viewpoint tight-money policies of the Federal Reserve Board tend to increase the probability of stock price sell-offs due to two negative implications, the opposite of those we noted above as existing with easier money:

1. Less money in circulation means that the sales and profits of companies may decline and that their dividends and earnings may be reduced, rendering the companies less attractive as investments.

2. Less money in circulation implies that the investor has less funds available to buy stocks.

A Brief Definition of Inflation

Inflation is often the primary reason why the Fed applies the credit brakes to end a boom. Technically inflation occurs when prices rise faster than productivity, but most people tend to think of inflation as the everyday prices that they pay for goods and services rising too fast, too soon. When you actually see the acceleration of prices, the debilitating effects of inflation are more apparent. For example, say the country is experiencing 7 percent inflation, which is what was actually occurring in the United States in 1969. This means that what you spent a dollar for that year would cost you about $1.07 the next year. Two years later the same item would cost you $1.15. Three years later the price would be about $1.23. In 1969 the average American family's income was around $10,000 annually. Most families usually spend most of what they earn on food, rent, medicine, clothing, transportation and education. If inflation were to continue at a reduced rate of five percent, in only ten years—by 1979—the average American family would need over $16,000 a year to buy the identical items. A new house selling for $30,000 in 1969 would cost over $50,000 in 1979.

5

The Fed in Action

Some of the Results of
Previous Federal Reserve Board Policy Decisions
to Influence Production, Employment and Prices

There have been approximately nine major boom periods in the United States since 1918. Nine times the Federal Reserve Board has voted to attempt to end these boom periods. Nine times they have generally succeeded, so their batting record is believed to be 1.000 percent to date.

But in 1951 the Federal Reserve Board made an important policy change. They severed their "invisible" tie with the U.S. Treasury. Between 1940 and 1951, economic history shows, the Federal Reserve System tended to be passive in its actions and subservient to U.S. Treasury policies. During that time the Fed's official posture was to keep U.S. government bonds—both short-term and long-term—from fluctuating extensively in price. This had the negative effect of inhibiting the Fed from regulating the volume of member bank reserves. Ultimately, through a chain of circumstances, this passive policy strongly contributed to a surge of inflation in 1950 and 1951, during the Korean "police action." More important to the investor is the fact that these events triggered the Fed's divorce from the U.S. Treasury, which economists call the Treasury–Federal Reserve Accord of 1951. Consequently, if you are interpreting the results of Fed decisions, you need to separate them into pre-1951 and post-1951. Pre-1951 analysis reveals Fed decisions to have been hobbled by its "marriage" to the U.S. Treasury. Post-1951 decisions show the Fed to be less concerned with the fluctuations of U.S. government bond prices and more actively attempting to dampen booms and soften busts, thereby contributing to the overall growth and stability of the nation's economy.

Following are highly condensed summaries of the Fed's record in influencing production, employment, interest rates and stock prices since 1918. The pre-1951 descriptions cover only their attempts to defuse boom conditions. The post-1951 descriptions additionally cover their stimulative actions to revive the economy. The descriptions are necessarily brief, being oriented toward the investor. Professional economists may very well take umbrage that statistical tables and a number of subtle actions that could possibly deepen the meaning and enlarge the interpretations have been omitted. Books and articles by the dozen explore these events in minute detail. These books are readily available to you if you choose to examine the fine points of each period more closely.

Pre-1951 Actions

Ending the 1919–20 Boom   At the end of World War I, around 1919 to 1920, there was an energetic postwar boom and inflation. The Fed voted to slow down credit extended by the banks. In 1920 and 1921, as the Fed cut off credit, interest rates rose to what were then fifty-year highs. A major business slump followed. Unemployment rose sharply. The stock market dropped 46 percent.

Ending the Late 1920's Boom   There was the "Roaring Twenties" boom and its accompanying inflation, which lasted until 1929. The Fed decided to bring it under control by making money tight. Events outside the control of the Fed, such as England's devaluing gold in 1931, compounded the economic woes. The worst depression in the history of our country followed. Millions became unemployed. The stock market dropped 89 percent.

Ending the 1936–37 Boom   In 1936 and 1937 an aggressive boom was underway. The Fed thought it was going too far too fast, with too much inflation, and slapped on the credit brakes. Interest rates moved up. A sharp business recession started. Unemployment rose by millions. Stock prices dropped 49 percent.

Ending the 1947–48 Boom   In 1947 and 1948 the postwar boom got underway. But strong inflationary pressures quickly developed because of the scarcity of goods. The Fed voted to reduce the lending power of banks. Consumer-credit controls were installed. Business sagged into a recession. Unemployment rose from about two million to almost five million. The stock market dropped around 20 percent.

Post-1951 Actions

Many Unknowns   In 1951 the Fed divorced itself from the U.S. Treasury and started to attempt to use its massive money-control powers to facilitate orderly economic growth for the nation. But the concept of "orderly growth" has proven difficult to accomplish—a few wild jokers always seem to be hidden in the deck and pop up at inopportune times. These unknowns, uncontrollables and variables were, and to this day continue to be:

- Unforseen changes in national and world economies, priorities and politics.
- Unexpected changes among national and world leaders and their individual personal goals.
- Advances in monetary know-how that void or modify previous Fed decisions.
- An unclosable and unavoidable time lag between the decision to act and the recognition of its consequences, known as the "recognition gap."
- The state of the confidence of the American consumer, causing him to spend or not to spend, and to save or not to save.
- The decisions of U.S. corporations to enlarge, modify, reduce or change their output.
- The decisions of U.S. labor unions to strike or not to strike and the varying sizes of labor settlements.
- Lack of knowledge of what other nations of the size and development of the United States have historically experienced.

Hence, the Fed finds itself captain of a giant ship of economics almost always sailing toward unknown horizons through uncharted waters. It guides the ship warily, sometimes moving too fast and at other times not fast enough, striving to avoid running aground.

With these variables in mind, here is a brief summary of the Fed's policies since 1951, *from the investor's viewpoint.*

Ending the 1952–53 Boom   As the Korean "police action" drew to a close, the nation was experiencing a major inflationary boom. The Industrial Material Price Index skyrocketed up over 80 percent in the nine months from April 1950 to December 1950. The Fed voted for tight money and the boom's days became numbered. The discount rate was ultimately raised to 2 percent by January 1953. As the boom peaked, 91-day Treasury bills were yielding 2½ percent, the highest in years. The stock market crested in January 1953 at Dow-Jones 295, up 84 percent in 41 months from its low of Dow-Jones 160 in August 1949. The leading economic indicators similarly topped out in January. Industrial production continued to rise until July 1953. Unemployment reached its lowest level of around 3 percent in August 1953.

The 1953–54 Aftermath of Tight Money   The stock market dropped 13 percent to bottom in September 1953 at Dow-Jones 255. The leading economic indicators registered their low point in December 1953. Industrial production touched bottom in February 1954. Unemployment doubled to touch 6 percent in August 1954.

Engineering the 1954 Recovery   Complications associated with the Korean situation—namely, the Eisenhower administration's actions to shift from a wartime to a peacetime economy—complicated the Fed's problem in engineering the recovery as war-oriented production was phased out. Money was continuously eased to where 91-day Treasury Bills were yielding under 1 percent by mid-1954. The discount rate was reduced twice to 1½ percent.

Ending the 1954–57 Boom   The engines of inflation heated up again as the boom rolled through 1955, 1956 and into 1957. The Fed tightened money gradually, raising the discount rate seven times so that by the summer of 1957 the rate stood at 3½ percent. The interest yield on 91-day Treasury bills reached 3½ percent in the autumn of 1957. The stock market crested in July 1957 at Dow-Jones 523, up 105 percent in 46 months from its September 1953 low of Dow-Jones 255. Industrial production peaked in July 1957 and unemployment receded to the 4 percent area by early 1957. The nation's economy then slowed down.

The 1957–58 Aftermath of Tight Money   The stock market fell almost 20 percent to bottom at Dow-Jones 417 in October 1957. The leading economic indicators bottomed in January 1958. Industrial production recorded its lowest figure in April 1958. Unemployment almost doubled to exceed 7 percent in May and June of 1958.

Engineering the 1958 Recovery   The Fed reduced the discount rate four times to 1¾ percent by the spring of 1958. Money was made more easily available at the banks to cause interest yields on 91-day Treasury bills to dip under 1 percent. The nation's economy began its upsurge in the spring of 1958.

Ending the 1958–59 Boom   The economic expansion continued through the remainder of 1958 and all of 1959 to crest in January 1960. The Fed raised the discount rate five times to a peak of 4 percent by the summer of 1959. Ninety-one day Treasury bills reflected the tight-money conditions with their yields rising to 4½ percent by January 1960. Such levels had not been seen since the early 1930's. The stock market topped out in January 1960 at Dow-Jones 688, up 65 percent in twenty-seven months from the low of Dow-Jones 416 in October 1957. Industrial production likewise peaked in January. The unemployment rate crested at 5 percent. Business conditions now began to deteriorate.

The 1960–61 Aftermath of Tight Money   The stock market sold off 18 percent to hold finally at Dow-Jones 565 in October 1960. The leading economic indicators bottomed in December 1960. Industrial production touched its low point in February 1961. Unemployment increased 40 percent to a reading of 7 percent by March 1961.

Engineering the 1961 Recovery   The Fed lowered the discount rate in two steps to a low of 3 percent during the summer of 1960. As money was made more easily available, interest yields on 91-day Treasury bills came down to a low of 2.1 percent by January 1961. In the spring of 1961 the economy started a major upward trek aided by tax cuts.

Ending the 1961–66 Boom   The Kennedy administration altered the tax schedule in an attempt to add impetus to the boom. The boom ultimately culminated in a severe inflationary surge in 1966. Consumer prices rose an aggressive 4.5 percent between August 1965 and November 1966. Throughout the economic upswing the Fed had been gradually tightening money, raising the discount rate three times to 4½ percent by January 1966. The Johnson administration, then in office, went on record as expressing disfavor with the increases in the discount rate. The yields on 91-day Treasury bills climbed steadily to reach six percent by late summer of 1966, the highest level in 40 years. The stock market crossed over the imaginary barrier of Dow-Jones 1,000 in February 1966. This proved to be its top, being up 77 percent from its low of Dow-Jones 565, 64 months earlier, in October 1960.

During that long up move two sharp stock market sell-offs occurred. The first sell-off started in November 1961 at Dow-Jones 741 and culminated in a panic in June 1962 at Dow-Jones 525, down 29 percent in seven months. There have been many Monday-morning-quarterback commentaries of that particular market drop, ranging from an overvalued market in which the Dow-Jones Industrial Average was selling twenty-four times earnings, to a loss of investor confidence because of a unique dialogue between President Kennedy and Roger Blough of U.S. Steel, and to S.E.C. stock market investigations. The second stock market sell-off started in May 1965 at Dow-Jones 944 and ended three months later in July 1965 at Dow-Jones 833, down 11 percent. The favorite explanation of a number of analysts for the 1965 decline continues to be the "disquieting similarities to the 1920's" speech of Federal Reserve Board Chairman William McChesney Martin.

Meanwhile, the Johnson administration was increasing the nation's involvement in Vietnam, causing increased expenses. Additionally, the Johnson administration couldn't resolve its dilemma as to whether or not to ask Congress for a tax surcharge to pay for the Vietnam expenses as requested publicly by the Fed and many economists. The leading economic indicators ultimately peaked in September 1966. Industrial production crested two months later, in November 1966, similarly with unemployment, which gave its lowest reading of 3.5 percent. From this point the nation entered what has been termed a "mini-recession."

The 1966 Aftermaths of Tight Money   The stock market sold off 26 percent to Dow-Jones 736 by October 1966. The leading economic indicators registered their low point in March 1967. Industrial production bottomed in June 1967. Unemployment increased over one-fifth to 4.3 percent by October 1967. In 1966 housing starts in the construction industry fell nearly 50 percent.

New economic lessons were learned by the Fed from near-panic conditions that erupted both in the normally staid bond market and in banking and insurance circles in August and September 1966. A month earlier, in July 1966, the Fed had lowered the yield on certificates of deposit offered by banks to reduce a rate war for public deposits between the banks and the savings-and-loans institutions. The reduced bank yield disenchanted savers, who astutely withdrew large deposits from the banks. These deposits were shrewdly relocated in higher-yielding instruments such as 91-day Treasury bills and corporate bonds. Cash-hungry business corporations, needing day-to-day capital, suddenly found the money well at the banks to be more like a dry hole. Result—*the credit crunch of 1966.*

Engineering the 1967 Recovery   The Fed lowered the discount rate to 4 percent by the middle of 1967. They reduced the yields on 91-day Treasury bills to 3½ percent by June 1967, an indication of easier money conditions. In the summer of 1967 the nation's economy resumed its upward path.

In April 1968, after one year of debate, Congress passed a tax surcharge. Then the Fed found itself in a dilemma between two conflicting economic theories. Classical economic theory held that the tax surcharge, by itself, could produce tight money, which in turn could trigger the unpleasantness of a business slowdown. New economic research data suggested that if the Fed overexpanded the money supply to blunt the slowdown possibilities of the tax surcharge, inflation would probably worsen. No one knew for sure what economic patterns would result as the Fed had never steered the economy through this unique set of conditions. The Fed voted to cast its lot with the classical economists and started to expand the money supply aggressively.

Ending the 1967–69 Boom   In the eyes of the Federal Reserve Board the inflationary pressures became overwhelmingly apparent by late 1968. Consumer prices had increased almost 8 percent from April 1967 to December 1968.

During that time the Johnson administration had attempted to sustain a "guns and butter" economy—keep the home folks happy and finance the Vietnam war. Unfortunately the administration's plans did not work out, and with greater misfortune, Vietnam's costs and involvements were underestimated. The Fed, concerned with mitigating the slowdown aspects of the tax surcharge, poured too much money into the economy (as they later publicly admitted).

Business boomed in late 1967 and 1968. The worst inflation in seventeen years took hold. In late 1968, with unprecedented publicity, the seven-member Federal Reserve Board of Governors (*all appointed by Democratic Presidents*) voted firmly to restrict credit with the announced aim of containing the inflation. The discount rate was raised four times, to 6 percent by the spring of 1969. The yield on 91-day Treasury bills rose to almost 9 percent by December 1969, demonstrating the intense tightness of money. Earlier, in January 1969, the Republican Nixon administration had taken office and had decided to aid the Fed by proposing a balanced budget, which reduced federal spending.

At this point in our summary the Composite Index of the New York Stock Exchange will replace the Dow-Jones Industrial Average in describing the movement of the stock market, as it more accurately reflects the up-and-down swings.

The New York Composite Index peaked in December 1968 at 61.27, up 55 percent from its low of 39.37, registered twenty-six months earlier, in October 1966. Unemployment rendered its lowest figure of 3.2 percent in February 1969. Industrial production topped out in July 1969. The leading economic indicators crested in September 1969. The business downturn was underway.

The 1969–70 Aftermath of Tight Money   The stock market as measured by the New York Composite Index sold off 35 percent by late May 1970 to 37.69 and also went under its October 1966 lows. (It's a statistical aberration that a stock price move from 40 up to 60 is a 50 percent increase, while a move from 60 down to 40 is a 33 percent drop.) The stock market decline lasted eighteen months and was the most severe in some thirty-odd years. The leading economic indicators bottomed in October 1970. Industrial production touched bottom in November 1970. Unemployment almost doubled, to a 6.2 percent reading by December 1970. Housing starts declined 33 percent, touching their low in January 1970.

Another chapter in new economic know-how was written for the Fed in 1970 concerning the bond market. Historically the bond market usually bottomed and rallied prior to the stock market. Such was not the case in 1970. The bond market, as measured by the Dow-Jones Average of forty bonds, registered its low of 64.36 in mid-August 1970, a number of months *after* the stock market registered its low.

Engineering the 1970–71 Recovery   The Fed reduced the discount rate five times to 4¾ percent by February 1971. Money was made readily available at the banks to cause interest yields on 91-day Treasury bills to dip under 3.4 percent in March 1971. The nation's economy started its uptrend in late 1970.

The knowledge and experience gained during the "1966 credit crunch" was well used by the Fed in June 1970, when the Penn-Central Transportation Company went bankrupt. The Penn-Central was forced into bankruptcy by its inability to refinance $152 million of its commercial paper. Such paper (corporate promissory notes) is usually an IOU, being short-term, and unsecured in that it is issued on "faith" with no assets pledged in case of default. The commercial paper market, amounting to almost $40 billion, was suddenly plunged into shock as well-financed corporations, which usually depended on the commercial paper market for day-to-day operating capital, found themselves unable to place their paper as cautious and injured buyers retreated to the side-lines. The makings of a major financial crisis were brewing. The Fed promptly resolved the problem by lifting the interest ceilings that banks might pay on short-term (eighty-nine days or less) certificates of deposit of $100,000 or more. The Fed-imposed interest ceiling at the banks had been 6½ percent and the next day, in open competition with commercial paper, the banks were offer-ing 8 percent plus. The crisis passed. In retrospect, it appeared to be the emotional low point of the 1969–70 tight money period.

The Behind-the-Scenes Role of the Fed Prior to the 1971 Wage and Price Freeze

On a quiet Sunday night, in mid-August 1971, via a nationwide television and radio broadcast, President Nixon startled and stunned the world by announcing that among other things he was:

* Ordering an immediate 90-day wage, price and rent freeze,
* Devaluing the dollar by cutting it loose from the historic $35-an-ounce price,
* Imposing a 10 percent surcharge on imports,
* Asking Congress to restore the investment-tax credit at a temporary rate of 10 percent, and to repeal the 7 percent auto-excise tax, and to speed tax cuts.

Administration spokesmen stated that the decisions announced by the President had been under study for many weeks and months. Wage and price control guidelines, and Phases 1 and 2, became part of the American scene.

President's Actions Appear More Prompted by Federal Reserve Board Nowhere in any of the official statements was any mention made of any connection between the actions that President Nixon ordered and those specific policies which the Federal Reserve Board wanted.

The authors hold the opinion that the Federal Reserve Board was the "secret power behind the throne" who for fifteen months, starting in May 1970, cajoled, prodded and pushed the Nixon ad-ministration toward the dollar devaluation and the wage and price freeze.

Former Federal Reserve Board Chairman William McChesney Martin had often called gold that "barbarous relic." It was during his reign that a two-tier gold program and a unique *paper-gold* system termed Special Drawing Rights was originated for international trade following much gold turmoil in the late 1960's.

But the institution of the wage and price freeze gives the investor an important insight into the Fed's powers. Within three months after assuming the chairmanship of the Federal Reserve Board, Dr. Arthur F. Burns publicly began the Fed's subtle, slow and ultimately successful campaign to get the Nixon administration to institute wage and price controls already authorized by Congress.

Witness the following.

In May 1970, at Hot Springs, Virginia, Dr. Burns for the first time publicly commented on the possibility of an incomes-policy by stating: "Providing that such a policy stops well short of direct wage and price controls, it might speed us through this transitional period of cost-push inflation."

The opening shot of a major campaign had been fired.

Dr. Burns Concedes 1970 Business Recovery Is Lagging In December 1970, in a major speech at Los Angeles, Dr. Burns conceded that the 1970 business recovery was not proceeding on schedule. He stated that new economic problems existed and that the economic know-how to resolve them was embryonic, nonexistent or politically unpalatable. He said in Los Angeles:

> What I see clearly is the need for our nation to recognize that we are dealing, practically speaking, with a new problem—namely, persistent inflation in the face of substantial unemployment—and that the classical remedies may not work well enough or fast enough in this case. Monetary and fiscal policies can readily cope with inflation alone or with recession alone; but, within the limits of our national patience, they cannot by themselves now be counted on to restore full employment, without at the same time releasing a new wave of inflation. We therefore need to explore with an open mind what steps beyond monetary and fiscal policies may need to be taken by government. . . .

Dr. Burns then carefully outlined a detailed 11-point plan to reduce inflation, including instituting a national incomes policy through the *creation of a high level price and wage review board* which could rule on the feasibility of wage and price increases.

The Federal Reserve Board Tells Congress that the U.S. Needs an Incomes Policy In February 1971, under questioning at a Congressional Joint Economic Committee hearing on Capitol Hill, Dr. Burns officially refused to commit the independent Federal Reserve Board to full support of President Nixon's economic growth target. Of greater significance to investors was his politically powerful statement that it was the "considered judgment of the seven-man Federal Reserve Board that the U.S. should have an incomes policy. . . ."

In March 1971, testifying again before the Senate Banking Committee, Dr. Burns strongly renewed his call for an "incomes policy."

The political winds were now shifting. Dr. Burns appeared to be acquiring a powerful ally, namely the newly appointed Secretary of the Treasury, John B. Connally. Although Mr. Connally hadn't publicly endorsed a wage-price review board, he was letting it be known that he was an "activist" and would probably look with favor on the creation of such a board. On the other hand, the Nixon administration maintained its official opposition to the whole concept, with George P. Shultz, Director of the Office of Management and Budget, the staunchest and most vocal opponent.

Conflict Between President Nixon and Dr. Burns Becomes Public In late June 1971, the differences of opinion between President Nixon and Federal Reserve Board Chairman Burns about an incomes policy emerged into the open. President Nixon publicly announced his adamant refusal to institute a wage-price review board. In testimony before a full session of the Congressional Joint Economic Subcommittee, composed of representatives and senators, Dr. Burns specifically quarrelled with the President's refusal, stating that "without an incomes policy, or stronger governmental action in the wage-price field, the pace of inflation won't abate." Dr. Burns also went on record as saying that the restoration of the 7 percent investment tax credit, repealed on President Nixon's initiative two years earlier, should be considered.

AFL-CIO President George Meany Indirectly Supports Dr. Burns
In mid July 1971, Dr. Burns suddenly acquired a major and
wholly unexpected ally. During a television interview, AFL-CIO
President George Meany said he would impose overall wage and
price controls on the nation if he were President Nixon. Mr.
Meany stated, "If I were in his position, I would impose controls
at this time. I don't see any other way this situation [inflation] is
going to get under control."

Open Rift Between White House and the Federal Reserve Board
By late July 1971, the economic rift between the Nixon administration and the Federal Reserve Board had widened considerably on what policy to pursue to reduce inflation. At the White
House, Press Secretary Ronald Ziegler declared that very good
inroads were being made against the nation's economic problems.
On national television, Treasury Secretary Connally contended
that substantial progress had taken place in the anti-inflation fight
during the first half of 1971. But on Capitol Hill, again in testimony before the congressional joint economics committee, Dr.
Burns implied that the Nixon administration was in error, stating,
"I wish I could report to you that we were making substantial
progress against inflation. I cannot do so. The rules of economics
aren't quite working the way they used to. Inflation is proceeding
at both an unacceptable and a dangerous rate. Let's not lose too
much time and give an incomes policy a fair try."

Fed Imposes Tight Money By late July 1971, money was tight in
the banks owing to Fed policies. The Nixon administration was
aware of these publicly available facts. The Federal Funds Rate*
touched 6½ percent. Ninety-one day Treasury bills rose above the
5.6 percent level, signaling tight money. The nation's banks reported a Net Borrowed Reserve position of almost $1 billion. The
Federal Open Market Committee voted to restrain the growth of
money. The prime rate had been raised twice to 6 percent. The
Fed raised the discount rate to 5 percent. And the stock market

---

* For explanations of the Federal Funds Rate, Prime Rate, Net Borrowed
Reserves, the Federal Open Market Committee, and other tools of the Fed,
see Chapters 7–11.

was declining. All the signs of tight money and a business slow-down were present.

The full reasons why the Federal Reserve Board was tightening money are subject to conjecture. Perhaps it felt that the money supply was expanding too fast and needed to be curbed. Perhaps they wanted to remind the administration of the Fed mandate to act as a watchdog over the nation's economic growth. Perhaps it was resigned to the assumption that the Nixon administration wasn't going to institute an incomes policy to help break the back of inflation. If such was the case, only the heavy-handed and re-cession-producing tight-money policies of the Fed could possibly do the job.

If the Fed's tight-money policies prevailed for a number of months, it was believed that President Nixon could face the uncomfortable probability of running for re-election in November 1972 in the midst of a recession. Perhaps President Nixon recalled that in his "Six Crises" book (New York: Doubleday & Co., Inc., 1962) he told how, years earlier in 1960, Dr. Arthur F. Burns, then his economics advisor, had predicted that Election Day in Novem-ber of 1960 would probably take place in a recessionary atmo-sphere. This was due to the then prevailing tight-money policy of the Fed. It is a matter of record that John F. Kennedy defeated Richard M. Nixon in a close election, with the 1960 recession serving as a major campaign issue.

Nixon Administration Considers Doubling the Size of the Federal Reserve Board   In the last week of July 1971, the Nixon adminis-tration "counterattacked." A close White House source "leaked" a political trial balloon hinting that President Nixon was considering asking Congress to double the size of the Federal Reserve Board and to put it under the direct, close control of the President, thereby curbing the Fed's independence.

This contemplated action to curb the Fed's power was the third such action proposed in the last ten years. In April 1962, President John F. Kennedy sent Congress a proposal to give each new Presi-dent the opportunity to select his own Federal Reserve Board chairman, with the chairman's term running for the same four years as the President's. That proposal was rejected. In January 1964, Representative Patman, Chairman of the House Banking and Currency Committee, opened hearings on moves to curb the independence of the Federal Reserve System. Those hearings died.

Many believed that if President Nixon's new proposal was actually put before Congress, it had the potential of igniting a controversy rivaling President Franklin D. Roosevelt's attempt in the 1930's to pack the Supreme Court.

In the first week of August 1971, the White House, apparently stung by the criticisms of its proposal, backed down and announced that President Nixon didn't intend to take under consideration any proposals for curbing the Federal Reserve Board's independence or increasing the number of its members.

President Nixon Adopts an Incomes Policy   The next week, on Sunday night, President Nixon went on national television and gave the Fed its often requested incomes policy by announcing a 90-day wage and price freeze and other major economic measures.

The Fed—After the 1971 Wage, Price Freeze   It is interesting to note that signs of easy money policies on the part of the Fed began to appear almost immediately after the President's proclamation. Within a week, the yields on 91-day Treasury bills dropped from 5.3 percent to 4.7 percent and by the first week of September it was under 4.5 percent. The banks found themselves amply provided with surplus funds so that the prime rate was reduced twice to under 5.5 percent by the middle of October. The Fed lowered its discount rate to 4¾ percent in the middle of November and reduced margin to purchase stocks from 65 percent to 55 percent in the first week of December. And the Federal Funds Rate trended down to under 5 percent. Practically all of the signs of major economic stimulation were present.

This should be enough to demonstrate to anyone the Federal Reserve Board's power—both direct and indirect—to influence production, employment and prices in the United States.

6

Five Guidelines to Aid You in How to Recognize Changes in Federal Reserve Policy

Five simple guidelines to aid you in spotting and interpreting changes in Federal Reserve policy are outlined in this chapter. The five guidelines, *used together,* consistently pinpoints shifts in Fed policy as the pendulum swings from easy money to tight money and back again to easy money. Each guideline is quite easy to understand. When one becomes fully acquainted with the five guidelines, he is normally able to keep abreast of the Fed's current policies by being a good reader of the day's news.

A complete chapter is later devoted to each guideline, explaining and illustrating each one in considerable detail. Additionally you will find specific detailed descriptions of how these guidelines have proven effective in the past so that you can use them to judge the future.

"Freedom-of-Information" Law Now Helps Investors to Interpret Federal Reserve Policy

Interpreting Federal Reserve policies became significantly easier in June 1967. At that time, in compliance with the "Freedom-of-Information" law that took effect on July 4, 1967 (a rather symbolic date), the Fed started to make available to the public the reports of its policy decisions. Figure 5 is a copy of *The Wall Street Journal* story indicating the actions that some leading U.S.

Court Fight Threatened If Reserve Board Panel Keeps Meetings Secret

Rep. Moss Says Free-Information Law Will Apply to Open Market Unit, Which Controls Credit

By a WALL STREET JOURNAL Staff Reporter

WASHINGTON — A leading Congressional sponsor of the recently enacted "freedom-of-information" law says the Federal Reserve System may face a court battle if—as it has often indicated—it wants to continue to keep secret the records of its Open Market Committee

Rep. Moss (D., Calif.) said the law, when it takes effect next July 4, "will apply to the Federal Open Market Committee." In response to a request for his views from Chairman Patman of the House Banking Committee, Rep. Moss said, "Any effort on the part of the Federal Reserve System . . . to impose restrictions on the availability of its records would be subject to review by the Federal courts upon complaint of any member of the public."

Rep. Patman (D., Texas) sent a copy of the Moss reply to Federal Reserve Board Chairman William C. Martin along with a letter asking that the minutes of the Open Market Committee be made available to Congress under the freedom-of-information law. Rep. Patman requested that the records and minutes of the committee be made available immediately to Congress because it was the clear intent of the bill "to remove the shrouds of secrecy" from the committee's operations.

The 12-man Open Market Committee meets in Washington every three weeks to decide whether to tighten or ease credit by selling or buying Government Securities in the open market. Immediate knowledge of the board's intentions would be extremely valuable to financial market men.

Currently, the board publishes a record of committee actions in its annual report and has made available to the public minutes of meetings which relate to discussion preceding action, through 1960. The reports are available in Washington and at the Federal Reserve Banks.

A board spokesman said that releasing information in other than the present manner could "defeat policy objectives" of the committee by providing speculators with advance knowledge of committee plans.

FIGURE 5

From *The Wall Street Journal,* August 15, 1966

Congressmen were willing to employ in mid-1966 to force the Fed to divulge its plans.

Federal Reserve Policy Decisions Published After a 90-Day News Blackout

Figure 6 contains unique data in that it is the *first* publication of Fed policies, which were formerly kept secret. Please note that the decision publicized in Figure 6 was ninety days old and was being revealed to the public for the very first time. The reasoning behind the ninety-day news blackout was that the Fed apparently convinced the congressional leaders that it was imperative to be secretive so as to prevent the plans to buy or sell billions of dollars of U.S. government bonds from going awry. Advance knowledge of the Fed's intentions could have permitted speculators to gain giant windfalls. Additionally the actual execution of the plans would probably have encountered difficulties in the money markets. Along these lines, in March 1967, a congressional committee voted to investigate an alleged information leak within the Federal Reserve System that involved $2½ billion in government bonds. The results of that investigation have never been disclosed.

Brief Description of the Five Guidelines

Guideline One: Know Whether the Federal Open Market Committee Is Voting for Easy Money or Tight Money This is the most accurate and factual guideline in that it is specific and straight from the horse's mouth. There is usually little, if any, judgment required on your part to ascertain current Fed policy. You are told what it is.

Guideline number one states: "Know whether the Federal Open Market Committee is voting for easy money or tight money." So the first question is: What is the Federal Open Market Committee?

The Federal Open Market Committee (hereafter referred to as "FOMC") is a major policy-making committee within the Federal Reserve System. The FOMC usually meets every three weeks. It was specifically created by an act of Congress in August 1935. Congress' intent was for the FOMC to direct open-market operations. The important effects of open-market operations on the investor will be touched when Guideline number five is explained in Chapter Eleven.

Reserve Board Acted With Near Unanimity On Easing of Credit
* * *
Formerly Secret Data Shows Only 3 Members Failed to Back Move in First Quarter

By a WALL STREET JOURNAL *Staff Reporter*

WASHINGTON—The Federal Reserve Board pursued with near unanimity a policy of easing credit to help a sluggish economy in the first quarter, newly released records of the board's open market committee disclosed.

In compliance with a "freedom of information law" that takes effect next week, the Federal Reserve said it plans to make available to the public reports of previously "supersecret" meetings of its open market committee 90 days after it meets. Previously, information on the meetings, held every three weeks, were made available only in the Federal Reserve Board's annual report to Congress.

At the meetings, the 12-man committee decides whether to tighten or ease credit by selling or buying Government securities in the open market. When it buys securities, it pumps money into the economy; selling has the opposite effect.

The policy directive resulting from the committee's Jan. 10 meeting was to conduct open market operations to ease conditions in the money market.

Three committeemen—former members Charles N. Sherpardson, Watrous H. Irons and William F. Treiber—dissented from this action. They preferred not to relax monetary restraint further at that time because of the balance-of-payments situation and the "desirability of awaiting further information" on Federal taxes before changing the monetary policy, according to the report.

The U.S. has a continuing balance-of-payments deficit, which occurs when foreigners acquire more dollars than they return to the U.S. in all transactions. The Federal Reserve Board, while moving to ease credit, has been wary of lowering too sharply short-term interest rates in the U.S., lest there occur a sudden outflow of dollars to higher-yielding investments abroad.

Lone Dissenter

In subsequent reports, there was almost no dissent. Only one committee member, Reserve Board member George W. Mitchell, voted against the Feb. 7 policy decision to maintain "prevailing conditions of ease in the money market." The committee noted "a continuing serious balance-of-payments problem" and advocated a position to foster "noninflationary economic expansion and progress toward a reasonable equilibrium" in the balance of payments, the report said. Mr. Mitchell argued for stronger action to ease the money market because he feared the possibility of an economic downturn in the first half.

The vote was unanimous for the March 7 policy statement, which was, in effect, to maintain the position of ease in the money market.

There weren't any dissenters from the April 4 committee directive adopting a "policy to foster money and credit conditions, including bank credit growth, conducive to combating the effects of weakening tendencies in the economy. . ." The committee directed that the board's open market operations be conducted to ease money-market conditions even further, the report showed.

Some Records Still Secret

In addition to the earlier release of open market committee reports, the Federal Reserve will make certain unpublished records available upon request. Under the old rules, unpublished records generally weren't made available to the public without express approval of the board and the open market committee. Some records, however, are exempt from disclosure under the law.

The open market committee is composed of the seven members of the Federal Reserve Board, the president of the New York Federal Reserve Bank, and, on a rotating basis, presidents of four of the other 11 district reserve banks.

FIGURE 6

From *The Wall Street Journal*, June 30, 1967

The FOMC is composed of twelve members. Eight are permanent and four alternate. The eight permanent members comprise the seven governors of the Federal Reserve Board, and the eighth is the president of the Federal Reserve Bank of New York, who also serves as the committee's permanent vice-chairman. Traditionally the FOMC's chairman is also the chairman of the Board of Governors. The presidents of the eleven other Federal Reserve Banks rotate as voting committee members in the four nonpermanent seats. As you can readily see from the makeup of the FOMC, its members are the key figures in the United States Central Banking System. Are they powerful? *Yes! They essentially control 85 percent of the money on deposit in U.S. banks.*

In 1963 the Federal Reserve Bank of New York published a pamphlet entitled *Open Market Operations.* The booklet described, in some detail, the inner workings and character of the FOMC. Selected excerpts from this booklet are given below. These excerpts rather fully divulge the FOMC's massive influence on the nation's economy and ultimately, as many now believe, on the stock market. It is important for the investor to be fully cognizant of the FOMC's wide range of powers. Quoting from the booklet:

> The Federal Open Market Committee, or FOMC as it is known, meets every 3 weeks as a rule, in Washington, D.C. These meetings have come to be the forum for exploring all aspects of the economy's performance and discussing what over-all monetary policy would be, which tools are most appropriate, and what the timing of their use should be. . . .
>
> Before each meeting of the FOMC, each President of each Federal Reserve Bank customarily meets with his staff to review the state of the economy and to discuss the most appropriate course for monetary policy to follow. A similar review takes place at the Board of Governors. . . .
>
> By the time the members of the Committee assemble in Washington, they are well prepared to deliberate. Each member of the Board of Governors and each Reserve Bank President then gives his views on current economic conditions and monetary policy. . . .
>
> The Chairman, as a rule, presents his appraisal last, after which he formulates the consensus of the meeting as to the relative degree of *ease or tightness* [authors' italics] which the committee wishes to foster in the national money market during the period until the next meeting.

In 1969 the booklet was revised and reprinted. The phrase "relative degree of ease or tightness" was deleted. The following vaguely worded phrase was used: "vote the directive that best embodies the Committee's intent." In the author's opinion, the original "ease or tightness" phrase more accurately describes the FOMC's power and actions.

Do you think your success as an investor in the stock market could be markedly increased if you became more aware of the decisions of the FOMC?

For most investors we believe the answer to this question is a resounding yes. The FOMC is considered by many astute investors to be the Fed's *key strategy* committee. The actual decisions to tighten money, which can cause a recession and a probable stock-market decline, or to loosen money, which may start a boom and a potential stock-market rally, are traditionally made when the FOMC meets.

The four remaining guidelines require you to use a little judgment so as to interpret Fed policy. The purpose of providing you with these four additional guidelines is to attempt to help you fill the information gap caused by the ninety-day news blackout. You will not always make the correct judgment using guidelines two through five. However, at the end of the ninety-day "secret" period, when the policy decisions of the FOMC are actually published, you should be able to check your accuracy. Today's stock market tends to be fast-moving. Hence, it is necessary for the alert investor to have these guidelines so as to make decisions.

Guideline Two: Public Comments by Members of the Federal Reserve Board of Governors   When any of the seven governors talks for the public record, he's quite often—but not always—giving his opinion on a major policy that may have originated in a meeting still in the "dark period."

Guideline Three: "Planted" News Items   At key turning points in Fed policy, reputable major newspapers and magazines sometimes publish news stories that quote a "senior Fed official," or an "anonymous banker" closely connected to the Fed.

Guideline Four: Short-term Interest-Rate Changes   You need to know if interest rates on 91-day Treasury bills and commercial paper are above or below the interest rates prevailing at the banks or savings-and-loan associations. This can tell you where the Fed may be "leading" the public to invest its cash and savings. If the bank interest rate is higher and thus more lucrative to the saver than the yield on 91-day Treasury bills and commercial paper rates, you may judge easy money. If the 91-day Treasury bills and commercial rates are more lucrative, you could possibly judge tighter money as money is drawn out of the banks.

Guideline Five: Know the Money Tools of the Fed and How They Work The Fed's primary tools, which they use to influence the supply of money and credit in the United States, are:

1. the discount rate
2. the prime rate
3. reserve requirements
4. bank interest rates (regulation Q)
5. margin requirements (regulations T and U)
6. open-market operations
7. reserves and borrowings
8. federal funds rates
9. money supply.

When analysts state that the Fed is doing something, they are usually referring to the policies of the Board of Governors and the FOMC. The knack of gaining the important insight into understanding the Fed is in knowing the "special money paths" through which the Fed channels its power and influence. The five guidelines, to be covered in detail in the next chapters, are designed to increase your knowledge of these paths. We shall discuss these guidelines primarily from the point of view of an investor. Extensive cause-and-effect relationships, elaborate descriptions of the mechanics of operation and economic arguments pro and con will be put aside. In the Selected Readings at the end of this book, those who elect to pursue any of the subjects in greater detail will find a number of worthwhile books listed.

7

Guideline One: Know If the Federal Open Market Committee Is Voting for Easy Money or Tight Money

How Do You Find Out If the FOMC Is Voting for Easy Money or Tight Money?

There are two ways of securing this important information.

First, you can subscribe to the *Federal Reserve Bulletin,* printed monthly by the Federal Reserve System, which publishes the policies decided at each FOMC meeting. However, you are faced with an unfortunate time lag. The "Record of Policy Actions of the Federal Open Market Committee" is published belatedly in the *Federal Reserve Bulletin* a number of weeks after the end of the ninety-day blackout period for each FOMC meeting. (For information on subscribing to the bulletin, refer to Selected Readings at the end of this book.)

Second, a number of reputable, major newspapers such as *The Wall Street Journal, The Los Angeles Times, The New York Times,* etc., often—*but not always*—publish the pith of the FOMC policy decisions, sometimes with a financial reporter's comments, as soon as the news blackout is lifted.

Figure 7 shows the news story published in *The Wall Street Journal* on February 25, 1969 that reported on the FOMC meeting of December 17, 1968. The sixth paragraph reads:

> The December 17, 1968 meeting of the Open Market Committee, the report made clear, was the one that launched the Reserve System into actively tightening credit.

Bank Reserves Boost Studied in December By Federal Unit in Its War on Inflation

By a WALL STREET JOURNAL *Staff Reporter*

WASHINGTON — The Federal Reserve Board disclosed that in mid-December it was considering an increase in commercial bank reserve requirements as a means of escalating its fight against inflation.

Because raising the percentage of deposits that banks have to keep idle immediately reduces their ability to lend, such action generally is regarded as the most drastic form of credit tightening that the board can use.

The official word that such a move was under consideration came in the board's regular release on deliberations of the system's "Open Market Committee," which includes the seven board members and five of the 12 district Reserve Bank presidents.

The report showed that, as of Dec. 17, some of the authorities favored a "moderate" increase in reserve requirements as well as a discount rate higher than the 5.5% the board approved later that same day, an increase of one quarter point. The discount rate is the interest charged by district Reserve Banks on temporary loans to member commercial banks.

Previous Boost 13 Months Ago

The most recent change in reserve requirements was in January 1968, when the ratio was raised to 17% from 16.5% against demand, or checking-account type, deposits at banks in larger cities, and to 12.5% from 12% at "country" banks; the increases affected only those with such deposits of more than $5 million.

The Dec. 17 meeting of the Open Market Committee, the report made clear, was the one that launched the Reserve System into actively tightening credit. All members except chairman William McChesney Martin, who was absent, voted to seek "firmer conditions in money and short-term credit markets." Basically, this involves selling Treasury securities from the system's portfolio in order to sop up funds that banks otherwise might lend.

The policy decision at that time was based on the finding "that over-all economic activity is expanding rapidly and that upward pressures on prices and costs are persisting," while the U.S. foreign-trade surplus remained "very small" and growth in the money supply was accelerating.

In view of the "unexpected strength" of the economy, the report showed, the committee unanimously decided on a "firmer" open market policy, but some favored a broader combination of policy actions "to dampen the prevailing inflation psychology." The committee was told that the board, itself, planned to "take action" on the discount rate shortly after that meeting "and also to consider the desirability of a moderate increase in member-bank reserve requirements."

November Deliberations Told

The apprehensive mood about inflation was in sharp contrast with that evinced at the previous meeting Nov. 26, on which the board also reported yesterday. At that time, a majority of the committee expressed belief that the economy "is moderating somewhat further from its rapid pace earlier in the year," and thought evidences of slower growth "were likely to become more pronounced in coming months." In arguing against a policy change then, the majority cited "the recent turbulence and continuing uncertainties in foreign-exchange markets" and the approach of "peak seasonal pressures" in financial markets.

So a majority, comprising the seven board members and Hugh D. Galusha, president of the Minneapolis district bank, voted to maintain "about the prevailing conditions" in money markets. Dissenting on grounds that the economy's expansion "was likely to remain excessive" under current policies were four district bank presidents—Alfred Hayes of New York, W. Braddock Hickman of Cleveland, Monroe Kimbrel of Atlanta and Frank E. Morris of Boston.

The policy record usually is released after a 90-day lag, but the mid-December session was covered along with the November one in a single report to complete the publication of calendar-year 1968 deliberations, a spokesman added.

FIGURE 7

From *The Wall Street Journal,* February 25, 1969

Length of News Blackout Varies

There are a number of points of pertinent interest in the article illustrated in Figure 7. On the date it was published (February 25, 1969) the stock market as measured by the Dow-Jones Industrial Average closed at 899. Fifteen months later, in late May 1970, the Dow reached its low of 631, down 268 points. Assuming that you accepted the principles of the influence of the Fed, you might have made decisions that would have changed your investment posture. Another point is that the news blackout for the December 1968 meeting lasted only *sixty days*. The facts are that the FOMC met in mid-December 1968. The news of its policy decisions was released in late February 1969, sixty days later, not ninety as usual. Hence, you should be constantly on the alert that there is nothing sacred about the ninety-day dark period. It is voluntary on the part of the Fed and self-imposed and has been shortened to suit their ends. In November 1968 some Fed officials considered reducing the secret period to sixty days but nothing came of it. The authors' opinion is that a thirty- to forty-five-day news blackout should suffice.

Examples of Newspaper Reports of Some "Turning Point" FOMC Meetings

Figure 8 contains a news story published November 11, 1969, describing the decision to continue the then existing tight-money policy that was agreed upon at the FOMC meeting held approximately ninety days earlier, in August 1969. The Dow closed at 779 that day with lower markets—as history bore out—yet to come. At that time much confusion existed in investors' minds as to whether or not the Fed was changing its policy.

Figure 9 shows the news story published May 12, 1970, that described the first official news that the FOMC had changed its policy from tight money to easy money. This easy money decision—of major import to investors—was made at the February 1970 FOMC meeting, about ninety days earlier. The Dow closed at 704 on May 12, 1970, and perhaps it's a coincidence that ten trading days later the bottom of the 1968–70 bear market was established.

Understanding the Format of FOMC Policy Directives

The format of "The Record of Policy Actions of the FOMC" as published in the *Federal Reserve Bulletin* tends to fit a mold. The first few pages discuss, in most enlightening detail, the prevailing economic climate, both domestically and internationally. Then comes the "meat and potatoes" information for the investor. The FOMC states its position about easy money or tight money in this manner:

The Committee agreed that it would be desirable at this time to . . .

whereupon it then outlines their general intentions. To accomplish their general intentions, the FOMC issues a policy directive to the Federal Reserve Bank of New York. The directive charts the path for Open Market Operations. As the directive may require the buying or selling of billions of dollars of U.S. government securities, you can well understand the need for the news blackout.

Understanding the Broad Language of FOMC Policy Directives

The FOMC tends to avoid making black and white statements about its intentions to ease or tighten money. Instead, the language used in its policy directives is couched in broad terms. If you understand these terms, you are closer to "speaking the language of the natives," and thus you increase your knowledge of their intentions.

Here is a brief explanation of some of the language used in some of the 1970–71 directives:

1. *maintain firm conditions in the money market* means "tight money" (January 1970 meeting).
2. *moderate growth in money and bank credit with a view toward somewhat less firm conditions in the money market* means "a trend toward easy money" (February 1970 meeting).
3. *the Committee seeks to promote some easing of conditions in credit markets and somewhat greater growth in money over the months ahead* means "easy money" (August 1970 meeting).

Open Market Group Of Federal Reserve Backed Tight Credit

Two Dissenters at Aug. 12 Meeting Of Committee Saw Restrictive Money Policy Being Heightened

By a WALL STREET JOURNAL *Staff Reporter*

WASHINGTON—The Federal Reserve System's Open Market Committee voted at its Aug. 12 meeting to retain firm credit policy, but two members dissented, arguing that this might have the effect of making monetary policy "more and more restrictive."

The two dissenters in the 10-to-2 vote were Reserve Board members Sherman J. Maisel and George W. Mitchell. The committee's statement said the dissenters felt "trends in monetary aggregates and the availability of credit were indicative of increased tightening that would be heightened if money market conditions were maintained at the levels called for in the directive favored by the majority."

Thus, "in order to guard against an undesired further tightening," the two members favored a directive that would have operations "moderate such contractive tendencies, if prospective declines in monetary aggregates should in fact occur, while maintaining the position of overall monetary and credit restraint."

Reports on the committee's deliberations are issued about 90 days after a meeting. To ease credit, the Federal Reserve generally buys existing Treasury securities on the market with newly created funds; when tightening credit, the system typically sells such securities from its portfolio, thus leaving commercial banks with less lendable cash.

The committee statement on the Aug. 12 meeting indicated that consideration of any change in policy was geared toward a possible easing rather than further restrictions. The committee agreed that any further increase in monetary restraint wouldn't "be warranted at present," the statement said, while "a majority of the members thought that action to ease market conditions would not be warranted now in view of the persistence of inflationary pressures and the risk that such action would encourage a new surge of inflationary expectations."

FIGURE 8

From *The Wall Street Journal*, November 11, 1969

Easier Credit Was Voted at Feb. 10 Meeting Of Reserve Board Open Market Committee

By a WALL STREET JOURNAL *Staff Reporter*

WASHINGTON — The Federal Reserve Board's Open Market Committee confirmed that it had voted to ease credit at its Feb. 10 meeting, with three of the 12 members dissenting.

The directive of the committee's majority said the open market operations should be "conducted with a view to moving gradually towards somewhat less firm conditions in the money market." But it quickly added that this move would be "modified promptly to resist any tendency for money and bank credit to deviate significantly from a moderate growth pattern."

The Federal Reserve in recent weeks, in fact, worked hard at reducing a large and unwanted bulge in monetary aggregates—money supply and bank credit— that had occurred in late March due to various technical factors. That operational action placed a tight pinch on the banking system and money market.

The Feb. 10 meeting was the committee's first under the chairmanship of Arthur F. Burns, who took over on Feb. 1. Mr. Burns already has indicated that the committee eased credit at that meeting.

Secret Meetings

Policy meetings of the committee are usually secret, and results aren't released for at least 90 days after the sessions have been held. To ease credit, the committee generally buys existing securities on the market with newly created funds.

The board said the committee concluded that "in light of the latest economic developments and current business outlook" it was "appropriate to move gradually toward less restraint." The majority said that money-market conditions should be "shaded in the direction of less firmness—with a view to encouraging moderate growth in money and bank credit over the months ahead."

But the committee said this move to easing "should be implemented cautiously with close attention to successive estimates of growth rates and the monetary and credit aggregates."

Dissenting from the directive were board members Andrew F. Brimmer; Alfred Hayes, president of the New York Federal Reserve Bank, and Philip P. Coldwell, president of the Dallas Reserve Bank. The Open Market Committee consists of the full seven-man board and five presidents of the 12 Federal Reserve banks.

Premature Move Feared

The board said the dissenters believed "any overt move toward less firm money market conditions was premature at this time and could strengthen market expectations of substantial easing."

The dissenters recognized some weakness in the economy but said they were "impressed by the strength of the inflationary expectations, the continuing increases in prices and wages, business plans for a large volume of capital spending, and the prospectively large balance-of-payments deficit."

Agreeing with the majority that some growth in the monetary and credit aggregates was desirable, the minority insisted that this objective could be "covered adequately" by a directive similar to the committee's January order.

At the Jan. 15 meeting, the committee said it would stress such measures as the money supply over its traditional view of money-market conditions, such as availability and cost of credit.

In conclusion, the dissenters said they "preferred not to relax restraint at this time because of the risk of encouraging resurgent growth in over-all demand before inflationary pressures and expectations have been adequately dampened."

In reaching the decision to ease credit, the committee noted that the Administration had forecast small budget surpluses in both the fiscal 1970 and fiscal 1971 budgets, although the dissenters expressed "concern about the prospects for adequate fiscal restraint." Recently, high Administration officials have conceded that both the fiscal 1970 and fiscal 1971 budgets are likely to show deficits.

FIGURE 9

From *The Wall Street Journal,* May 12, 1970

4. *maintaining the recently attained money market conditions* means "no change" (December 1970 meeting).

5. *to attaining temporarily some minor firming in money market conditions* means a shift away from "easy money" towards *"tight money"* (April 1971 meeting; see Appendix I, Arrow No. 1).

6. *to achive more moderate growth* means to dampen further the growth of the nation's money supply (August 1971 meeting).

In Appendix I, you will find a completely unedited example of a "Record of Policy Actions of the FOMC" as it actually appeared in the *Federal Reserve Bulletin* for July 1971.

Individual Votes of the Twelve Members of the FOMC Are Noted

An interesting aspect of the FOMC policy directives is that the voting position of each of the twelve members is noted. Additionally the dissenting voters may have the reasons for their position officially noted in detail.

The Importance of Guidelines Two Through Five in Helping You to "See Into" the News Blackout Period

As mentioned earlier, the key purpose of guidelines two through five is to help you see into the sixty to ninety day news blackout. To give you an analogy, a good physician seeks to diagnose a patient's illness by analyzing the symptoms. Laboratory tests will confirm the preliminary diagnosis or cause the physician to look elsewhere. So it is with guidelines two through five. For example, you know from the news story published in late-February 1969 (Figure 7) that the FOMC decided in mid-December 1968 to tighten money. Your knowledge of guidelines two through five could have helped you significantly in spotting this major policy shift to tight money *prior* to the news officially being published.

Example of the Value of Guidelines Two Through Five

Sometimes the major newspapers do not publish the policy decisions of the FOMC. Unfortunately this lapse can occur even at key turning points in money policy. How then can you protect yourself? The authors believe that your main protection is a thorough knowledge of guidelines two through five.

A pertinent, glaring example of the major newspapers' and magazines' dropping the ball in reporting the news on a major change in the FOMC policy occurred in early July 1971. Here are the particulars. On Tuesday, July 6, 1971, the Dow-Jones news ticker, which is the "broad news tape" displayed in most brokerage offices to a select few, reported that the FOMC had voted *temporarily to tighten money*. This important policy decision was made at the FOMC's meeting in early April 1971. This was the FOMC's first shift toward tight money since late 1968, and it had major implications for the serious investor.

Yet the majority of newspapers and magazines did not carry a single line of type referring directly to this FOMC meeting or to the temporary tight-money policy. If you had been aware of guidelines two through five, you probably would have "sensed" this important policy change, and you might have taken steps affecting your investments.

On July 6, 1971, the Dow closed at 892. Lower markets loomed ahead. By late November 1971 the Dow touched 793, down almost 100 points in about five months.

8

Guideline Two: Public Comments by Members of the Federal Reserve Board of Governors

Pay Heed When a Governor Speaks

When one of the seven members of the Board of Governors talks for the record, he is quite often—but not always—announcing or giving his opinion on a major shift in money policy that has originated in a FOMC meeting that's still blacked out. It tends not to be a Madison Avenue thing—let's run the idea up the flagpole and see who salutes. The FOMC or the Board of Governors has usually voted on a firm policy. Often enough, one of the governors is spreading the word. Hence, when one of them speaks publicly—*pay heed*.

Prior to 1968 Fed officials tended to be close-mouthed. But in that year they became significantly more public-relations conscious. As you will recall from *The Wall Street Journal* story reproduced as Figure 7, in mid-December 1968 the FOMC voted for tight money, with the policy directive becoming publicly available in late February 1969. It is important to note that in December 1968 and January 1969 the seven Federal Reserve governors held public news conferences with magazines and newspaper reporters to announce, defend and explain their mid-December 1968 tight-money decision.

Public Statements That Were Available in January 1969

Here are some public statements during that particular blackout period which were available for investors to interpret.

The January 20, 1969, issue of *U.S. News and World Report* contained two major articles on the Fed. The first article, headlined "Crackdown on Inflation Begins" above a recent group photograph of the seven-member Board of Governors (who had previously tended to avoid publicity), succinctly stated their inflation-breaking objectives.

The second article was an exclusive question-and-answer interview* with George W. Mitchell, a Federal Reserve Board governor. Here are some of the pertinent questions with Mr. Mitchell's answers in full:

Mr. Mitchell, is the Federal Reserve Board determined to get inflation under control?

Yes, indeed. We mean business in breaking the inflation psychology that has developed. We will proceed, however, in an orderly way.

How quickly can inflation be brought down to the 2 percent level?

The aim is to reduce inflation as quickly as possible without plunging the country into a business recession. I do not expect a credit crunch like the one in 1966. Our policy of credit restraint is forceful, but it is also gradual. Economic growth might be retarded for a year or more before the needed change in climate takes place.

Are you saying the money squeeze may last that long?

Yes, that could happen. We will need restraint—either tight money or restraint on the fiscal side from stiffer taxes or reduced federal spending. And we will need it as long as escalating prices and inflationary psychology persist.

What are the practical effects of your squeeze on credit?

Banks are having to ration loans to their customers. State and local governments are having to defer projects because financing is not available. Banks are being more selective in all types of loans, including consumer loans. And, of course, the cost of borrowed money is very high.

---

* Copyright © 1969 by *U.S. News & World Report*.

Is the Board willing to take a mild recession in order to get inflation under control?

I think we can get things under control without pushing the country into an actual slump. But there is an element of risk. You are talking about quite a bit of fine-tuning when you talk about slowing the economy by exactly the right amount. Such a course obviously runs the chance of slowing things a little too much, and thus bringing on a recession.

Would a pause in business activity bring higher unemployment?

Without a doubt, a cooling of the boom will cause unemployment to rise. We must accept that as inevitable to some degree. It is important to remember, however, that unemployment is extremely low. Over all, the jobless rate is 3.3 percent of the work force—counting teen-agers and Negroes, where unemployment is high. Among married men, the heads of families, unemployment is only 1.4 percent of the work force—no real unemployment at all. You can give everyone a job—trained and untrained—if you work the economy at forced draft, as we did in World War II. The trouble is that you also get serious inflation. The answer to today's unemployment problem is training to prepare the teen-agers and the Negro jobless for work they can handle. The answer is not an inflationary boom to try to keep unemployment at rock bottom.

Are you determined to get speculation under control as well as inflation?

There is some adjustment now taking place in the stock market that is cooling speculative fervor. This has been going on, actually, for several weeks. A simmering down of the stock market speculation will play a part in cooling the economy.

The events of 1969 and 1970 showed Mr. Mitchell's comments to be prophetic. On January 20, 1969, when this interview was published, the Dow-Jones Average closed at 931. The lack of investors who promptly took Mr. Mitchell at his word is seen by the paradoxical evidence that the Dow-Jones Average rose steadily for the next sixteen trading days, up to 952.

Other Pertinent Public Comments, 1969 Through 1971

In late June 1969 Federal Reserve Board Chairman William McChesney Martin made a public statement that there will be "*a*

good deal of pain and suffering" before the U.S. eliminates inflation. The sophisticated investor could judge that as of that June
date no easing of the tight-money policy was yet in sight as the
highest-ranking Fed official was inferring its continuation.

In early December 1969 a Federal Reserve Board governor,
Andrew F. Brimmer, publicly stated that the Federal Reserve
Board should *"remain steadfast"* in its policies because it has yet
"to win the battle against inflation." The December 3, 1969, issue
of *The Wall Street Journal* carried Mr. Brimmer's comments. Mr.
Brimmer further stated that he couldn't speak for others on the
seven-member board, but that he was *"personally deeply troubled"*
by arguments that efforts against inflation should be relaxed or
abandoned for fear of a recession.

From Mr. Brimmer's *"remain steadfast"* comments, as of December 2, 1969, the investor could construe that the policy of the
Fed was still one of tight money. On that December day in 1969,
when any number of investors had an opportunity to read Andrew
Brimmer's comment, the Dow-Jones Average stood at 793, with
its major lows still months ahead.

Another example of a public comment by a Fed official being
useful to a knowledgeable investor concerns the statements by the
new Federal Reserve Board chairman, Arthur F. Burns, who, on
March 18, 1970, testified before the Senate Banking Committee.
The next day *The Wall Street Journal* headlined the story:

Burns Indicates Federal Reserve Has Eased Credit:
He Hopes Banks Will Lower Prime Rate Fairly Soon

As history evolved, Arthur Burns' public comments gave an
accurate peak under the ninety-day blackout curtain. In Figure 9
you will note the mid-May 1970 news item reporting the FOMC's
policy shift toward easy money decided on months earlier, in their
February 1970 meeting. On that March day, *during the blackout
period,* Mr. Burns was telling it as it was. The stock market
hovered at Dow-Jones 767. A year later (March 18, 1971) the
Dow-Jones was at the more elevated level of 916, up over 148
points. However, in the immediate ten-week period following Dr.
Burns's statements, the market fell over 136 points. Quite obviously comments by Fed officials tend to be more significant from
a long-term point of view rather than the short-term.

In late November 1971, usually closed-mouth Fed officials

simultaneously gave public interviews on both the East and West Coasts that were highly optimistic about 1972 economic prospects. In San Francisco, a member of the seven-man Federal Reserve Board, Sherman J. Maisel, stated that the substantial rise in general economic activity predicted by the majority of Republican and Democratic economists for the United States for 1972, would seem to indicate a *"need"* for the nation's money supply to expand at a 6 percent to 8 percent rate. In Washington, D.C., Dr. Arthur F. Burns would neither support nor take exception to his associate's estimates. Dr. Burns stated, *"I'm on a moderately expansive path, and I'll get it there."* In addition, Dr. Burns said he couldn't discern any basic economic reasons for the current drop in stock prices.

On that November day when the two members of the Federal Reserve Board spoke, the Dow-Jones Average touched an intraday low of 793, down over 16 percent from its April 1971 peak of 951. Perhaps it's a coincidence, but immediately, a strong market rally started. In the next six trading days, the Dow rose to around 860, up almost 70 points. By early-April 1972 the Dow-Jones Average exceeded 960.

1966 Example

Another pertinent example of guideline two working for you had occurred a number of years earlier. In late December 1966 the Fed sent a letter to its member banks "terminating" its request that the member banks should slow down their commercial loans. In short, the Fed was giving the green light to banks to extend credit and write loans. Quite obviously, to accomplish this the Fed had to be ready to make credit easily available to the banks. When the Fed publicly took this easy-money stance via its letter (December 28, 1966), the Dow-Jones Average read 788, and within twenty-four months it rose over 200 points. This particular peek into the Fed's thinking is worth noting because at the time the FOMC meetings were totally secret. It was not until six months later, in June 1967, that the FOMC information started to become publicly available on a somewhat regular basis.

Current Style of Public Comments

The year 1970–71 saw one individual on the Federal Reserve Board emerge as the chief spokesman. That individual is its chairman, Dr. Burns. As though by a gentlemen's agreement, the other governors tend to defer to him and avoid making public comments. Additionally, and perhaps more important to the investor, a national forum is usually made available to Dr. Burns to voice his comments. That forum is the Senate Banking Committee in Washington, D.C. Dr. Burns has appeared on numerous occasions to voice discreetly the Federal Reserve's current point of view on a number of domestic and international economic problems.

Unfortunately not enough newspaper and TV editors consider Dr. Burns' appearances before the Senate Banking Committee as "newsworthy."

9

Guideline Three: "Planted" News Items

In January 1969 there appeared a number of unique news items about the Fed. All the articles were variations on the same theme—the serious bent of the Fed to tighten money.

Figure 10 illustrates the headlined portion of a major article published on January 13, 1969, in *The Wall Street Journal*. The article assertedly described the Fed's current tight-money thinking. It included quotes by a *"ranking analyst,"* an *"insider,"* a *"key planner,"* a *"financial overseer,"* and other authorities. Yet no Fed official or individual was quoted by name.

Another "planted" news item apparently was published on January 27, 1969. *The Wall Street Journal* printed a veiled interview with an anonymous banker about the Fed's projected tight-money plans under a headline that read:

Reserve System's Plan for Cooling
Inflation is Outlined by Banker.
Year or More of Firm Restraint on Bank Lending,
Retention of 10% Surtax Included in Formula.

The article outlined in some detail the possible duration of tight money. The banker, *The Wall Street Journal* reported, "wished to remain anonymous," and "is particularly close to the thinking at the New York Reserve Bank." *The Wall Street Journal* story stated that the banker's analysis reflected the "unanimity of sentiment prevailing at the other Federal Reserve Banks and on the Federal Reserve Board itself."

For guideline three to be of any help to you, it is necessary that you do your homework by reading extensively.

The Fed's Warning
Tight Credit Policy
Aims at Inducing Firms
To Use More Restraint

Board Fears Deep Downturn
May Follow Heavy Outlays
On Plants and Inventories

But Some Foresee 'Overkill'

By RICHARD F. JANSSEN
Staff Reporter of THE WALL STREET JOURNAL
WASHINGTON—The word from the Fed to the nation's businessmen: Go slow.

That's the message the Federal Reserve Board, by holding to a tight-credit course, is trying to get across to the many business executives it fears are poised to plunge into excessive inventory and factory-building activity.

While increases in such investment are usually healthy for the economy, the monetary strategists worry that the businessmen's sense of timing is seriously awry now, with expansion plans taking concrete form just when consumers are about to slow their spending.

"Businessmen have their eye on the prospect of long-term prosperity, but the consumer is beginning to look at his paycheck," comments a ranking analyst. If unsold goods start piling up on shelves and new factories start gathering dust, he warns, "there can be a painful correction"—the first recession in eight years.

It's partly to discourage commercial banks from fueling extra business investment right now that the board has been pursuing a tighter credit policy since late November, close observers say. The same reasoning makes the monetary authorities inclined to tolerate the stiff 7% "prime" interest rate that banks are now charging on loans to their best customers, even though last week's increase came as a surprise to Federal Reserve chiefs here.

Further Moves

What's more, the measures already taken by the board, if not effective enough, seem sure to be buttressed by further moves. What more might it do? An insider answers with another question: "What does it really take to shake more people into realizing" that they ought to "reconsider" their ambitious investment plans?

The possible responses by the Federal Reserve: A further rise in the discount rate on loans to its member banks, currently at a relatively reasonable 5.5%; increases in bank reserve requirements, which would force banks to keep more funds idle; and tightening in the reserve system's open-market operations, which typically involve selling Treasury securities to absorb lendable funds from banks.

The board's basic target is the inflation and the accompanying "inflationary psychology" that are increasingly plaguing the nation. It's largely the desire to buy and build before things get even costlier, officials suspect that's spurring businessmen now into actions that may worsen inflationary strains and risk a serious downturn.

FIGURE 10

From *The Wall Street Journal,* January 13, 1969

10

Guideline Four: Short-Term Interest-Rate Changes

Here is the key question embodied in guideline four: Are the interest rates on 91-day Treasury bills and commercial paper above or below the interest rates prevailing at the banks or savings and loan associations?

The answer: You should be able to judge where the Fed is "leading" the public to invest its cash and savings. This guideline took on much greater significance after the "credit crunch" of 1966 when savers withdrew billions of dollars from banks and savings-and-loan associations in search of higher interest. Savers want the most mileage for their dollars, specifically the largest possible yields.

Interest should be considered as rent for the use of someone else's money. One definition of credit is use of someone else's money who rents it to you for a certain period of time for a fee (called "interest").

One characteristic of a boom is increased demand for credit. The laws of supply and demand prevail. With more people and businesses demanding to borrow money on credit, and less of it available, the higher the rent, or interest, banks and the public can command.

The Fed has full control over the amount of interest a bank may pay on its life blood, namely savings deposits. The Fed possesses the power arbitrarily to raise or lower this rate of interest or yield.

This control is exercised through Regulation Q, which will be briefly covered in discussing guideline five in the next chapter. Of greater significance to the investor is the fact that the Fed does *not* have direct legal control over *all* interest rates. Yet the interest these other securities pay tends to be "moved" up or down by actions of the Fed.

Question: What are 91-day Treasury bills?

The answer: Ninety-one-day Treasury bills are obligations (IOUs) of the U.S. government as issued by the U.S. Treasury Department. They are also called "three-month Treasury bills." The terms are interchangeable. The bills are sold weekly at public auction. The relative ease or tightness of money determines the current percent yield. If less money is generally available, the moneylender (generally the public), who are the buyers of the bills, can demand that the seller (the U.S. Treasury) pay a higher interest return. In the last 15 years the yields on 91-day (three-month) Treasury bills have varied from 1 percent to over 8 percent.

Question: What is commercial paper?

Answer: Commercial paper is a promissory note (IOU) issued by a corporation which is the borrower. The public (including other corporations) are the moneylenders. All commercial paper has a maximum life limit of nine months (270 days). The reason that 270 days is the maximum is that any corporate loans *over* this period have to be registered with the Securities and Exchange Commission. Therefore, commercial paper can become obligations of corporations yet remain exempt from registration. The amount of commercial paper outstanding in 1970 varied between $30 billion and $40 billion. A major market exists to "connect" the lenders and the borrowers. The interest yield from prime commercial paper has ranged from 1½ percent to 9 percent in the last fifteen years.

Question: How does the Fed influence the interest rate on 91-day Treasury bills and commercial paper?

Answer: Generally by either "flooding" money or restricting its flow into banks via Open Market Operations (to be explained in the next chapter). The Fed also employs the laws of supply and demand. By sharply increasing the amount of cash lying dormant in banks and thus available to be loaned, the Fed permits normal market forces to "arm-twist" the banks to reduce continually the level of interest rates to where the use of this cash becomes attractive to borrowers. The going market yield on three-month bills and commercial paper freely changes as both the available supply of money and the demands of borrowers undergo changes. It is important to note that the Fed admits it has major control over short-term interest rates and confesses it possesses little control over long-term interest rates (see Figure 11). You should note the wide swings in three-month Treasury bills as compared to the shallow moves of corporate AAA bonds, which are considered to be long term.

Figure 12 is an important chart for the investor, as it illustrates a quarter century of percent yields. Note especially (1) the yield paid on three-month Treasury bills and (2) the average annual interest yield available at the local commercial bank for savings deposits. Since 1954, as can be readily seen from Figure 12, the Fed has "flooded" the banks with money on five different occasions, driving down the interest yields on 91-day Treasury bills and commercial paper *below* yields these same banks were paying on savings deposits. At these special times the Fed appeared to be "leading" the public to deposit its funds in the banks. The five recent periods that the Fed engaged in these major easy-money actions are:

1. 1954
2. 1958
3. 1960 through 1963
4. 1967
5. 1971–72.

It should appear to be more than a coincidence that these years were periods associated with economic recession and generally *low stock prices,* and the Fed was believed to be attempting to engineer the subsequent economic recovery.

Recent Examples of Guideline Four Working for You

In July 1966 the Fed attempted to dampen an interest-rate war that erupted between commercial banks and savings-and-loan

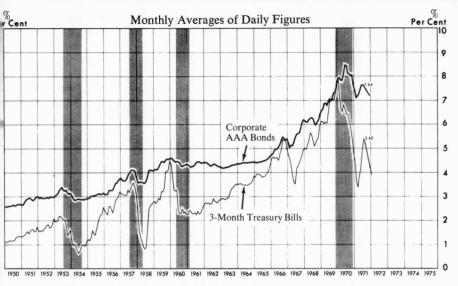

Shaded areas indicate economic recession periods.

FIGURE 11: SELECTED INTEREST RATES: THREE-MONTH TREASURY BILLS VERSUS CORPORATE AAA BONDS.

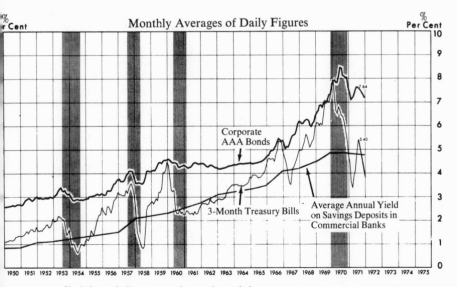

Shaded areas indicate economic recession periods.

FIGURE 12: A QUARTER CENTURY OF SELECTED PERCENT YIELDS.

associations. The "war" broke out as each institution raised interest yields (within the legal limit) to attract savings. The Fed reduced to 5 percent the highest interest rate the banks could pay on some certificates of deposits (called "CDs") and cut others to 4 percent. At the same time, high-quality corporate bonds were yielding almost 6 percent. Ninety-one-day Treasury bills were yielding 4.98 percent; however, a few weeks later they rose to yield over 5¼ percent. To the astonishment of Fed officials, an exodus of money from the banks and savings-and-loan associations into higher-yielding securities started with a vengeance. The technical economic term for this astute action on the part of the saver to search for higher yields is *disintermediation*. The year 1966 was the first time this sort of thing had happened in twenty years. Banks were forced to reduce their loans. The stock market as measured by the Dow-Jones Average dropped from its mid-July 1966 figure of 884 to its low of 744 within three months.

In late December 1966 the yields on 91-day Treasury bills were "adjusted" to where they were paying under 4.8 percent. Additionally the Fed rescinded its "request" that banks refuse business loans. Under the easy-money conditions then known to be prevailing, the stock market (Dow-Jones Average) rose 200 points in the next two years.

In December 1968 the yield on 91-day Treasury bills was permitted to rise to 6¼ percent. The yield on commercial paper moved up to 6½ percent. The very best yield that commercial banks could offer was 6 percent on the singularly large $100,000 CDs. The astute American saver promptly started his search for higher yields. New York City banks reported almost immediate withdrawals of over $1 billion. Over $10 billion was withdrawn from banks nationwide in the next eight months. The Fed's plan to draw savings out of the banks to reduce the money available to be loaned was being accomplished. The yields on 91-day Treasury bills stayed above 5 percent until late November 1970, a unique tight-money period that lasted almost twenty-four months. In retrospect, December 1968 was the high-water mark of that particular up cycle of the stock market, with the Dow-Jones reaching over 985.

You should be aware that the investment attractiveness of 91-day Treasury bills to the small saver was watered down in late

February 1970. At that time the Federal Home Loan Bank Board reported that savings-and-loan associations were experiencing a near record *outflow* of money as savers withdrew their funds to relocate them in higher yields. In response to these pressures the U.S. Treasury Department boosted the size of the 91-day Treasury bill unit to $10,000 from $1,000. Additionally, banks posted a "service charge" of up to $15 to handle requests to buy a 91-day bill. Both of these actions tended to freeze out the small investor.

By early December 1970, when the yields on three-month Treasury bills were permitted to fall under 5 percent, confirming easy-money conditions, the American saver started strongly to shift his funds back into the banks and savings-and-loan associations. In the single month of December 1970, the savings-and-loan associations reported a net *inflow* of over $1 billion, a significant change from the outflow of a few months earlier. Also, in early December 1970, the stock market as measured by the Dow-Jones Average hovered around 765. It rose over 170 points in the next five months, to surpass 950 by April 1971 in a rally that astounded and confounded analysts.

Question: How does an investor keep informed about the current percent yield on three-month Treasury bills and commercial paper?

Answer: There are three ways, all easy.

First, check the business section of the newspaper each Tuesday to find out the interest yields that resulted from the bill auction held the previous day, Monday. If Monday is a holiday, the auction is held Tuesday, and Wednesday's newspaper should tell the tale (see Figure 13).

Second, subscribe to the free bulletins published by the various Federal Reserve District banks (see Selected Readings, Appendix II).

Third, check Financing Business, a section of *The Wall Street Journal,* which contains a digest headed "Money Rates," which discloses the going free-market interest rates for money. Practically all rates, except 91-day Treasury bills, are shown. Figure 14

Yields Continue to Fall At Treasury's Auction Of Short-Term Issues

By a WALL STREET JOURNAL *Staff Reporter*

WASHINGTON—Yields continued to fall on the Treasury's latest issues of short-term bills.

The average return to investors on the 13-week bills dropped to 3.307% from 3.407% at the previous week's auction and was the lowest since the 3.253% at the Aug. 5, 1963, sale.

The average yield on the companion issue of 26-week bills dropped to 3.359% from 3.467% the previous week and was the lowest since the 3.355% at the July 15, 1963, auction.

Yields are determined by the difference between the purchase price and face value. Thus, higher bidding narrows the investor's margin of return while lower bidding widens the yield. The percentage rates are based on the discount from par and are calculated on a 360-day year rather than the 365-day year on which yields of bonds and other coupon securities are figured.

	13-Week	26-Week
Applications	$2,905,855,000	$2,537,750,000
Accepted bids	1,900,095,000	1,400,270,000
Accepted at low price	66%	38%
Accepted noncompet'ly	254,595,000	83,000,000
Average price (Yield)	99.164 (3.307%)	98.302 (3.359%)
High price (Yield)	99.179 (3.248%)	98.325 (3.313%)
Low price (Yield)	99.156 (3.339)	98.287 (3.388%)
Coupon equivalent	3.39%	3.47%

The 13-week bills are in addition to those dated Dec. 10, 1970 and mature June 10, 1971. The 26-week bills are dated March 11, 1971 and mature Sept. 9, 1971.

FIGURE 13

From *The Wall Street Journal,* March 9, 1971

illustrates two examples. Figure 14-A (February 1970) shows a tight-money period. Figure 14-B (March 1971) illustrates the easy-money period one year later. Notice the large drop in interest rates that took place in the 13-month span from February 1970 to March 1971. Ask yourself if such a dramatic change could have occurred solely because of free-market conditions, Or was the Fed the mastermind with its hand on the throttle? The Fed itself answers this most pertinent question. Quoting the 1969 edition of the Federal Reserve booklet *Open Market Operations:*

> The FOMC has delineated the operational ranges [*percent yields*], for such money market indicators as the Federal Funds rate, and the 3-month Treasury bill rate. At various times the committee may be particularly concerned with one of these variables—for example, the (interest) level of the 3-month bill.

* * *

Money Rates

NEW YORK – Bankers acceptance rates quoted by one dealer: One to 180 days, 8⅝% to 8½%.

Federal funds in an open market: Day's high 9⅝%; low 9⅜%. Closing bid 9⅜%; offered 9½%.

Call money lent brokers on stock exchange collateral by New York City banks, 8⅜% to 9%; by banks outside New York City, 8⅜% to 9%.

Call money lent on Governments to dealers by New York City banks, 9¾% to 10%; to brokers by New York City banks, 8⅜% to 9%; to brokers by banks outside New York City, 8⅜% to 9%.

Commercial paper placed directly by a major finance company was: 30 to 89 days, 8¼%; 90 to 270 days, 8%.

Commercial paper sold through dealers: 30 to 270 days, 8½% to 9%.

Certificates of deposit: Rates paid at a major New York City bank, 30 to 59 days, 6¼%; 60 to 89 days, 6½%; 90 to 179 days, 6¾%; 180 to 359 days, 7%; 360 and out 7½%.

Eurodollar rates in London include one, two, three, four, five and six months, 9 7-16% to 9 9-16%.

* * *

FIGURE 14A

From *The Wall Street Journal,* February 3, 1970

* * *

Money Rates

NEW YORK — Bankers acceptance rates quoted by one dealer: one to 180 days, 3⅞% bid, 3¾% offered.

Federal funds in an open market: Day's high 3½%; low 3%. Closing bid 3%; offered 3¼%.

Call money lent brokers on stock exchange collateral by New York City banks, 5¼% to 6%; by banks outside New York City, 5¼% to 6%.

Call money lent on Governments to dealers by New York City banks, 3⅞% to 4%; to brokers by New York City banks, 5¼% to 6%; to brokers by banks outside New York City, 5¼% to 6%.

Commercial paper placed directly by a major finance company was: 30 to 89 days, 3¼%; 90 to 179 days, 3⅞%, 180 to 270 days, 4%.

Commercial paper sold through dealers: 30 to 270 days, 3⅞% to 4⅝%.

Certificates of deposit ($100,000 or more): Rates paid at a major New York City bank, 30 to 59 days, 3½%; 60 to 89 days, 3⅝%; 90 to 119 days, 3¾%; 120 to 179 days, 4%; 180 to 269 days, 4⅛%; 270 to 359 days, 4⅜%; 360 days, 4½%.

Eurodollar rates in London include one month, 4 11-16% to 4 13-16%; two months, 4⅞% to 5%; three months, 5% to 5⅛%; four months, 5 7-16% to 5 9-16%; five months, 5 9-16% to 5 11-16%; six months, 5⅝% to 5¾%.

* * *

FIGURE 14B

From *The Wall Street Journal*, March 8, 1971

11

Guideline Five: Know the Money Tools of the Fed and How They Work

The Fed's Main Tools

The Fed's main tools to influence business conditions in the United States via changing the supply of money and credit in the 50 states, are considered to be:

1. the discount rate
2. the prime rate
3. reserve requirements (Regulation D)
4. bank interest rates (Regulation Q)
5. margin requirements (Regulations T and U)
6. open market operations
7. reserves and borrowing
8. federal funds rate
9. money supply.

A working knowledge and understanding of the first five of these tools usually can give the investor an immediate and often accurate peek behind the Fed's 90-day blackout curtain. The remaining four tools require the investor to know something about their individual cause-and-effect relationship so as to appreciate fully their significance and power. A professional economist could easily build a logical case that one or two of these items are not truly "tools" of the Fed, but, instead, mirror the results of the Fed's actions. This point is conceded. However, this information is oriented toward investors who wish to be cognizant of Fed actions so as to make investment decisions; hence both the "tools" of the Fed and the waves they cause are lumped under one heading.

The subject matter in this guideline lends itself nicely to a few questions and answers.

The Discount Rate

What is the discount rate? This is the rate of interest that a local Federal Reserve District bank charges its member banks for loans. It is the interest rate that the Federal Reserve Bank of San Francisco, for example, charges the Bank of America, or that the Federal Reserve Bank of New York charges the Chase Manhattan Bank. Since 1946 the discount rate has varied from 1 percent to 6 percent.

What is the effect of changes in the discount rate on easy money or tight money? Increases in the discount rate are signs of tightening money; reductions in the discount rate are indications of the easing of money.

How may an investor promptly interpret the Fed's position toward easy money or tight money by knowing the changes in the discount rate? Changes in the discount rate are usually decided when the FOMC meets and are immediately and publicly announced in a press release. This is in contrast to the policy directives of the FOMC meetings, which are not publicly revealed until sixty or ninety days later (see Figure 7). In the FOMC meeting in mid-December 1968, in which tight money was voted, the discount rate was raised to 5½ percent. This increase was made public the same day—an immediate signal that tighter money was becoming the name of the game. Hence there was no need for investors to sit patiently through the FOMC blackout period to find out about this major policy shift toward tight money. In early April 1969 the discount rate was raised further to 6 percent, signaling even tighter money. The discount rate stayed at 6 percent until mid-November 1970, when it was lowered to 5¾ percent, signaling easier money. And then, during the next three months, the discount rate was reduced in four steps, to 4¾ percent, with each reduction signaling further leaning of the FOMC toward easier money. In mid-July 1971, the Fed raised the discount rate to 5 percent which signaled tight money. After President Nixon imposed the wage price freeze, the discount rate was lowered in two steps to 4½ percent in November and December 1971. The key point here is that the *current thinking* of the Fed is promptly divulged when the discount rate is raised or lowered.

Does a single change in the discount rate signal a major policy shift? No. In ending the 1954–57 boom the Fed raised the discount rate seven times. The 1958–59 boom was choked off after the discount rate had been raised five times. The 1961–66 boom required three increases. The reverse is also true. The 1961 recovery was accompanied by two drops in the discount rate. The 1970 recovery found the discount rate being reduced five times.

Does there appear to be any significance to the investor concerning the timing of Fed changes in the discount rate? Yes. Since 1954 the Fed has changed the discount rate thirty-eight times as of November 1971. The rate has been increased twenty-two times and reduced sixteen times. The *first* lowering of the discount rate, an important easy-money sign, appears to possess the most significance in timing for the investor. Since 1954 this all-important first cut has tended to coincide with the bottom areas of stock market declines, generally affording the investor *the* major buying opportunity. Here is the record of the stock market's price action since 1954, following that very first cut in the discount rate:

1. On February 5, 1954, the Fed cut the discount rate from 2 percent to 1¾ percent. On that day the Dow-Jones Average read 293. Twelve months later the Dow-Jones Average closed at 409, up 116 points, or 39 percent. This cut was the first of two.

2. On November 29, 1957, the Fed reduced the discount rate from 3½ percent to 3 percent. That day the Dow-Jones Average closed at 449. One year later, it closed at 560, up 111 points, or 24 percent. This was the first of four cuts.

3. In early June 1960 the discount rate was dropped from 4 percent to 3½ percent (June 3, 1960). The Dow-Jones Average read 628 on that day. A year later it closed at 703, up seventy-five points, or 12 percent. This was the first of two cuts.

4. In early April 1967 the Fed lowered the discount rate from 4½ percent to 4 percent (April 7, 1967). In one year the Dow-Jones Average rose from 853 to 884, up thirty-one points, or 3 percent. This was a single cut.

5. In late August 1968 the discount rate was reduced from 5½ percent to 5¼ percent (August 29, 1968). In three months (to November 29, 1968) the Dow-Jones Average rose from 894 to 985, up 101 points, or 10 percent. But over the span of one year (to August 29, 1969) the Dow-Jones Average declined from 894 to 836, down fifty-eight points, or 6 percent. This was also a single reduction.

6. On November 10, 1970, the Fed announced a discount rate cut from 6 percent to 5¾ percent. This was the first of five cuts. In the next six months the Dow-Jones Average rose from 777 to 932, up 155 points or 20 percent.

7. On November 10, 1971—a year later—the Fed reduced the discount rate from 5 percent to 4¾ percent. In the next five months the Dow-Jones Average rose from 826 to 971, up 143 points or 17 percent.

Prime Rate

What is the prime rate? The prime rate is the lowest interest rate that a bank charges its public customers for loans. More specifically, it is the interest rate that major banks such as the Bank of America and Chase Manhattan levy against their best and most credit-worthy borrowers. Here is the sequence. The Bank of America may borrow money from the Fed at the discount rate. The Bank of America may then loan this money to its largest and best customers at a higher rate, which is called the "prime rate." Less credit-worthy customers are charged even higher interest rates than the prime. Each bank makes it own decision when to alter its prime rate. However, astute investors realize that the Fed tends to be "pulling the strings" behind the scenes. A variation called the "floating prime rate" was introduced by major New York banks in late 1971.

Does there appear to be any significance to the investor concerning the timing of when the banks change their prime rate? No. In 1954, 1957, 1960 and 1968 the banks lowered their prime rate after the Fed reduced the discount rate. But in 1967, 1970 and 1971 the banks reduced their prime rate prior to the Fed's cutting the discount rate. History indicates that usually the Fed moves first.

Reserve Requirements

What is meant by "reserve requirements"? Reserve requirements are the cash that a bank is not allowed to lend. The public, who deposit money in the banks, generally have the legal right immediately to withdraw its money. The banks are prepared for these withdrawals, having established cash reserves. The Federal Reserve Board, as we have seen, has the legal power to specify the amount of cash reserves. These reserves may be deposited with the local Federal Reserve District bank or may be held as cash in the bank's own vault.

From the investor's point of view, what is the importance of changes in reserve requirements? Increases in reserve requirements signal tighter money. The bank is forced to "idle" cash and is not permitted to use it for commercial loans. Decreases in reserve requirements "free" money for loans and usually mean easier money conditions.

Does the Fed have sole authority over establishing reserve requirements? Yes, but only for the member banks, in which approximately 85 percent of the nation's monies are deposited. The Banking Act of 1935 permits the Federal Reserve Board of Governors to change reserve requirements at their own discretion within certain high and low limits. A recent, pertinent example of a change in the reserve requirements, which alerted investors to tighter money conditions, took place in early April 1969. The Fed raised reserve requirements, indicating continuation and intensification of the then prevailing tight money conditions. On the other hand, in August 1970 the Fed lowered reserve requirements, adding emphasis to its announced easy money policy. The decision to change reserve requirements is traditionally made at the FOMC meetings and is promptly and publicly announced in a press release. So here again the investor gains an important insight into the Fed's *immediate thinking* by being aware of the cause-and-effect relationship of changes in the reserve requirements.

Bank Interest Rates (Regulation Q)

What is Regulation Q? Regulation Q gives the Fed the sole authority to vary the legal maximum interest rate that commercial banks may pay on the monies deposited by the public in time and savings accounts. (The highest interest that a savings-and-loan association or a savings bank may pay is also regulated, but by a different agency.)

From the investor's point of view, what significance should be attached to changes in bank interest rates by means of Regulation Q (known as "Reg Q" in the banking industry)? You must determine whether changes in the interest rate banks may offer to depositors are encouraging savers to increase or decrease their savings deposits. The investment principle of importance here is this: if interest-rate changes encourage the saver to *increase* his deposits, then the banks should have more money to lend, and this is a sign of easy money.

A most useful example of this principle came about in June 1970 in a unique manner. The Fed, using their Reg Q powers, removed the interest-rate ceiling on those CDs of $100,000 or more maturing *only* in the thirty- to eighty-nine-day range. (The thirty- to eighty-nine-day maturity range means that the lender's funds are committed for this period of time.) The Fed was attempting to direct the massive lending powers of the banks toward filling a sudden, ominous vacuum in the commercial-paper market.

The intent of the Fed was to avoid a potentially dangerous credit crisis triggered by the unexpected Penn-Central bankruptcy. Overnight, Penn-Central's commercial paper became valueless. The $30 billion commercial-paper market found itself paralyzed in a state of fear. Who might go into bankruptcy next?

Interest rates competitively offered by the banks on the "freed" CDs promptly rose above the Reg Q fixed rate of 6 percent to the free-market "stratospheric" level of 8¾ percent, where they competed effectively with the then prevailing rates on commercial paper. The easy money investment implications to the investor were evidenced by the sudden and overwhelming inflow of billions of dollars into commercial banks via this newly opened CD avenue. In the nine-week period from the end of June 1970 to August 1970, bank holdings of CDs increased over 50 percent, from $13 billion to $20 billion. Months later, by March 1971, the level approached $29 billion, and the competitive yield offered by the banks had been forced down to 4 percent to meet market conditions. As of this writing the interest ceiling on the "freed" CDs had not yet been reinstated by the Fed. The authors believe that, if the Fed were to reinstate the ceilings, it would be a convincing sign of tightening money. This singular use of the Fed's Reg Q powers was unique in that all other bank interest rates were deliberately left unchanged and should highlight the pinpoint selectivity of the Fed's Reg Q powers.

Margin Requirements

What are margin requirements? Margin is the use of borrowed money to buy stocks and bonds. The investor borrows the money from a brokerage firm or from a bank. The securities purchased serve as the collateral. The Fed possesses the full power to change the *percentage* of money that a brokerage firm or a bank may lend to the investor. Congress gave this power to the Fed in 1934. The percentage of money that a brokerage firm may lend for security purchases is controlled by Regulation T, while banks are under the control of Regulation U. Since 1934 the Fed has varied the margin requirements on stock purchases between 25 percent and 100 percent.

What is an example of margin? Let us assume that you buy 100 common shares of Company XYZ at $100 a share, or $10,000. For the sake of this illustration, it is assumed that it is permissible to buy Company XYZ's shares on margin, although some stocks are restricted. Let us further assume that it is April 1970. The margin requirement is 80 percent. You may put up the entire $10,000 in cash and own the 100 shares of XYZ outright, or you have the option of putting up only 80 percent cash, or $8,000. The remaining $2,000 is a loan and is borrowed at the prevailing interest rates.

What is the overall significance of changes in margin requirements? If margin requirements are raised, you may correctly think that the Fed is attempting to curtail the purchase of stocks, usually to curb speculation and to tighten money. If margin requirements are reduced, you may assume that the Fed is encouraging the purchase of stocks and the borrowing of money from banks. The important action of lowering margin requirements generally coincides with other easy-money directives. This investment principle was made evident in early May 1970, when the Fed *lowered* the margin requirements for stock purchase from 80 percent, to 65 percent. This meant that you then needed to put up only $6,500 in cash if you elected to buy Company XYZ's stock on margin. It was now legal for you to borrow the larger sum of $3,500.

Does there appear to be any significance to the timing of when the Fed changes margin requirements for stock purchases? Yes! The timing of the *reductions* in margin requirements, rather than the increases, appear to have greater import for the investor. Since 1955 the Fed has changed margin requirements ten times. Margin has been increased six times and lowered four times. Following is the record of stock market price movements for the four recent times that the Fed has lowered margin requirements. You'll see that the reductions generally occurred near the bottoms of major stock market sell-offs and usually offered the investor a significantly attractive buying opportunity.

1. On January 15, 1958, the Fed cut stock margin requirements from 70 percent to 50 percent, and on that day the Dow-Jones Average read 445. Twelve months later, in mid-January 1959, the Dow-Jones Average closed at 594, or up 33 percent.

2. In late July 1960 the Fed reduced margin from 90 percent to 70 percent, and the Dow-Jones Average closed at 605 (July 28, 1960). One year later, the Dow-Jones Average closed at 705, up 100 points, or 16 percent.

3. On July 9, 1962, the Fed reduced margins from 70 percent to 50 percent. The Dow-Jones Average closed that day at 590, and one year later it closed at 714, up 134 points, or 23 percent.

4. On May 5, 1970, margin was reduced from 80 percent to 65 percent. In one year the Dow-Jones Average rose from 718 to 939, up 221 points, or 30 percent.

5. On December 3, 1971, margin was reduced from 65 percent to 55 percent. In four months, the Dow-Jones Average rose from 859 to 971 up 112 points or 13 percent.

Open-Market Operations

Is it important to the investor to know about open-market operations? Yes! Open-market operations are perhaps the least known, the least understood—*but the most powerful tool*—available to the Fed. Through the singular use of this one tool, without resorting to any other instrument, the Fed can impose either tight- or easy-money conditions throughout the U.S. banking system.

What are open-market operations? They are the buying and selling of U.S. government bonds and bills. In 1935 Congress created the FOMC specifically for this purpose. In 1968 Congress further granted the Federal Reserve System the authority to buy and sell all federal government agency securities, which it began to do in 1971.

Are U.S. government securities the primary vehicle used by the FOMC for open-market operations? Yes! At the end of 1970 almost $250 billion in marketable U.S. government securities were available to be traded. These securities first saw the light of day when the U.S. Treasury needed to borrow to finance past budget deficits. A major portion of these securities is in the hands of the public, namely individuals, insurance companies—and particularly commercial banks, which hold over $63 billion.

Is there a primary "nerve center" where the FOMC does its buying and selling of U.S. securities? Yes. Currently only the Federal Reserve Bank of New York is permitted to perform open-market operations. It receives its instructions from the FOMC by means of the secret policy directive. Currently the approximate size of the Fed's holdings of U.S. government securities is over $62 billion.

How does the FOMC tend to foster easy-money conditions by means of open-market operations? The Fed buys U.S. government bonds and bills from the banks. To pay for the securities, the Fed "writes" a check against itself. This check is deposited in the banks. Then the banks have that money to lend. Technically the bank's reserves position has been increased, enlarging its financial base for writing loans.

How is money tightened by means of open-market operations? The Fed sells U.S. government securities and bills to the banks. To pay for the securities the banks give money to the Fed. Then the banks have less money to lend to the public. Technically the bank's reserve position has been decreased. Another way is for the

Fed to fail to bid for 91-day Treasury bills at the weekly auction. By the Fed's abstaining, the public can buy the bills and to pay for them, the public must withdraw monies from banks. This reduces bank cash, which in turn has the tight-money effect of lowering bank lending capacity. One way of understanding open-market operations is to think of the Fed as being able to change the bank's lendable cash into unlendable bonds and then back again into lendable cash.

How do you find out if the Fed is buying or selling? The information is usually released each Thursday by the Federal Reserve Bank of New York when it publishes the *Federal Reserve Report*. Leading newspapers carry the report on Friday. Unfortunately no great significance can be read into any one report, as the figures presented are usually part of an overall trend.

If no great significance can be gained from individual reports, how can you decide if the Fed is buying or selling? The impact of open-market operations tends to be "seen" through changes in sensitive short-term interest rates such as those on 91-day Treasury bills, commercial paper and the Federal funds, which will be explained a little later. For example, if the Fed is continually *selling* securities (tightening money by reducing bank cash), then the following will usually occur: The yield on 91-day Treasury bills and other short-term instruments may rise and the prime rate may be increased. On the other hand, if the Fed is continually *buying* securities (easing money by increasing bank cash), then you may expect short-term yields to decline along with the prime rate.

How much importance does the Fed give to open-market operations? A great deal. The 1969 edition of *Open Market Operations,* published by the Federal Reserve Bank of New York, states:

> The Federal Reserve System uses open-market purchases and sales of U.S. government securities as its most flexible means of influencing bank reserve positions and the availability of bank credit.

Reserves and Borrowings

What is meant by "excess reserves"? A bank with excess reserves is in the enviable position of being able to make more loans. Its reserves—specifically the idle cash held to comply with the reserve requirements—exceed what is necessary.

What is meant by "borrowed reserves"? A bank with borrowed reserves tends to be fully loaned out and has overextended itself. Having insufficient reserves of its own to cover its deposits, it is in violation of Fed reserve requirements and has been forced to obtain "borrowed reserves" to bring itself into compliance with the prevailing reserve requirements. Borrowed reserves are also known as "federal funds."

How does a bank go about obtaining borrowed reserves? There are three ways:

First, the deficient bank may borrow the "excess reserves" from other banks by paying the prevailing federal-funds rate (to be explained).

Second, the deficient bank may borrow directly from its Federal Reserve District bank at the discount rate.

Third, the deficient bank may be forced both to call in loans and to stop making new loans so as to build up its existing reserves to bring itself into line. This is the most drastic.

What is meant by "net free reserves"? "Net free reserves" describes a certain reserve-requirement condition of the total U.S. banking system usually associated with easy-money policies. In particular, it means that on a national banking basis the banks have more "idle" money than necessary to protect their deposits. Consequently the banks have more money to lend.

What is meant by "net borrowed reserves"? This is the opposite of net free reserves. On a national basis the banks tend to be short on cash to meet the reserve requirements to protect their deposits. Thus, they have been forced to borrow from the Fed at the discount rate. This condition tends to be associated with tight money.

How do you find out if the U.S. banking system is in a net-borrowed-reserve or a net-free-reserve position? The Federal District Bank of New York estimates the current condition in its weekly report.

Do net borrowed reserves always indicate tight money and the possibility of a stock-market sell-off? No. Refer to Figure 15. In

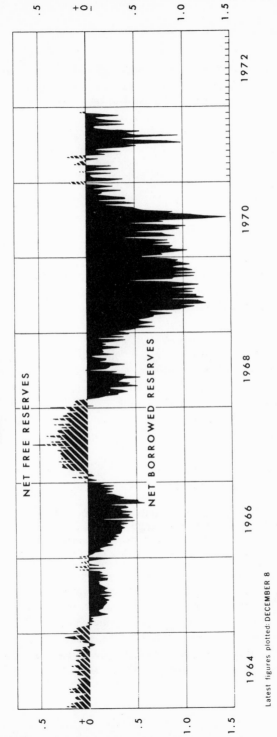

Billions of dollars

WEEKLY AVERAGES OF DAILY FIGURES

NET FREE RESERVES

NET BORROWED RESERVES

1964   1966   1968   1970   1972

.5   +0   .5   1.0   1.5

Latest figures plotted: DECEMBER 8

BOARD OF GOVERNORS OF THE FEDERAL RESERVE SYSTEM

FIGURE 15: EXCESS RESERVES AND BORROWINGS OF MEMBER BANKS.

1965, 1968, 1970 and 1971 the Fed consistently kept the U.S. Banking System in a net-borrowed-reserve position. The record shows that in those years the stock market as measured by the Dow-Jones Average generally rose. But on the other hand, harsher net-borrowed-reserve positions coexisted in 1966 and 1969 with *other* stringent tight-money conditions, and stock prices generally suffered. Hence net borrowed reserves by themselves don't always signal tight money.

Federal Funds

"Federal funds" is a shorthand phrase essentially interchangeable with the term "excess reserves." Federal funds are borrowed by those banks which are currently overextended when they are in a deficient reserve position so as to bring their deposit/reserve ratio into compliance. On the other hand, banks not fully loaned out, and therefore temporarily flush with reserves, continually offer to loan their excess reserves as "federal funds" on an overnight basis.

What is the federal-funds rate? The federal-funds rate is the interest rate that the banks with excess reserves levy against banks that need to borrow the excess bank reserves (federal funds) to bring themselves into compliance with reserve requirements. Since 1963 the federal-funds rate has varied between 2¾ percent to over 9½ percent.

Can an investor use the federal-funds rate to judge tight or easy money conditions? Yes! Quoting a Federal Reserve publication:

> The rate at which Federal funds are bought and sold is one of the most sensitive indicators of pressure on bank reserves. When general credit conditions are tight, for example, Federal funds are usually scarce, and the Federal funds (interest) rate may well rise above the discount rate.

Refer to Figure 16. Two interest rates are shown. One is the Federal Reserve discount rate; the other is the federal-funds rate. Notice how in periods of tight money and generally declining stock prices (1966 and 1969–70) the federal-funds rate rose substantially above the discount rate. Also notice that during easy money periods the federal-funds rate and the discount rate tend to

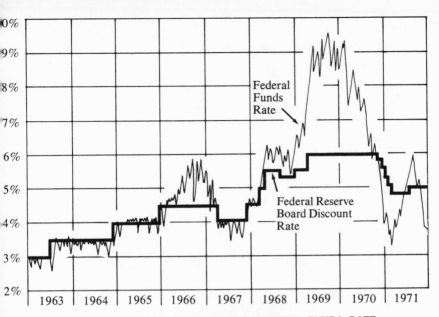

FIGURE 16: DISCOUNT RATE VERSUS FEDERAL-FUNDS RATE.

hover together and criss-cross frequently. The investment principle of importance here is:

- easy money conditions generally prevail if the federal-funds rate and the discount rate are close together;
- tight money conditions may be existing if the federal-funds rate is significantly *above* the discount rate.

Is it easy for the Fed to control the federal-funds rate? Yes. The secret policy directives of the FOMC to the trading desk at the Federal Reserve Bank of New York usually specify certain targets for the federal-funds rate. In a revealing, behind-the-scenes report, issued in early 1972, the New York bank reported that they could "hit" a federal-funds rate with considerable precision using open-market operations.

How do you find out what the federal-funds rate is each day? Refer to Figure 14. The going rate on federal funds is published daily in *The Wall Street Journal* in the Money Rates summary of the Financing Business section.

Money Supply

What is meant by "money supply"? This is the amount of money in circulation in the U.S. at any given time. At the outset, note that the phrases "money supply" and "money stock" tend to be interchangeable. The Fed uses three means to measure the money stock. Figure 17 illustrates these current methods. They are referred to as "M-1," "M-2" and "M-3" by the Fed and most economists. These designations are also used in the FOMC policy directives.

Who controls the supply of money and credit in the U.S.? The Federal Reserve Board by means of its use of open-market operations and its power to control the amount of coin and currency put into circulation through the Federal Reserve Banks.

Why is it important for the investor to be aware of changes in the money supply? Recent research indicates that as goes the money supply, so tends to go the stock market. Refer to Figure 18, which illustrates the money stock (M-1) in the U.S. since 1952. Please note that there are seven places in Figure 18 where the money-supply curve flattened out. These seven flat periods, which graphically describe no growth in the U.S. money supply (M-1) were not accidental. The records clearly indicate that these flat periods directly resulted from Federal Reserve policies produced in the FOMC meetings. If you jog your memory a bit, you may recall that investors experienced sharp stock market sell-offs in those years.

How did the "connection" between money supply and stock prices come to the attention of investors? In the authors' opinion, it started in the early 1960s. The first date of importance is 1963. The now renowned Professor Milton Friedman of the University of Chicago published a landmark economic study. It had the rather cumbersome title *The Relative Stability of Monetary Velocity and the Investment Multiplier in the United States, 1897–1958* (Englewood Cliffs, N.J.: Prentice-Hall, 1963). The thesis of the study was that the boom-bust cycle of American business seemed to dovetail with the up-down shifts of the nation's money supply. The most glaring example was the 1929–32 period. The Federal Reserve Board of that era permitted the money supply to shrink 30 percent. In essence, this meant that in 1932 there were 30 percent fewer dollars in circulation than in 1929. In a number of

FEDERAL RESERVE   statistical release

H.6

MONEY STOCK MEASURES
IN BILLIONS OF DOLLARS

For Immediate Release
December 16, 1971

Date	Seasonally Adjusted M1 — Currency plus demand deposits 1/	Seasonally Adjusted M2 — M1 plus time deposits at commercial banks other than large CD's 2/	Seasonally Adjusted M3 — M2 plus deposits at nonbank thrift institutions 3/	Not Seasonally Adjusted M1 — Currency plus demand deposits 1/	Not Seasonally Adjusted M2 — M1 plus time deposits at commercial banks other than large CD's 2/	Not Seasonally Adjusted M3 — M2 plus deposits at nonbank thrift institutions 3/
1970--November	213.6	414.3	628.1	215.4	414.9	628.1
December	214.8	418.2	634.1	221.2	423.5	639.4
1971--January	215.3	423.1	642.5	221.4	428.3	647.9
February	217.7	430.4	653.7	215.6	427.8	650.8
March	219.7	437.1	664.2	217.5	435.7	663.2
April	221.2	441.5	672.9	222.3	443.7	675.6
May	223.8	446.6	681.5	219.9	443.7	678.6
June	225.5	450.6	688.6	223.7	449.1	687.5
July	227.4	453.4	694.5	226.0	452.0	693.3
August	228.0	454.5	698.0	224.9	451.7	694.8
September	227.6	455.6	701.4	226.2	454.3	699.8
October	227.7	458.3	706.7	227.5	458.0	706.3
November p	r 227.7	r 460.8	r 711.7	r 229.6	r 461.4	r 711.7
Week ending: 1971--Oct. 27	228.5	459.6		227.0	458.1	
Nov. 3	227.8	459.4		229.8	461.2	
10	227.1	459.4		228.9	460.3	
17	227.5	460.6		230.1	461.6	
24	r 227.7	r 461.7		r 228.3	r 460.3	
Dec. 1p	r 227.7	r 462.1		r 230.7	r 463.2	
8p	228.5	463.2		232.5	465.8	

1/ Includes (1) demand deposits at all commercial banks other than those due to domestic commercial banks and the U.S. Government, less cash items in the process of collection and F.R. float; (2) foreign demand balances at F.R. Banks; and (3) currency outside the Treasury, F.R. Banks and vaults of all commercial banks.

2/ Includes, in addition to currency and demand deposits, savings deposits, time deposits open account, and time certificates of deposits other than   p - Preliminary
negotiable time certificates of deposit issued in denominations of $100,000 or more by large weekly reporting commercial banks.   r - Revised

3/ Includes M2 plus the average of the beginning and end of month deposits of mutual savings banks and savings and loan shares.

FIGURE 17

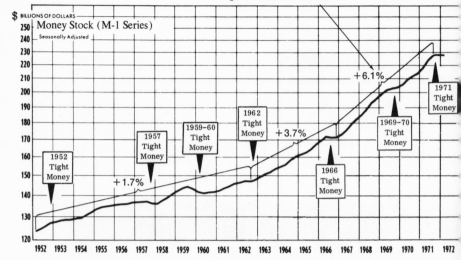

Average Annual Growth Rate

FIGURE 18: MONEY STOCK (M-1 SERIES).

academic circles the catastrophic 1929–32 depression and stock market crash is now viewed as a failure of aggressive money leadership on the part of the Federal Reserve System.

The next date of importance is 1964. Using Milton Friedman's data as a springboard, Mr. Beryl W. Sprinkel published a penetrating book for investors called *Money and Stock Prices* (Homewood, Ill.: Dow-Jones–Irwin, Inc., 1964). This book attempted to show that the major up-down movements of the stock market were connected with the up-down movements of the nation's money supply. The pith of the book is summed up by these sentences from page 119:

> Changes in monetary growth [monetary supply] lead changes in stock market prices by an average of about 15 months prior to a bear market and by about 2 months prior to bull markets. . . .
> Leads of 15 months and 2 months appear to give the best investment results, but the leads might well change in the future.

The next date of importance is 1967, when the FOMC policy directives concerning easy money and tight money were first published. From that point on an investor became more fully armed.

From Friedman's data the investor was made aware of the connection between the boom-bust cycles of American business and the up-down shifts of the money supply. From Sprinkel's data the investor was made aware of the bear market–bull market cycle of stock prices as influenced by the up-down movements of the money supply. From the published data of the FOMC the investor was made more aware of the policy shifts toward easy money or tight money.

The logic appears to be this: Tight money deals the stock market a one-two punch. Punch number one is that the profits of companies generally recede, rendering them less attractive as investment. Punch number two is that there is usually less money to purchase stocks. Result: stock prices tend to decline. On the other hand, easy money acts with a positive force. With more money in circulation, the companies' profits generally increase and there is additional cash to invest. Result: stock prices tend to rise.

In 1971 Mr. Sprinkel published a complete revised and updated edition of his book called *Money and Markets: A Monetarist View* (Homewood, Ill.: Richard D. Irwin, Inc., 1971). In his new book Mr. Sprinkel offers the opinion that the lead time of downward changes in the money supply over declining stock prices has been dramatically shortened from the average of 15 months mentioned in his earlier book. The reasons appear obvious. The knowledge gap has been significantly narrowed.

The investment principle of importance here is:

- decisions by the Fed to expand the money supply often start stock market rallies;
- decisions by the Fed to contract the money supply may trigger stock market sell-offs.

Is money supply the "magic" answer? No one knows. Professor Friedman is on record as saying that he sincerely believes that through his research he has found the "magic" formula for keeping the U.S. economy on a steady upward course. The essence of his formula is that the central bank (the Fed) should expand the money supply at a steady rate. The Fed, with Arthur Burns as chairman, has partially embraced this notion. In the spring of 1970 the FOMC policy directives stated that the money supply should grow at a 4 percent rate. The targeted growth rate was upped to 6 percent by late 1970. By the spring of 1971 the money supply was expanding at an 11 percent rate. Friedman's research has polarized economic thinking. Friedman's "school" is broadly called the "monetarists," and also the "Chicago School of Money theorists." The opposing camp is called "Keynesian," after John M. Keynes, who wrote *The General Theory of Employment, Interest and Money* (New York: Harcourt, Brace and World, Inc., 1936). Keynesian economic theory is also called the "new economics." In Selected Readings, Appendix II, are listed a number of books in which you can explore the pros and cons of each economic theory.

What is the policy of money supply expansion in other nations? The central banks of other industrial nations apparently elect to expand their money supply more aggressively than the United States. Below, in Table B, are tabulated the recent growth rates of the money supply in some major industrial nations.

TABLE B

Money Supply Growth Rates of Other Nations (1971)

1.	Belgium	14%	6. Japan	29%
2.	Canada	25%	7. Netherlands	16%
3.	France	8%	8. Switzerland	18%
4.	Germany	14%	9. United Kingdom	11%
5.	Italy	12%	10. United States	6%

(Source: Federal Reserve Bank of St. Louis)

Is it easy for the Fed to precisely control the money supply growth rate? Apparently not. During 1970 and 1971, the FOMC directed the trading desk at the Federal Reserve Bank of New York to achieve a specific growth rate in the nation's money supply (M-1). However, 1971 witnessed erratic growth rates. In 1972, the New York bank reported that maintaining a specific money supply growth rate was a "peculiarly elusive target." Part of the blame was attributed to the four- to six-month time lag in acquiring accurate statistics, which forced the Fed to operate in the dark.

12

The Eight Significant Characteristics
of an Undervalued Stock

So far you have been provided with essential data intended to help you gain the all-important "sense of feel" that characterizes successful investors. Briefly reviewed: You were shown (1) the money-accumulation power available through compounded growth; (2) the stock market's recurring cycle of fear, confidence and greed; and (3) the guidelines intended to help you interpret the behind-the-scenes actions of the Fed to judge the economy.

Profit-Estimate Sheet

Once you have made the decision to buy stocks, the question arises: *What stocks should you buy?*

In Robert Peisner's personal investment activities, and in managing stock portfolios for a large number of conservative investors, he has developed a "Profit-Estimate Sheet" (Figures 19A–19D). The purpose of the Profit-Estimate Sheet is both to organize an investor's thinking and to make sure that he covers the more pertinent information about a potentially undervalued stock that he is examining as a possible investment. It is a checklist. More importantly, the Profit-Estimate Sheet contains the eight significant characteristics you might think of as "tests." These tests were devised by the authors over a period of years to help determine when conservative stock appeared to be *currently* undervalued.

PROFIT ESTIMATE SHEET

designed by

ROBERT N. PEISNER

CONSERVATIVE GROWTH - LOW PRICE/EARNINGS RATIO - HIGH DIVIDEND % YIELD

SECTION ONE - BASIC DATA

1) Date of Analysis . . . . _____

2) Company: _____

3) Exchange & Symbol . . . . Exchange:_____; Symbol:_____

4) Primary Industry: _____

5) Continuous cash dividends paid since:. . . . . _____

6) Number shares of stock outstanding: . . . . _____

7) Number of institutions holding:. _____

8) Number of shares institutions hold: . . . . _____

9) % shares institution hold (line 8_____ divided by
line 6_____) . . . . _____ %

10) Source of historical investment data:_____

FIGURE 19A: PROFIT-ESTIMATE SHEET
SECTION ONE.

SECTION TWO - HISTORICAL EARNINGS AND STOCK DATA

	(A) FISCAL YEAR ENDING - MONTH	(B) 1st QTR ENDING	(C) 2nd QTR ENDING	(D) 3rd QTR ENDING	(E) 4th QTR ENDING	(F) FISCAL YEARLY EARN	(G) $ DIV	(H) STOCK PRICE HI LO	(J) PRICE/ EARN RATIO P/E HI LO	(K) $ ANNUAL SALES
11)										
12)	,19									
13)	,19									
14)	,19									
15)	,19	E	E	E	E	E	E	E	E	E

SECTION THREE - CURRENT DATA

16) Today's stock price: . . . . $_____

17) Indicated current cash dividend per share: . . . . $_____

18) Current Yield: (line 17 $_____ divided by line 16 $_____; Caution if under 4.5%): . . . . [ ] OK ___% CAUTION

19) Most recent quarterly earnings report: Qtr_____ Month_____ Fiscal Year_____

20) Latest 12 months earnings (Addition of 4 most recent quarters) . . . . . $_____

21) Current dividend protection ratio (line 20 $_____ divided by line 17 $_____; Caution if protection ratio less than 1.4): . . . . [ ] OK CAUTION

22) Current (P/E) Price/Earnings Ratio (line 16 $_____ divided by line 20 $_____; Caution if P/E is more than 15 to 1): . . . . . . [ ] OK P/E CAUTION

FIGURE 19B: PROFIT-ESTIMATE SHEET (CONTINUED) SECTION TWO AND THREE.

SECTION FOUR - CRITERIA FOR FUTURE ESTIMATES

23) (A): Average LOW Price/Earnings Ratio (P/E) last 2 years
(13J LO_____ plus 14J LO_____ divided by 2 equals_____);
(B): JUDGMENT - use LOW P/E of . . . . _____ P/E

24) (A): Average HIGH Price/Earnings Ratio (P/E) last 2 years
(13J HI_____ plus 14J HI_____ divided by 2 equals_____);
(B): JUDGMENT - use HIGH P/E of (but not more than 1-1/2 times
P/E of 23B): . . . . _____ P/E

25) Enter estimated HIGH (HI) and LOW (LO) Price/Earnings Ratio in box 15J

26) Estimated earnings per share for fiscal year ending 19_____;   OK
(Caution if less than line 20; Enter in box 15F) . . . . $_____   CAUTION

27) Source of estimate _____

28) Estimated quarterly earnings (fill in boxes 15B, 15C, 15D and 15E)

29) Estimated dividends per share for fiscal 19_____; (Enter in box 15G) . $_____

30) Estimated dividend protection ratio (line 26 $_____ divided by   OK
line 29 $_____; Caution if less than 1.4): . . . .   CAUTION

SECTION FIVE - ESTIMATED LOSS VERSUS GAIN

31) Estimated 19_____ LOW stock price
(line 23B_____ LOW P/E x line 26 $_____) . . . . $_____ LOW

32) Estimated 19_____ HIGH stock price
(line 24B_____ HIGH P/E x line 26 $_____) . . . . $_____ HIGH

33) Enter estimated HIGH (HI) and LOW (LO) stock prices in box 15H

34) Estimated loss per share (line 16 $_____ minus line 31 $_____) . $_____

35) % Potential Downside Risk (line 34 $_____ divided by   OK
line 16 $_____; Caution if more than 20%). . . . .   % CAUTION

36) Estimated profit per share (line 32 $_____ minus line 16 $_____) $_____

37) % Potential Upside Gain (line 36 $_____ divided by line 16 $_____) _____ %

38) Gain to Loss Ratio (line 36 $_____ divided by line 34 $_____;   OK
Caution if less than 2 to 1) . . . .   CAUTION

**FIGURE 19C: PROFIT-ESTIMATE SHEET (CONTINUED)
SECTION FOUR AND FIVE.**

SECTION SIX – PROFIT ESTIMATE FOR STOCK (100% CASH)

39) Assume a cash investment of . . . . $_____

40) Number of shares purchaseable (line 39 $_____ divided by
line 16 $_____): . . . . _____ SH.

41) Estimated gross profit (line 36 $_____ x line 40 _____ SH) . . . . $_____

42) Commissions: a) Buy $_____ b) Sell $_____ c) SUM of a + b . . $_____

43) Estimated net CAPITAL GAINS profit (line 41 $_____ minus
line 42c $_____). . . . . $_____

44) Dividends received per year (line 29 $_____ x line 40_____ SH) . . $_____

45) Total dividends received (line 44 $_____ x _____ years) . . . . . $_____

46) Total estimated return from capital gains and dividends
(line 43 $_____ + line 45 $_____). . . . . $_____

47) ESTIMATED ANNUAL % NET GAIN (line 46 $_____ divided by
line 39 $_____; Caution if less than 25%). . . . . | | OK
| | % CAUTION

SECTION SEVEN – MARGIN PROFIT ESTIMATE

48) Current Stock Margin requirements set by FRB or Exchange . . . . . . _____ %

49) Assume same number of shares as line 40 . . . . _____ SH.

50) Cash required to purchase shares per line 49 (line 39 $_____ x
line 48 _____%). . . . . $_____

51) Amount of margin loan (line 39 $_____ minus line 50 $_____). . . $_____

52) Margin call when stock price is (1ine 16 $_____ x _____%) . . . . $_____

53) Approx. cash required for one margin call (line 51 $_____ x
_____%). . . . . $_____

54) Maximum $ amount of margin calls (same as line 51; amount of loan) . . . $_____

55) Margin interest costs for one year (line 51 $_____ x _____%). . . $_____

56) Total estimated return from capital gains and dividends
(line 46 $_____ minus line 55 $_____) . . . . $_____

57) ESTIMATED ANNUAL % NET GAIN USING MARGIN (line 56 $_____
divided by line 50 $_____) . . . . _____ %

IT IS ADVISED THAT A PERSON UNABLE TO KEEP AN ADEQUATE CASH RESERVE, OR UNABLE
TO HONOR ONE OR MORE MARGIN CALLS, NOT PARTICIPATE IN ANY MARGIN PURCHASES.

FIGURE 19D: PROFIT-ESTIMATE SHEET (CONTINUED)
SECTION SIX AND SEVEN.

The eight tests are designed to help you estimate a stock's future price action!

The Profit-Estimate Sheet has seven sections and 57 lines. It is necessary both to fill in and to calculate specific investment information about an individual stock in completing the 57 lines. Eight of these lines are of major importance. The calculations are easy, requiring only simple arithmetic. With practice you can complete the Profit-Estimate Sheet on any one stock in ten to fifteen minutes. However, when you first start, it may take you up to two or three hours. Since you are investing your hard-earned money, it should be time well spent and not to be begrudged.

The authors are in the process of employing a computer program to more speedily "zero in" on the potentially undervalued stocks.

You will find a chapter devoted to each of the seven sections, explaining and illustrating it in significant detail. Briefly these sections are:

Section One: Basic Data
Section Two: Historical Earnings and Stock Data
Section Three: Current Data
Section Four: Criteria for Future Estimates
Section Five: Estimated Loss Versus Gain
Section Six: Profit Estimate for Stock (100 percent cash)
Section Seven: Margin Profit Estimate

Historical Patterns Tend to Repeat

The key to estimating a stock's future price action by means of this technique lies in discovering consistent, logical patterns that appear to exist in the stock's *recent* past performance. The eight characteristics highlight the particular past patterns the authors consider pertinent. The success of this stock-selection method depends upon these *recent* past patterns repeating themselves. Yet there is no assurance, and it is beyond logic, for you either to assume or to expect that *every* stock selected by this method will perform exactly as it has in the past. Yet, with sufficient regularity, the future price action of the stocks brought to your attention by this technique tends to mirror their past performances so as to make this particular stock-selection method worthy of investigation.

The Eight Key Lines

The eight lines of major importance on the Profit-Estimate Sheet spotlight for you the eight significant characteristics of a potentially undervalued stock. Please note that in the Profit-Estimate Sheet these particular eight lines are circled to make them stand out. Also note that each of these lines requires that you calculate an answer, which you are to insert in the answer box. And note, too, that next to the answer box are printed "OK" and "Caution." It is an either/or decision. Only one condition can apply per answer. Your choice between "OK" or "Caution" for each answer should be rather clear-cut.

Here is the investment principle: *If you uncover a stock that gives you eight "OK" signals, then the probabilities favor your having found a potentially undervalued stock.*

If you receive even one soliary "Caution" signal, you are advised to purchase with caution or, better yet, hold your funds until you uncover a stock that receives eight OKs.

Brief Description of the Eight Characteristics

The eight tests are of sufficient importance to be brought to your attention with a preliminary explanation. Their position in the Profit-Estimate Sheet is noted by the accompanying line numbers. In the chapters to come you will be shown step-by-step where to find the specific, readily available investment information so that you can easily calculate each of these characteristics. Refer to Figures 19A–19D on pages 106–109.

Line 18—Current Dividend Yield
Should Be 4.5 Percent or More

The current dividend yield of the stock you are examining should exceed 4.5 percent to give you an OK signal. If the yield is under 4.5 percent, you have a Caution signal. Additionally the cash dividends should have been paid for a consecutive number of years, without any recent *decrease* in the dividend payout.

Line 21—Current Dividend Protection Ratio
Should Be 1.4 or Higher

The latest twelve-month earnings per share divided by the latest twelve-month cash dividend payout should work out to a ratio of

1.4 or more. A ratio of 1.4 means that the company is reporting net earnings per share of $1.40 for each $1.00 in cash dividends paid to the stockholders. This may also be called the "dividend protection ratio." The higher the ratio, the greater the earnings available to protect, support and possibly cause the current dividend to be increased. A ratio of 1.4 or higher rates an OK. A ratio of less than 1.4 is a Caution signal, indicating the possibility of a dividend cut.

Line 22—Current Price/Earnings Ratio Should Be Less Than 15 to 1

The current market price of the stock divided by the latest twelve-month earnings per share produces for you the price/earnings ratio for the stock. Price/earnings ratio is usually noted in the investment world by the symbol "P/E," which will be used in this book. If the current P/E exceeds 15 to 1, the stock may be entering an overvalued stage under the criteria in this book and signals Caution. P/Es under 15 to 1 are OK.

Line 26—Estimated Earnings Per Share for the Next Fiscal Year Should Equal or Exceed the Latest Twelve-Month Earnings

This characteristic is to alert you that the future earnings of the company may be faltering. Stock market history consistently indicates that decreased earnings often, and unfortunately, lead to falling stock prices and to dividend cuts. The stock under analysis gets a Caution rating if the estimated earnings per share for the coming fiscal year are *less* than the latest twelve-month earnings. An OK is awarded if competent research gives you an estimate of no change or of a potential increase in earnings.

Line 30—Estimated Dividend Protection Ratio Should Be 1.4 or Higher

This is a necessary follow-up to the characteristic noted in line 26. Its key importance is to help you monitor a stock that you may already have purchased. If the earnings estimates for the next fiscal year indicate a decline in earnings, this ratio will indicate that the current cash dividend payout of the stock that you already own may be in jeopardy because of inadequate earnings and could be vulnerable to a dividend cut. If the ratio calculates out to 1.4 or higher, you can assume the current cash dividend is adequately protected and rates an OK. On the negative side, a ratio below 1.4 gives you a Caution signal.

Line 35—Potential Downside Risk Should Not Exceed 20 Percent

By the time you reach this point in the Profit-Estimate Sheet you will have already estimated the lowest logical price that the stock might normally touch in a decline. This information is important in that it permits you to estimate your potential downside risk. However, you must be aware that market conditions could force the stock price down to even lower levels.

If the "calculated" downside risk is more than 20 percent, the Caution signal applies as this stock may not be sufficiently depressed in price to merit your consideration and possible purchase. If the downside risk is less than 20 percent, you mark it OK.

Line 38—Gain-to-Loss Ratio Should Be More Than 2 to 1

At this state in the Profit-Estimate Sheet you have already projected the potential price appreciation from the stock's current market price. You have also estimated the "probable" low price. You should want the gain-to-loss ratio to be in your favor. The authors are inclined toward a minimum gain-to-loss of 2 to 1. More specifically, the stock should clearly show that its potential price gain is better than two times its possible loss, based upon your interpretation of its past performance. If the gain-to-loss ratio is 2 to 1 or higher, in favor of the gain, the stock is rated OK. Under 2 to 1 signals Caution.

Line 47—Estimated Annual Percent Net Gain Should Be More Than 25 Percent

When you have reached this point in the Profit-Estimate Sheet, you have reached the eighth and crucial test. You should want the combined total appreciation of the estimated price rise and the dividend income to add up to at least 25 percent. Why bother to invest in a stock that indicates a profit potential of less than 25 percent for your hard-earned money? Ideally, you may uncover a number of "undervalued" stocks that project a potential gain of up to 40 percent, 50 percent or more.

Additionally, if you elect to use margin—being aware of the greater risks and rewards—you may discover "undervalued stocks" in which gains exceeding 100 percent may be fundamentally estimated. (See line 57 of the Profit-Estimate Sheet.)

And now on to showing you how to fill out the all-important and hopefully rewarding Profit-Estimate Sheet.

13

The Profit-Estimate Sheet in Action— Section One: Basic Data

Example: Standard Oil of California (SD—NYSE)

To illustrate the Profit-Estimate Sheet in action, let us make an analysis of an actual stock. We will use Standard Oil of California. The stock market symbol for Standard Oil of California is "SD," and it will be used throughout this discussion.

Let us review some facts. In December 1968 SD's share price was 73. It's cash dividend was $2.57, or a 3.5 percent yield. But in March 1970 SD had declined to 45. It's cash dividend had been increased to $2.76. Because of the much lower price (of 45) SD's yield then calculated out to 6.1 percent. Was it possible that in March 1970 SD might check out in the Profit-Estimate Sheet with eight OKs?

Two Important Investment Questions

Before putting the Profit-Estimate Sheet to work on any stock you should attempt to find the answers to two important investment questions:

1. *How do you interpret the current mood of investors?*
2. *How do you interpret the Federal Reserve Board's current policy towards easy money or tight money?*

Your accurate answers to these questions should help you immensely in judging whether or not you should consider making an investment.

A Return Look at March 1970

SD is being analyzed from its market price in March 1970. Hence, the two important questions noted above need to be rephrased:

1. How might you have interpreted the mood of investors in March 1970?

Answer: You have essentially three choices, i.e., fear, confidence or greed. The prevailing mood in March 1970 may be interpreted from rereading Chapter Two, "You, Your Emotions, and the Stock Market." Point EE in Figure 3 appears to apply best. The investor's mood in March 1970 — you might think — appeared to be fear.

2. Using the five guidelines, how might you have interpreted the Federal Reserve Board's money policies in March 1970?

Answer: Let us assume that you were prone to agree with the overall principle that Fed money policies tended to exert influence on the stock market. Let us also assume that you did your homework to keep yourself up to date on the Fed's activities. And let us further assume that you were astutely using the five guidelines to attempt to get a "peek" behind the ninety-day news blackout of the policy decisions of the FOMC.

Rereading Chapters Five through Ten, and first using guideline one, you would have come to the conclusion that tight money was still the prevailing official policy. So it is necessary for you to use guidelines two through five in the hope of "sensing" a policy change in the making.

Let us now put guidelines two through five to work. Using guideline four, you would have noticed that the interest rates on 91-day Treasury bills had dropped from near 9 percent in January 1970 to the high 6 percent range in March 1970. A good sign. But too vague and not specific enough, in the authors' opinion.

Using guideline five, you would have noticed that the interest rate on Federal funds (guideline five–*h*) had dropped from about 9½ percent in January 1970 to under 7½ percent by March 1970. Another good sign. But again too vague and not sufficiently specific, from the authors' point of view.

Using guideline five–*i* (Money Supply), you would have noticed that a low point was reached in the nation's money supply in mid-February 1970. A bad sign in that the money-supply trend appeared downwardly oriented. This seemed to contradict the good signs just mentioned.

Two additional positive signs occurred within days of each other. Using guideline two, you might have noticed that on March 18, 1970, Federal Reserve Board Chairman Arthur Burns hinted strongly before the Senate Banking Committee that the FOMC was starting to ease credit.

Additionally, on March 25, 1970, the major New York banks lowered the prime rate from 8½ percent to 8 percent (guideline five–*b*).

Summing up: In March 1970 you had only "signs" that the Fed was ending its tight money policy and appeared to be beginning an easy money policy. You did not have factual confirmation from an official FOMC policy directive. If you had wanted to get a jump on other investors and were willing to accept the risks, the authors believe that you could have used the guidelines to interpret that the Fed appeared to be switching toward an easy money policy.

The Authors' Position

The answers to the above questions may appear to possess the overtones of Monday-morning quarterbacking, but such is not the case. Figures 20A and 20B illustrate a Profit-Estimate Sheet on SD, dated March 9, 1970, which Robert Peisner calculated and distributed at that time. He has since slightly revised the physical format of the Profit-Estimate Sheet to increase its efficiency. The new, revised format is illustrated in Figures 19A–19D. Additionally, Figure 21 illustrates a market commentary dated April 1, 1970, headed "Federal Reserve Board—A Change to Easier Money" written by Robert Peisner as his personal interpretation of question 2. Figure 22 illustrates the first paragraphs of a market commentary dated January 27, 1969 entitled "Suggested Stock Market Strategy for 1969" written by Robert Peisner as his personal view of the then prevailing market climate and the trend toward tight money.

How to Find the Pertinent Investment Data for the Profit-Estimate Sheet

To fill out the Profit-Estimate Sheet properly, it will be necessary for you to obtain specific investment data. The major part of

CONSERVATIVE GROWTH - LOW PRICE/EARNINGS RATIO - HIGH DIVIDEND % YIELD

BUSINESS: STANDARD OIL OF CALIFORNIA is one of the 5 largest international oil companies. In 1968, 56% of profit came from Western Hemisphere operations. Markets oil & gas products on west coast and southeastern part of U.S. F-310 "additive" has received good reception and test reports are positive. Changes in oil depletion allowance expected to hold down increase in profits this year. 47,800 employees. 247,000 stockholders.

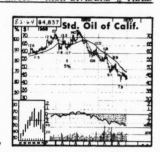

Chart: Courtesy R. W. Mansfield Company

1) Date of Analysis . . . .   March 9, 1970

2) Company: ___Standard Oil of California___

3) Exchange & Symbol. . . . . Exchange: __NYSE__ ; Symbol: __SD__

4) Primary Industry: _____Oil_____

5) Today's Stock Price: . . . . $ 45

6) Current Cash Dividend per Share: . . . . $ 2.80

7) Current Yield: (line 6$ _2.80_ divided by line 5$ _45_ ;
   Caution if under 5%) . . . . | 6.2 % | OK ~~CAUTION~~ |

8) Continuous cash dividends paid since:.   1911

9) Number shares of stock outstanding . . . .   84 MIL

10) Number of institutions holding:.   360

11) Number of shares institutions hold:. . . . .   5.8 MIL

12) % shares institutions hold (line 11 _5.8_ divided by
    line 9 _84_)   7   %

13) Source of historical investment date: __S & P #2106 February 20, 1970__

QUARTERLY EARNINGS ($) REPORTS AND STOCK DATA

	(A) FISCAL YEAR ENDING - MONTH	(B) 1st QTR ENDING	(C) 2nd QTR ENDING	(D) 3rd QTR ENDING	(E) 4th QTR ENDING	(F) FISCAL YEARLY EARN	(G) $ DIV	(H) STOCK PRICE HI	(H) LO	(J) PRICE/ EARN RATIO P/E HI	(J) LO	(K) $ ANNUAL SALES
14)	December	Mar.	June	Sept.	Dec.							
15)	Dec. ,1967	1.18	1.27	1.16	1.22	4.83	2.38	61	51	12	10	$3.2 BIL
16)	Dec. ,1968	1.28	1.34	1.34	1.36	5.32	2.57	73¼	54	14	10	$3.6 BIL
17)	Dec. ,1969	1.34	1.36	1.31	1.34	5.35	2.76	75	48¼	14	9	$3.8 BIL
18)	Dec. ,1970	1.33 E	1.36 E	1.32 E	1.39 E	5.40 E			42¼			$4.2 BIL E

(Over)

FIGURE 20A

CURRENT DATA

19) Most recent Quarterly Earnings Report: Qtr 4th Month Dec. Fiscal Year 1969

20) Latest 12 month earnings (Addition of 4 most recent quarters). . . . $ 5.35

21) Latest 12 month dividends (less extras): . . . . $ 2.80

22) Current earnings-dividend ratio (line 20$ 5.35 divided by
line 21$ 2.80 ; Caution if protection ratio less than 1.4): . . . . | 1.9 | OK ~~CAUTION~~

23) Current Price/Earnings Ratio (line 5$ 45 divided by
line 20$ 5.35 ; Caution if more than 13 to 1): . . . . | 8 P/E | OK ~~CAUTION~~

24) (A): Average HIGH Price/Earnings Ratio (P/E) last 2 years
(16J HI 14 plus 17J HI 14 divided by 2 equals 14);
(B): JUDGMENT - use HIGH P/E of: . . . . 12 P/E

25) (A): Average LOW Price/Earnings Ratio (P/E) last 2 years
(16J LO 10 plus 17J LO 9 divided by 2 equals 9½);
(B): JUDGMENT - use LOW P/E of: . . . . 8 P/E

FUTURE EARNINGS ESTIMATE

26) Estimated earnings per share for fiscal year ending 19 70 ;
(Caution if less than line 20): . . . . $ 5.40 | OK ~~CAUTION~~

27) Source of estimate: Standard & Poor's Forecaster February 20, 1970

28) Estimated quarterly earnings (fill in line 18 above in quarterly
earnings boxes.)

29) Estimated dividends per share for fiscal 19 70 : . . . . $ 2.80

30) Estimated earnings-dividend ratio (line 26$ 5.40 divided by
line 29$ 2.80 ; Caution if less than 1.4): . . . . | 1.9 | OK ~~CAUTION~~

GAIN VS RISK POTENTIAL FOR STOCK

31) Estimated 19 70 HIGH stock price (line 24B 12 PE x Line 26$ 5.40)$ 64

32) Estimated profit per share (line 31$ 64 minus line 5$ 45). . . . $ 19

33) % Potential Upside Gain (line 32$ 19 divided by line 5$ 45). . . 42 %

34) Estimated 19 70 low stock price (line 25B 8 PE x line 26$ 5.40)$ 43 Use actual low of 42¼

35) Estimated loss per share (line 5$ 45 minus line 34$ 42¼). . . . . $ 2-3/4

36) % Potential Downside Risk(line 35$ 2-3/4 divided by
line 5$ 45 ; Caution if more than 15%): . . . . | 6 % | OK ~~CAUTION~~

37) Gain to Risk Ratio (line 32$ 19 divided by line 35$ 2-3/4 ;
Caution if less than 2 to 1) . . . . | 6 to 1 | OK ~~CAUTION~~

PROFIT ESTIMATE FOR STOCK (100% CASH)

38) Assume a cash investment of. . . . . $ 4,500

39) Number of shares purchaseable (line 38 $ 4,500 divided by
line 5 $ 45): . . . . 100 SH.

40) Estimated gross profit (line 32 $ 19 x line 39 100 SH). . . $ 1,900

41) Commissions: a) buy $ 41.50 b) sell $ 45.40 c) sum of a + b . . . $ 87

42) Estimated net profit (line 40 $ 1,900 minus line 41c $ 87). . $ 1,813

43) Dividends received per year (line 29$ 2.80 x line 39 100 SH). . $ 280

44) Total dividends received (line 43 $ 280 x 1 years) . . . . $ 280

45) Total estimated income received (line 42 $ 1,813 +
line 44$ 280). . . . . $ 2,093

46) Estimated % gain (line 45 $ 2,093 divided by line 38 $ 4,500 ;
Caution if less than 25%). . . . . | 46 % | OK ~~CAUTION~~

FIGURE 20B

From   ROBERT N. PEISNER
            MANAGED ACCOUNTS
            VICE PRESIDENT   April 1, 1970

SUGGESTED STOCK MARKET STRATEGY FOR 1970 - CONSERVATIVE GROWTH STOCK

FEDERAL RESERVE BOARD - A CHANGE TO EASIER MONEY

It is my opinion that the 1969 stock market sell-off is just about over. It is also my opinic
that major buying opportunities in quality issues are now currently available. The Federa
Reserve Board is the government's watchdog over the economic health of the country. In
the past few weeks the usually close-mouthed Federal Reserve officials have made many
public statements to announce that they are ending their tight-money policy and are changi
to an EASIER MONEY policy.

1970 - PROBABLE RISING STOCK MARKET

In my opinion, there exists a strong probability that 1970 will witness a rising stock mark
due to this EASIER MONEY policy. Mr. Arthur Burns, the new Chairman of the Federal
Reserve Board, in answering questions of Senator Proxmire of the Senate Finance Commit
(as published in The Wall Street Journal, 3-19-70), stated that he (Burns) believed the
nation's money supply should be kept expanding at a 2%-to-6% range at the present time.

We, therefore, have it from the highest authority (Chairman Burns) that the Federal Reser
Board's current thinking is for the nation's money supply to increase 2% to 6% in 1970, a
distinct change from the now-ending tight-money policy. The nation's largest banks follow
Mr. Burns' statement by dropping the prime interest rate from 8-1/2% to 8%.

POSSIBLE REPLAY OF 1962 AND 1966: SPOTLIGHT ON CONSERVATIVE GROWTH STOC

A look back into stock market history shows that CONSERVATIVE GROWTH STOCKS start
to move up first, following the market declines of 1962 and 1966. These first-to-rise stoc
had -- in my opinion -- certain identifiable characteristics, as follows:

1. A large, well-entrenched company.
2. A steep decline in stock price over the last year or so.
3. A current price "basing" pattern indicating the price decline to have ended.
4. A large, well-protected dividend with its corresponding high yield (over 5%+.)
5. An historically low Price/Earnings Ratio (under 13 to 1.)
6. A probable increase in sales and Earnings-per-Share for the coming year.

Enclosed you will find a "Profit Estimate Sheet" on such a Conservative Growth Stock whic
highlights these characteristics.

FIGURE 21: FEDERAL RESERVE BOARD:
A CHANGE TO EASIER MONEY.

GROWTH SECURITIES MANAGEMENT

SUGGESTED STOCK MARKET STRATEGY FOR 1969

EDERAL RESERVE BOARD - THE WATCH-DOG

is our opinion that "storm clouds" are gathering over the stock market for the first six onths of 1969. These storm clouds will tend to produce an environment in which it will e difficult for growth stocks to rise aggressively until some time in the summer. The ederal Reserve Board is the government's watch-dog over the economic health of the untry. In the past few weeks, the usually close-mouthed Federal Reserve officials have en making many public statements that the economy is over-expanded and needs to be educed to manageable proportions. It could be compared to an athlete who has gained gnificant weight and needs to go on a diet.

nce 1919, there have been nine periods of prosperity or "boom." The current period of osperity is the ninth. In the previous eight, the Federal Reserve Board has severely ghtened down on the credit screws to stop the boom. They were successful each time. s each economic boom tapered off, the stock market declined, only to usually rise higher the next economic boom.

ere is why we feel the Federal Reserve Board will be successful in stopping this ninth oom, causing difficult times in the stock market for the first six months of 1969, and en producing a major buying opportunity.

1) The Federal Reserve Board has tightened credit to the point that commercial banks are at their tightest money situation since 1959. Unfortunately, Federal Reserve analysts have announced that they still see no more than faint, fragmentary and inconclusive signs of any cooling of the economy. More credit tightening may therefore be expected.

2) This coming February and March, taxpayers will be surprised at how much they owe when they make out their 1968 tax returns due to the new surtax. We feel they will be less prone to spend.

3) In March, France and England are expected to announce negative economic news, thereby contributing to the generally bleak economic climate that we anticipate to be prevalent at that time.

ere are some economic signs to look for that the Federal Reserve Board is succeeding "braking" the economy, setting the stage for a major stock market rally.

1) Unemployment should rise from its current historically low level of 3.3% to 3.5%, 3.6% or higher.

2) New issues of top quality bonds will sell lower than the current historically high rate of 7%+.

3) The Federal Reserve Board will lower the discount rate.

FIGURE 22

your "raw data" can be secured simply and quickly. You have two primary sources of information. Both are usually free.

Public Libraries: The first source of information is your local public library. A well-stocked, up-to-date library should carry every copy of *The Wall Street Journal* for the past five or ten years, as well as various investment advisory services such as Standard & Poor's, Moody's, The Value Line, etc.

The easiest way for you to locate the investment data that you are looking for is to use Standard & Poor's, which is a national service that makes up a detailed "Stock Report" on most companies listed on the New York Stock Exchange and the American Stock Exchange and companies traded over-the-counter (O-T-C). Each Stock Report describes one company and lists the "lion's share" of statistical data about that company that you will normally need to fill out the Profit-Estimate Sheet. Standard & Poor's periodically updates the information.

The Stock Reports can be ordered from Standard & Poor's Corporation, 345 Hudson Street, New York, N.Y. 10014, or obtained at your broker's office.

Stock Brokerage Offices: The second source of information are the various New York and American Stock Exchange member brokerage offices located throughout the country. Most of these brokerage offices normally maintain up-to-date financial libraries that include Standard & Poor's. It is an open-door policy of the New York and American Stock Exchanges that you are welcome to visit these offices. They want you to feel free to walk in and browse around and ask for free statistical investment information.

Example of a Standard & Poor's Stock Report

In Figures 23A and 23B, you have the front and reverse sides of a typical Stock Report for a company as issued by Standard & Poor's for a stock listed on the New York Stock Exchange. We are using SD. The actual physical format of the Stock Reports describing stocks listed on the American Stock Exchange and those traded O-T-C are somewhat different.

Standard Oil of Calif.

SD¹　　　　　　　　　　　　　　　　　　　　　　　**2106**

Stock—	Price Feb. 5'71	Dividend	Yield
COMMON.........................	53¼	²$2.80	²5.3%

RECOMMENDATION: This well-balanced, major international oil company derives some 57% of its profits from Western Hemisphere operations. Relatively fast growth in demand abroad should tend to fortify profit prospects for the foreign divisions, supported by the important 30% interest in Aramco, the principal Saudi Arabian crude producer, and by Iranian, Indonesian and other diversified crude sources. Additions to refining capacity, crude development and other expansion should enhance the company's North American prospects. The shares have basic attraction.

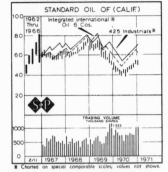

³**GROSS OPER. INCOME (Million $)**

Quarter:	1970	1969	1968	1967	1966
March.....	1,135	1,053	1,004	822	741
June......	1,167	1,105	1,032	923	817
Sept.	1,195	1,108	1,047	1,014	831
Dec.		1,124	1,073	1,031	813

Sales and other revenues for 1970, based on the preliminary report, rose 8.8% from those of the preceding year, with the company's gross worldwide production of crude oil and natural gas liquids up 11% to a new high. Natural gas sales increased some 7%, and sales of refined products advanced strongly some 10%. Aided by improved product and crude oil prices in the late months of 1970, and use of newly added supertankers, profit margins for the year as a whole held up well; despite greater interest expense and a heavier tax provision, net income rose some 0.2% to a new peak. Share earnings were equal to $5.36, compared with $5.35 for the preceding year.

PROSPECTS

Near Term—Revenues for 1971 are expected to rise further, with increases in crude output contributing. Sources of crude were extensively diversified in the past year, including new or expanded sources in Canada, South America, Indonesia, Nigeria, Alaska, Australia and in the U. S. onshore and offshore. Gasoline sales should extend the company's relatively favorable momentum in this division, with the new additive contributing, along with introduction of leadfree and low-lead gasoline in the domestic service stations in 1970.

The addition of eight supertankers in 1970 is expected to reduce costs in this division with four more being added in 1971. Higher taxes in producing areas abroad may well be offset in large part by increases in prices in consuming areas. On balance, prospects favor earnings improvement in 1971 from the $5.36 a share of 1970. Dividends should continue at $0.70 quarterly.

Long Term—Prospects are enhanced by the improving domestic position and strong representation in international areas.

RECENT DEVELOPMENTS

The company's worldwide gross production of crude and natural gas liquids in 1970 rose 11% to 2,558,000 barrels daily, and product sales rose 10% to 1,920,000 barrels daily. The company reported significant discoveries offshore California, the Gulf of Mexico, in Iran and Indonesia. Three finds in Indonesia may prove of major importance. The new Grand Bahama Island 250,000 barrel a day refinery, 35% owned, has been placed in operation, with low-sulphur fuel oil shipments now available.

DIVIDEND DATA

Dividends in the past 12 months were:

Amt. of Divd. $	Date Decl.	Ex-divd. Date	Stock of Record	Payment Date
0.70...	Apr. 29	May 5	May 11	Jun. 10'70
0.70...	Jul. 29	Aug. 4	Aug. 10	Sep. 10'70
0.70...	Oct. 28	Nov. 4	Nov. 10	Dec. 10'70
0.70...	Jan. 27	Feb. 4	Feb. 10	Mar.10'71

⁴**COMMON SHARE EARNINGS ($)**

Quarter:	1970	1969	1968	1967	1966
March.....	1.22	1.34	1.28	1.18	1.16
June........	1.27	1.36	1.34	1.27	1.26
Sept.	1.38	1.31	1.34	1.16	1.10
Dec.	1.49	1.34	1.37	1.22	1.21

¹Listed N.Y.S.E. & Pacific Coast, Midwest & Honolulu S.E.; also traded Cincinnati, Boston, Detroit & Phila.-Balt.-Wash. S.Es.
²Indicated rate. ³Includes excise taxes. ⁴Adj. for 5% stk. divds. each paid in 1967 & 1969.

STANDARD N.Y.S.E. STOCK REPORTS　　　　　　　　　**STANDARD & POOR'S CORP.**

Published at Ephrata, Pa. Editorial & Executive Offices, 345 Hudson St., New York, N.Y. 10014

Vol. 38, No. 29　　　　　　　Thursday, February 11, 1971　　　　　　　Sec. 21

FIGURE 23A

Courtesy Standard and Poor's Corporation

(11A) (K) (F) (G) (H) (J)

2106 STANDARD OIL COMPANY OF CALIFORNIA

INCOME STATISTICS (Million $) AND PER SHARE ($) DATA

Year Ended Dec. 31	[5]Gross Oper. Inc.	[1]% Op. Inc. of Gross	[1]Oper. Inc.	[4]Depr., Depl. & Amort.	Net Bef. Taxes	Net Inc.	[2]Common Share ($) Data: Earns.	*Cash Generated	Divs. Paid	Price Range	Price-Earns. Ratios HI LO
1971--	-----	---	-----	-----	-----	-----	---	---	0.70	--------	-----
1970--	-----	---	-----	-----	-----	[6]454.80	[6]5.36	---	2.80	54⅞-38	10- 7
1969--	3,825.0	17.2	657.36	312.91	590.39	453.79	5.35	9.04	2.76½	75 -48¼	14- 9
1968--	3,634.8	18.6	677.94	314.03	569.43	451.83	5.33	9.22	2.57	73¼-54¾	14-10
1967--	3,298.6	19.4	640.91	283.36	513.09	409.39	4.83	8.34	2.38	61⅜-51⅜	12-10
1966--	2,698.3	22.0	593.94	252.65	500.65	401.24	4.73	7.72	2.26½	78 -50	16-11
1965--	2,442.5	23.0	561.16	280.11	455.99	391.23	4.67	7.36	2.06	72⅜-60¼	15-13
1964--	2,285.7	21.0	480.21	259.22	393.36	345.29	4.17	6.75	1.82	66⅜-50⅜	16-12
1963--	2,202.5	19.4	427.86	247.57	356.75	322.07	3.88	6.28	1.72½	59⅞-50¼	15-13
1962--	2,150.9	20.1	432.26	237.49	348.79	313.78	3.78	5.79	1.65	50 -41	13-11
1961--	2,046.5	20.1	411.91	217.03	335.09	294.41	3.53	5.61	1.57	44½-36¾	13-10
1960--	1,663.4	22.7	378.34	198.83	302.41	266.11	3.30	5.27	1.57	40¼-31⅜	12- 9

PERTINENT BALANCE SHEET STATISTICS (Million $)

Dec. 31	Gross Prop.	[3]Capital Expend.	Cash Items	Oil Inventories	Receivables	Current Assets	Current Liabs.	Net Workg. Cap.	Cur. Ratio Assets to Liabs.	Long Term Debt	[2]($) Book Val. Com. Sh.
1969--	6,594.6	775.15	231.0	291.8	1,034.2	1,668.1	991.3	676.8	1.7-1	635.98	52.34
1968--	6,153.6	650.78	356.9	281.5	894.0	1,645.4	873.2	772.2	1.9-1	603.64	49.82
1967--	5,834.0	643.31	229.2	271.4	869.1	1,476.0	795.9	680.1	1.9-1	554.73	46.43
1966--	5,339.7	554.84	178.0	205.7	723.5	1,207.0	647.4	559.6	1.9-1	290.06	41.58
1965--	5,014.4	653.93	136.8	198.7	612.6	1,043.0	625.4	417.6	1.7-1	216.33	38.58
1964--	4,582.3	569.91	172.2	186.7	519.4	971.0	478.0	492.9	2.0-1	216.30	35.62
1963--	4,273.0	465.78	203.9	183.6	445.9	916.6	450.9	465.7	2.0-1	183.22	35.15
1962--	4,028.4	546.42	202.3	186.6	399.2	871.4	434.1	437.3	2.0-1	184.90	32.68
1961--	3,752.1	474.90	219.9	164.8	347.4	819.8	393.8	426.0	2.1-1	171.60	30.42
1960--	3,371.7	388.08	217.0	134.7	317.5	753.8	324.0	429.8	2.3-1	172.80	28.27

[1]Aft. all tax except inc. taxes, but bef. cost of unproductive wells. [2]Adj. for 5% stk. divs. in 1969, 1967, 1964, 1963, & 1962. [3]Incl. exploratory expenditures & investments. [4]Incl. all prop. chgs. [5]Excl. product excise taxes. [6]Preliminary.
*As computed by Standard & Poor's.

(4) → **Fundamental Position**

Standard Oil of California is the leading Pacific Coast oil unit, is prominent on the East Coast, and has important foreign interests. Operations in the Western Hemisphere account for an estimated 57% of consolidated net income, with the Eastern Hemisphere accounting for 43%. Major Eastern Hemisphere interests include 50% of the Caltex group, 30% of Arabian American Oil and a 7% stake in the Iranian Consortium.

Including company's interest in affiliates, gross production of crude and natural gas liquids in 1969 on a worldwide basis rose to 2,300,612 barrels daily, from 2,115,024 barrels daily a year earlier. Western Hemisphere production for the company's account eased to 690,470 barrels daily for 1969 from 706,974 barrels daily for 1968; Eastern Hemisphere production rose to 1,610,142 barrels daily from 1,408,050 barrels daily. Output is approximately 38% from Saudi Arabia, 24% from the U. S., 13% from Indonesia, 8% from Iran, 8% from Libya, 3% from Canada, and 6% from other countries. Sales of natural gas (all Western Hemisphere) rose 4% in 1969 to 1,581,274 Mcf. daily from 1,519,174 Mcf. daily for the prior year.

As of December 31, 1968, net proved crude and liquids reserves were estimated at 4,739 million barrels, including 2,126 million barrels in the U. S. Proved net reserves of natural gas in the Western Hemisphere were placed at 9,256 billion cubic feet. At December 31, 1967, other Western Hemisphere crude reserves were put at 603 million barrels, Europe and Africa 1,652 million, Iran 1,652 million, and through affiliates Middle East 20,390 million and Sumatra 868 million.

Worldwide sales of petroleum products, including equity in affiliates, rose to 1,744,770 barrels daily in 1969, up 6.2% from 1,642,273 barrels daily in 1968. Of 1969 product sales, some 58% was in the Western Hemisphere, mainly U. S. Refinery runs in 1969 averaged 1,560,455 barrels daily, up from 1,455,032. Refined products are sold through some 25,000 Chevron hallmark outlets in the Western Hemisphere, including about 1,200 units operated by the company, the largest such system. In the Eastern Hemisphere, sales are partly through the Caltex affiliate mostly east of Suez, and partly in Europe through Chevron Oil Europe. Chemical sales in 1969 eased to $268.1 million from $278.2 million in 1968. Chemical divisions include Oronite (industrial chemicals) Ortho (agricultural) and Polymer (plastics).

Paid each year since 1911, common dividends averaged some 50% of available net in the five years through 1970. ← (5)

Finances

To finance expansion of foreign activities, including those in Europe, the company early in 1968 sold $50,000,000 of 5% convertible debentures of Chevron Overseas. Capital outlays in 1971 may exceed 1970's $800 million.

CAPITALIZATION

LONG TERM DEBT: $635,975,000, incl. $50 million of 5% debs. conv. into com. at $62.14 a sh.

COMMON STOCK: 84,837,251 shs. ($6.25 p.). ← (6)

Incorporated in Del. in 1926. **Office**—225 Bush St., San Francisco 94120. **Pres**—H. J. Haynes. **Secy**—H. L. Severance. **Treas**—H. D. Armstrong. **Dirs**—O. N. Miller (Chrmn), W. M. Allen, D. L. Bower, J. E. Gosline, J. R. Grey, H. J. Haynes, J. T. Higgins, G. M. Keller, J. A. McCone, J. E. O'Brien, G. L. Parkhurst, R. A. Peterson, E. H. Wasson. **Transfer Agents**—Company's office; Chase Manhattan Bank, NYC; Montreal Trust Co., Vancouver, B.C. **Registrars**—Crocker-Citizens National Bank, San Francisco; First National City Bank, NYC; National Trust Co., Vancouver, B.C.

FIGURE 23B

Courtesy Standard and Poor's Corporation

Special Markings

Figures 23A and 23B show a Stock Report of SD, specially marked by the authors. You will note that there are circled numbers with arrows pointing toward selected data in the Stock Report. These numbers refer to lines on the Profit-Estimate Sheet. The intent is to help you locate the specific investment data in the Stock Report so as to fill out the particular lines in the Profit-Estimate Sheet. The Stock Report illustrated was printed in February 1971. The purpose of using this *updated* sheet is to show you the before-and-after statistics on SD.

Section One: Basic Data; How to Fill It Out

Let us now begin our analysis of SD. In Figure 24 you will find the Basic Data section of the Profit-Estimate Sheet completely filled out. The analysis has the intent of determining if SD in March 1970 possessed eight OKs so that you might elect to qualify it as an undervalued stock. The results produced by this sheet are identical to what is illustrated in Figures 20A and 20B.

The analysis starts at line 1 in Figure 24.

CONSERVATIVE GROWTH - LOW PRICE/EARNINGS RATIO - HIGH DIVIDEND % YIELD

SECTION ONE - BASIC DATA

1) Date of Analysis . . . . March 9, 1970

2) Company: _____ Standard Oil of California _____

3) Exchange & Symbol . . . . Exchange: NYSE ; Symbol: SD

4) Primary Industry: _____ Oil and Gas Products _____

5) Continuous cash dividends paid since:. 1911

6) Number shares of stock outstanding: 84,800,000

7) Number of institutions holding:. 361

8) Number of shares institutions hold: 5,946,000

9) % shares institution hold (line 8 5,946,000 divided by
line 6 84,800,000) . . . . 6.9 %

10) Source of historical investment data: _____ Standard & Poor's #2106 _____

FIGURE 24

LINE 1: Date of Analysis: March 9, 1970.

Enter the current day, month and year in which you are making the analysis.

LINE 2: Company: Standard Oil of California.

Refer to circle 2 in Figure 23A. Enter the exact name of the company. (It is surprising the number of investors who do not know either the specific name or the spelling of the name of companies in which they own stock.)

LINE 3: Exchange & Symbol: Exchange: NYSE; Symbol: SD.

Refer to circle 3 (Figure 23A). Enter the "SD," for Standard Oil of California. (All stocks on the various exchanges are identified by ticker symbols of from one to four letters to identify each stock on the quote boards and ticker tapes worldwide as it is being traded.)

On which of the stock exchanges is SD traded? Notice in Figure 23A that next to the symbol SD is placed a little "1." This directs your attention to a footnote on the Stock Report, indicating that SD is listed on the New York Stock Exchange, the Pacific Coast Stock Exchange and other regional exchanges. This information could be important to you. There sometimes occurs the necessity to buy or sell quickly. Knowing where the stock is traded can be helpful. For example, the New York Stock Exchange is currently open for trading from 10:00 A.M. to 3:30 P.M. (Eastern Time). But the Pacific Coast Stock Exchange is open for trading from 10:00 A.M. to 5:30 P.M. (Eastern Time), which is an additional two hours after the close of the New York Stock Exchange. If you lived in New York, and the time was 5:00 P.M. and if you wanted immediately to execute a trade in SD, you could not use the New York Stock Exchange, but the Pacific Coast Exchange would be open for your business for another half-hour.

LINE 4: Primary Industry: Oil and Gas Products.

Refer to circle 4 in Figure 23B, which is on the back of the Stock Report. The first paragraph of the "Fundamental Position" tells you what SD does. The remainder of this section tells you other pertinent information about SD, its specific products and recent activities.

LINE 5: Continuous cash dividends paid since: 1911.

Refer to circle 5 in Figure 23B. SD has paid dividends continually for fifty-nine years.

The purpose of lines 5, 6, 7, 8 and 9 is to give you brief, but very pertinent information about the "solidity" of the company you are analyzing.

LINE 6: Number of shares of stock outstanding: 84.8 million.

Refer to circle 6 in Figure 23B. The 84.8 million shares outstanding are a significant amount. It tells you that SD should be able to absorb substantial waves of buying or selling without showing a major change in price. Hence, you should be able, quickly and easily, to buy or sell large quantities of stock. This investment principle is called *liquidity*. In the "jargon" of the stock world, SD is known as a "High-Cap" stock. "High-Cap" means "highly capitalized," or having a large number of shares outstanding.

LINE 7: Number of institutions holding: 361.

LINE 8: Number of shares institutions hold: 5,946,000.

Lines 7 and 8 will be explained together. Much of the data to follow came from Robert Peisner's book *How to Select Rapid Growth Stocks*.

The figures on institutional holdings are published monthly. They are published by Standard & Poor's in its monthly publication the *Stock Guide*. This handy tabulation of data can be ordered from Standard & Poor's on a single-copy or subscription basis, or can be readily consulted at your broker's office or public library. Most major brokerage houses have Standard & Poor's put an individualized cover on the *Stock Guide* to advertise the brokerage house.

Two items of information about institutions given in the *Stock Guide* are:

1. the number of institutions holding the stock in question; and
2. the total number of shares held by the institutions.

Figure 25 shows a reprint of a typical page from the February 1970 issue of the *Stock Guide*.

The important column you are looking for is indicated by **Arrow** 1, a star, and the abbreviation "Inst. Hold.," which means "Institutional Holdings." The column is divided into two parts, each with a vertical row of figures.

(1)

STANDARD & POOR'S CORPORATION

(2)

INDEX	Ticker Symbol	STOCKS NAME OF ISSUE (Call Price of Pfd. Stocks)	Market	Earns & Div Rank-ing	Par Val.	★ Inst. Hold Cos	Shs. (000)	STOCK CHARACTERISTICS Principal Business	PRICE RANGE 1936-68 High	Low	1969 High	Low	1970 High	Low	Feb. Sales in 100s	February, 1970 O-C Recent Bid Ask High	Low	Last	% Div. Yield	P-E Ra-tio
1	SB	Standard Brands, Inc.	[3]NYS, De	A+	No	90	1225	Diversified line food products,	54⅞	a2¾	51½	42¼	54	45⅜	1548	54	45⅜	53⅜	2.8	20
2	Pr	$3.50 cm Pfd (100) vtg	NYS•	AA	No	29	40	distills gins, whiskey	102	58⅜	63	50⅛	55	51½	2.7	53⅝	52½	53⅝	6.5	..
3	SBP	Standard Brands Paint	NYS	B+	1	4	65	Discount strs; mfr own paint	a23⅛	a3½	32	20⅛	37¼	28¼	1307	37¼	29½	35	1.0	30
4		Standard Computer Corp	UNL	NR	No	...	....	Multi-lingual computer sys	....	....	18½	11	20½	16	....	....	16B	16¾A	....	d
5	STT	Standard Container Co.	ASE	NR	1	1	20	Ammun boxes, cans; met prod	15⅛	10½	16	9⅛	11⅞	10	126	11¼	10	10¾	....	8
6	SNC	Standard Coosa-Thatcher Co.	ASE	NR	10	1	n/a	Cotton yarns & threads	42	a7½	29	22⅛	22¾	22	20	22¾	22	22⅝	5.7	7
7	SDR	Standard Dredging Corp.	ASE, MW	B−	1	...	....	Flood control and harbor	29⅛	1	17¾	10	12⅞	10¼	142	12⅜	11¼	12	1.7	13
8	Pr	$1.60 cm Pfd (33)	ASE¶, MW	B	20	...	....	improvement work	30	7¾	25	20⅞	20⅞	18¾	11	20	18¾	20	8.0	..
9	STL	Standard International	NYS, PC	B+	No	1	22	Pub, med, consumer, techn'l	27⅜	a7¾	27⅜	14¼	17	14	286	15½	14	14⅜	‡1.7	11
10	SKO	Standard Kollsman Ind.	NYS, MW, PB	B	1	7	106	TV, missile el'tronics; Casco	53¼	5¾	31¼	10½	13¾	11	277	11¾	11	11⅛	....	19
11	SMM	Standard Metals Corp.	ASE, PC, SL	B−	3¢	...	....	Uranium; precious, basemetals	14¾	a¾	13⅝	4	8½	4½	864	6⅞	5⅞	6⅜	‡...	d
12		Standard Milling, Cl A non-vtg	UNL	B−	1	...	....	Makes flour & feed; mdse grain	5⅝	2⅛	5¾	2¾	3	2¾	....	....	3B	3½A	5.7	11
13	SMP	Standard Motor Products, Cl A	ASE	B+	2	1	18	Ignition & fuel system parts	23⅜	6⅞	21¼	14	24¼	19⅜	544	24¼	19⅜	24	3.1	13
14	SD	Standard Oil Co. of California	[1]NYS, Ho	A+	6¼	360	5877	Integrated international oil	86	a4⅛	75	48¼	53⅛	42¼	9687	48½	42¼	47½	‡5.9	9
15	SN	Standard Oil Co. (Indiana)	[1]NYS	A	12½	426	4335	Dominant refiner in midwest	67½	a5	70¾	44	48⅞	37½	6325	44	37½	41¾	5.5	9
16	J	Standard Oil Co. (New Jersey)	[2]NYS	A+	7	906	12919	World's leading oil company	92⅞	a5	85⅜	60⅜	63⅛	49⅞	17926	57½	49⅞	54	6.9	9
17	SOH	Standard Oil Co. (Ohio)	[3]NYS, MW	A	5	108	1327	Oil refining, marketing in	75⅞	a2¼	119⅞	65¼	85	59¼	5360	77½	59¼	75⅞	3.6	14
18	Pr	3¾% cm A Pfd (100:SF100) vtg.	NYS, MW•	AA	100	21	21	Ohio area; plastics and	104	63½	68	51	56	52¼	15	56	54	55½	6.8	..
19	Pr B	4% cm Cv B Pfd ([6]150)	NYS	AA	100	3	3	petrochems products	108½	93½	167	100	123	89½	1	89½	89½	89½	4.5	..
20	SPF	Standard Pacific Corp.	ASE, PC	NR	25¢	2	130	Home & comm'l constr franch	23	¼	21¼	7½	11¾	7⅝	579	11¾	7⅝	10½	....	28
21	SPK	Standard Packaging Corp.	[5]NYS	B	1	6	490	Advertising specialties; flex	39⅝	a¾	20⅜	8⅝	10¾	7½	1156	9⅛	7½	8	....	11
22	Pr C	$1.60 cm Cv Pfd (33) vtg	NYS	.....	1	...	....	pkg; dstr consumer prod	117	9⅞	61	33	34½	27	9	30	27	30	5.3	..
23	SDP	Standard Pressed Steel Co.	NYS, PB	B	1	31	530	Major mfr indust. fasteners	a37⅜	a5½	28	11	14¼	9¾	1492	11⅞	9¾	10	4.4	14
24	SPD	Standard Products Co.	ASE	B	1	...	....	Parts for auto industry	33¾	a1¾	31¾	21⅜	27⅝	23⅛	15	25	23⅞	24	5.0	7
25	STU	Standard Prudential Corp	NYS	NR	1	6	57	Diversified industrial &	21⅞	2	15¾	9⅝	11⅜	10	798	11⅜	10½	11	6.0	21
26	Pr	$0.10 cm [8]Cv Pfd ([9]16.80) vtg	NYS	.....	No	1	4	financial corp.	30	25⅛	29½	19½	25⅜	21½	70	25⅜	24	25	0.4	..
27		Standard Register Co.	UNL	B	50¢	6	49	Business forms, handling eq	39¾	a11¼	31¾	23½	31	26½	....	....	28¾B	29¾A	3.4	15
28		Standard Screw Co. (aa)	UNL	B+	10	5	69	Faucets, fasteners, fuel inject	34	a3¼	35¾	26	31¼	21¾	....	....	29B	30A	4.7	12
29	SWD	Standard Shares, Inc.	ASE	.....	1	...	....	Investment trust; lge hld'gs	35¾	a1/32	34⅝	26	28⅝	27	90	28¼	27	27¾	‡...	..
30	STH	Standard-Thomson Corp.	ASE	B	1	1	3	Components for aircraft, auto,	a18	a⅝	16½	11	14	11	221	14	11⅛	13⅛	....	9
31		5½% cm Pfd (13; SF 12½)	UNL	B	12½	1	10	bldg, home appliances	12¾	4	10	5½	8	7	....	....	7B	....	9.8	..
32		Stange Co.	UNL	NR	1	2	5	Processor of natural spices	33	a1¾	45	20½	26¼	23	....	....	26¼B	27A	0.7	31
33	SAC	Stanley Aviation Corp.	ASE	B−	10¢	1	1	Equip for military aircraft	23½	a2	17¾	5	7⅛	4⅞	98	5⅞	4⅞	5½	....	18
34		Stanley Home Products non-vtg	UNL	B+	2½	1	15	Home sale household items	48½	a6⅞	35	17½	25½	21¼	....	....	25¼B	26A	3.5	15
35	SWK	Stanley Works (The)	NYS	B+	10	14	369	Mfr full line hardware prod	56	a4⅞	54	41⅝	44½	37⅝	300	41	37⅝	39½	3.5	11
36	SRY	Stanray Corporation	NYS, MW	B	1	9	200	Mfr railway equip & parts	34	6⅜	33⅞	13⅜	16¾	13⅛	209	14½	13⅝	14	4.3	9
37	SKU	Stanrock Uranium Mines	ASE, TS	C	1	2	119	Uranium mining in Ontario	5 5/16	⅛	6 1/16	1 13/16	2⅝	1 15/16	654	2 3/16	2	2 1/16	....	d
38	STK	Stanwick Corp.	ASE	NR	10¢	...	....	Engr & mgmt serv organ; govt	....	....	15½	3⅞	5¾	4	111	4½	4	4	....	13
39	SMS	Stapling Machines Co.	ASE	B	No	1	15	Machs to wirebound cont'nrs	33¼	11¼	23½	16½	18½	16	65	17⅛	16	16	5.0	14
40	STR	Star Supermarkets	ASE	B	1	...	....	Food mkts, Rochester NY area	21¾	6¼	15⅞	9	10½	9¼	56	10	9¼	9¼	6.5	8

Uniform Footnote Explanations—See Page 1. Other: [1]Bo, Ci, De, MW, PB, PC, TS. [2]Bo, Ci, De, MW, PB, PC. [3]Bo, Ci, MW, PB, PC, TS. [4]®$1.56, '68. [5]MW, PB, PC. [6]104 after 1-15-71, then 50¢ less annually to 100. [7]®$0.49, '69. [8]From Jul. 1, 1970. [9]From 10-1-70. t—^$0.15, '65; ^$0.01, '66; ^$0.02, '67. u—Partial year. v—□$3.43, '68. x—□$0.18, '65; ^$0.18, 66; ^$1.75, '67; □$0.18, '68. aa—Plan name change to Stanadyne Inc.

FIGURE 25

Courtesy Standard and Poor's Corporation (from *Stock Guide*)

One row is headed "Cos.," for "Companies." The other row is headed "Shs. (000)," for "Number of Shares Held in Thousands of Shares."

Refer to Arrow 2 in Figure 25. This is Index line 14. Using SD as an example, read across the SD line. Under the column "Cos." you find "361." This means that 361 separate and individual institutions, as of February 1970, owned SD stock.

How many shares did the 361 institutions hold? Under the column "Shs. (000)" you see "5946." This number means 5,946,-000 shares.

When a stock is said to be in "strong hands" the stock is thought to be held by people who are professional, sophisticated, patient and knowledgeable. One set of published statistics that reflects, in a broad sense, the appeal of a stock to this important type of buyer are the statistics on *instituitonal holdings.* Institutions currently account for more than 60 percent of the dollar volume traded on the New York Stock Exchange.

The figures published monthly by Standard & Poor's cover the activities of more than 2,500 institutions. These institutions include mutual funds, bank trusts, investment companies, fire, casualty and life insurance companies, pension funds and retirement systems.

Another reason for dealing in stocks that are in "strong hands" is the irrefutable fact that the institutions tend to hold only the stock of companies of good and proven quality. Many institutions have large research departments that employ full-time professional economists and security analysts, who generally investigate the companies thoroughly before an investment is made.

Rule of Thumb: If the stock is not suitable for the institutions to buy, it is probably not suitable for you to buy. You should want your stock to be generally favored and bought by the institutions. But here's a note of caution. The price volatility of these "conservative stocks" can sometimes be disconcertingly high due to the excessive concentration of such stocks in institutional hands. On bad news, a number may decide to sell. Here is an example: On November 16, 1971, Chesapeake & Ohio was trading at 61. Suddenly, the New York Stock Exchange suspended trading in the stock on word from the company that an important news announcement was pending. The news was that the Board of Directors of Chesapeake & Ohio voted to omit the regular $1.00 quarterly cash dividend. Immediately, sell orders appeared. The New York Stock Exchange continued the trading suspension. The next day, November 17th, the stock opened for trading at 47, *down 14 points*. There was no in-between price for an investor to get out.

LINE 9: % shares institutions hold [line 8; 5,946,000 divided by line 6: 84,800,000]: 6.9%.

What percentage of the total amount of stock do the 361 institutions hold? You know from line 6 that SD had 84,800,000 shares; 5,946,000 is 6.9 percent of 84,800,000.

LINE 10: Source of historical investment data: Standard & Poor's 2106.

Note the two circled 10s in Figure 23A. SD is currently No. 2106 in Standard & Poor's files. The purpose of this line is to serve as a memory jogger to permit you easily to recheck your figures if necessary.

14

The Profit-Estimate Sheet in Action— Section Two: Historical Earnings and Stock Data

Now you are ready to examine the stock's historical data. The purpose is to extract certain pertinent criteria. There are diverse opinions among analysts as to how much historical data should be used. The authors' opinion is that the "here and now" is most important. The values assigned to stocks five, ten or fifteen years ago should be viewed as relics from antiquity. The reason is that such values resulted from the unique mix of the then prevailing economic, market and emotional climate. The authors elect to look back no more than three years.

In Figure 26, you will find "Section Two—Historical Earnings and Stock Data" of the Profit-Estimate Sheet completely filled out. It provides you with a quick, yet precise look at the more pertinent investment data concerning SD as of March 1970. It also provides you with the answers to these important questions:

1. What is SD's fiscal year?
2. What has been the trend of quarterly earnings?
3. What has been the trend of yearly earnings?
4. What cash dividends have been paid?
5. What have been the stock's high and low prices each year?
6. What has been the price/earnings ratio range each year?
7. What has been the trend of annual sales?

A "box structure" is provided so that this important investment data may be easily seen.

Line 15 Projects the Future

A look at line 15 in Figure 26 shows that each of the boxes contains an "E." The "E" stands for "Estimated." You will be estimating what values should be in those boxes and projecting the *future* performance of the stock. Only time will tell the accuracy of your projections. To fill in line 15 fully, it is necessary to complete Sections Three and Four of the Profit-Estimate Sheet. Ultimately box 15H will be crucial. In box 15H you will be estimating the high and low price range of the stock for the coming year. The stock prices that you calculate should indicate if the potential profit outweighs the investment risk.

Earnings Per Share

One of the underlying theories of this stock-selection technique is that the company's dividend should be well protected. How is it possible for you to know this important financial condition about a company? For one thing, you must know and understand earnings per share.

Earnings per share tells you how much money the company is making or losing in terms of one share of stock.

Earnings per share is easy to figure. And since earnings per share is so important to the correct operation of this method, it is necessary that you understand *how* the earnings for a company are figured.

SECTION TWO - HISTORICAL EARNINGS AND STOCK DATA

	(A) FISCAL YEAR ENDING - MONTH	(B) 1st QTR ENDING	(C) 2nd QTR ENDING	(D) 3rd QTR ENDING	(E) 4th QTR ENDING	(F) FISCAL YEARLY EARN	(G) $ DIV	(H) STOCK PRICE HI LO	(J) PRICE/ EARN RATIO P/E HI LO	(K) $ ANNUAL SALES
11)	December	March	June	Sept.	Dec.					
12)	Dec. ,1967	1.18	1.27	1.16	1.22	4.83	2.38	61 51	12 10	$3.2 BIL
13)	Dec. ,1968	1.28	1.34	1.34	1.36	5.32	2.57	73¼ 54	.14 10	3.6 BIL
14)	Dec. ,1969	1.34	1.36	1.31	1.34	5.35	2.76	75 48¼	14 9	3.8 BIL
15)	Dec. ,1970	1.33 E	1.36 E	1.32 E	1.39 E	5.40 E	2.80E	64 42¼ E	12 8 E	

FIGURE 26

We can use SD as an example. In 1969 SD reported a net profit of $453,800,000. To change this enormous figure to simple earnings per share, you must know how many shares of common stock SD has outstanding. Refer to circle 6 on the Standard & Poor's Stock Report in Figure 23B. SD has 84,800,000 shares of stock outstanding. Divide the net profit of $453,800,000 by the 84,800,000 shares of stock. The result is $5.35 earnings for each share of SD stock.

Earnings per share is one of the more important money figures to describe a company's financial health. Practically all analysts use it. It is so important that it is usually calculated for you.

A convenient source of information on earnings is the "Digest of Earnings Reports" column published in *The Wall Street Journal*. Figure 27 is a reprint of part of this column for January 29, 1970. The quarterly, semiannual and annual earnings reports are digested in this column as they are issued. Perhaps some 150 reports may be printed on a given day. The importance of these reports for the serious stock buyer cannot be overemphasized. It is up to you as a careful investor to check the "Digest" daily and to note the earnings and sales data on those stocks in which you are interested. The research vice-presidents of many Stock Exchange firms normally turn to this column as the very first order of business of the day.

Also there is the element of speed here. The earnings per share figures are published only once in the "Digest of Earnings Reports" column. There is no second time. It is up to you to be attentive to catch it. The fact that most company executives are creatures of habit and tend to release earnings reports at about the same time each quarter is often a help in knowing about when to expect them to appear.

What Is the Difference Between Earnings Per Share and Cash Dividends?

It is important to eliminate the confusion between cash dividends and earnings per share.

For the calendar year of 1969 SD paid out $23,744,000 in cash dividends. To find what the cash dividend per share of stock was, divide $23,744,000 by 84,800,000 shares: The result is $2.80 cash dividends per share ($.70 per quarter).

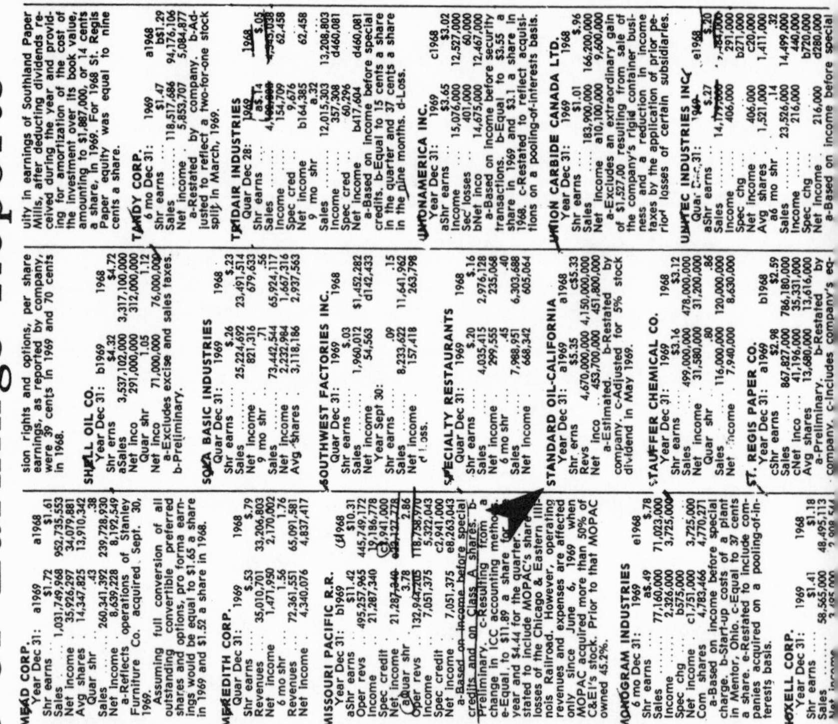

Digest of Earnings Reports

TODAY'S INDEX

FIGURE 27: HOW TO FIND "DIGEST OF EARNINGS REPORTS."

From *The Wall Street Journal* (January 29, 1970)

As noted, SD's earnings per share was $5.35 in 1969. The cash dividend per share was $2.80. If you owned one share of SD for the entire year of 1969, you received $2.80 in cash dividends.

Cash dividends are a distribution of profit. Therefore they are normally paid out of net profit. *Net profit is earnings per share.* SD's cash dividend of $2.80 per share came out of the earnings per share of $5.35. Refer to circle 5 in Figure 23B. The line reads: "common dividends averaged some 50% of available net in the five years through 1970."

At this point a student of the stock market could ask what happened to the remaining $2.55 per share ($5.35 minus $2.80) which amounts to $216 million (84,800,000 shares times $2.55). SD put it back into the company for research and development, new plant expenditures, oil exploration, etc. In the next chapter you will find additional information about dividends.

The Importance of Earnings Per Share

A company's earnings per share indicate how much profit it is making. When earnings per share rise from one year to the next, it means the company is richer and stronger because it is making more money. The company may therefore be able to increase its dividend. Its stock is normally worth more on the open market. On the other hand, if the earnings per share go down, the company is more likely to cut its dividend and the stock should normally be worth less. By knowing the trend of the earnings per share, you know if the company's earning power is strengthening or weakening. And, more important, you can judge whether the current dividend is well protected, whether it may be increased, or whether it is likely to be cut.

The Importance of Quarterly Earnings per Share

Every three months most of the companies listed on both the New York Stock Exchange and American Stock Exchange report their earnings per share for the current quarter. To the investor, this means that every dollar spent and every dollar earned by the company is reported to you quarterly.

Every company has an accounting period of one year. The United States Government, for taxation purposes, requires this. Normally, it is the calendar year January through December.

However, it can be any 12-month period. SD's fiscal year coincides with the calendar year. Its quarters end March 31, June 30, September 30 and December 31. The report for the first quarter (January, February, March), called the "March quarterly report" in the language of Wall Street, is normally reported in April.

Quarterly Earnings Are Reported in the "Digest of Earnings Reports"

In Figure 28 you can see how SD's earnings for the quarter ending March 31, 1970, were reported in the "Digest of Earnings" column of *The Wall Street Journal* on April 30, 1970. (Arrow 1).

R.E.D.M. CORP.

Quar Mar 31:	1970	1969
aShr earns ..	$.15	$.10
Sales	5,679,000	5,655,000
Income	89,000	63,000
bTax credit .	75,000	56,000
cNet inco ...	164,000	119,000
Com shares	1,271,000	1,117,000

a-Based on income before tax credit. b-From tax-loss carryforwards. c-Equal to 13 cents a share in 1970 and 10 cents in 1969.

RICHARD D. IRWIN INC.

Year Feb 28:	1970	1969
Shr earns	$1.01	$.81
Sales	11,638,993	9,917,194
Net income .	1,285.666	1,013,820

RICHARDSON CO.

Quar Mar 31:	1970	1969
Shr earns	$.31	$.61
Sales	31,609,000	31,730,000
Net income .	746,000	1,183,000

Assuming conversion of preferred shares, per share earnings would be 30 cents in 1970 and 47 cents in 1969.

RIC INTERNATIONAL

Year Dec 31:	1969	a1968
Revenues ...	$4,677,218	$2,470,192
Loss cont op	1,492,686	86,809
Loss disc op	166,181	b1,603
Loss	1,658,867	85,206
Spec chg ...	d881,951	
Net loss ...	2,540,818	85,206

a-Restated by company. b-Income. d-Reserve for estimated losses from a subsidiary and reduction of certain asset valuations.

ROBERTS CONSOL INDUS.

Quar Mar 29:	1970	1969
Shr earns ...	$.39	$.35
Sales	7,198,000	7,4 ,000
Net income .	276,000	,000

ROBINS INDUSTRIES CORP

Quar Mar 31:	1970	1969
Shr earns	$.01	$.07
Sales	770,835	621,031
Net income .	5,205	26,701

SAFEGUARD INDUSTRIES INC.

Quar Mar 31:	1970	a1969
Shr earns	$.19	$.16
Sales	17,358,400	12,713,200
Net income .	724,000	610,500
Shares	3,811,485	3,711,895

a-Restated to reflect all acquisitions on pooling-of-interest basis.

SONOCO PRODUCTS CO.

Quar Mar 31:	1970	a1969
Shr earns	$.67	$.69
Sales	31,411,711	31,224,529
Net income .	1,558,913	1,594,547

a-Restated to reflect consolidation of three subsidiaries.

SPARTON CORP.

Quar Mar 31:	1970	1969
Shr earns ...	$.34	$.53
Sales	8,511,991	8,576,202
Net income .	288,189	473,230
9 mo shr ..	.93	1.13
Sales	23,574,369	27,702,845
Net income .	807,682	1,089,283

SPECIALTY RESTAURANTS

Quar Mar 31:	1970	1969
Shr earns ...	$.18	$.12
Sales	4,398,020	3,194,258
Net income .	278,115	192,467
9 mo shr ..	.63	.53
Sales	12,386,971	9,497,946
Net income .	946,457	797,531

STANDARD INT'L CORP.

Quar Mar 31:	1970	e1969
Shr earns ...	$.34	a$.33
Sales	28,126,948	27,462,496
Income	1,281,612	1,260,686
Spec credit		b326,568
Net income .	1,281,612	c1,587,254
9 mo shr ...	.99	a.94
Sales	82,227,327	81,352,852
Income	3,816,579	3,683,532
Spec credit .		b1,856,921
Net income .	3,816,579	c5,540,453
Avg shrs	3,769,741	3,820,596

a-Based on income before special credit and adjusted for a 5% stock dividend in December 1969. b-From sale of foreign subsidiary and portion of a domestic subsidiary. c-Equal to eight cents a share in the quarter and $1.42 a share in the nine months. e-Restated to include acquisitions on a pooling-of-interests basis.

STANDARD OIL CO-CALIF'

Quar Mar 31:	1970	1969
Shr erns	$1.22	a$1.34
Revenue	1,211,000,000	1,114,000,000
Net inco	103,642,000	113,579,000

a-Adjusted for 5% stock dividend in May 1969.

STAR SUPERMARKETS INC.

12 wk Mar 28:	1970	1969
Shr earns	$.36	$.40
Sales	20,830,455	19,907,435
Net income .	203,990	226,483

Sales	17,025,000	13,379,000
Net income .	972,000	693,000
9 mo shr .	1.82	a1.20
Sales	46,759,000	36,432,000
Net income .	2,651,000	1,738,000

a-Adjusted for 20% stock dividend in May 1969.

UNICARE HEALTH SERVICES

9 mo Feb 28:	1970	1969
Shr earns ...	a$.16	$.11
Revenues ...	17,795,341	6,094,634
Income	918,834	634,194
Spec credit .	b303,830	
Net income .	c1,222,664	634,194

a-Based on income before special credit. b-From sale of a wholly owned subsidiary. c-Equal to 42 cents a share.

UNITED MERCHANTS & MFRS

Quar Mar 31:	1970	1969
Shr earns ...	$.54	$.85
aSales	178,026,000	175,443,000
Net income .	3,259,000	5,183,000
9 mo shr .	2.52	2.83
aSales	540,682,000	522,242,000
Net income .	15,321,000	17,219,000

a-Excludes factoring volume.

VOPLEX CORP.

Quar Mar 31:	1970	1969
Shr earns ...	$.23	a$.22
Sales	1,941,120	2,136,551
Net income .	102,559	100,207

a-Adjusted to reflect 100% stock dividend in February 1970.

WARD FOODS INC.

Quar Mar 31:	1970	a1969
Shr earns ...	$.15	$.49
Sales	105,900,000	91,000,000
Net income .	462,000	1,531,000

a-Restated by company.

ZENITH LABORATORIES INC.

Quar Mar 31:	1970	a1969
Shr earns ...	$.22	$.04
Sales	2,681,000	1,219,000
Net income .	136,000	24,000
Avg shares	616,797	551,317

a-Restated by company.

ZIONS UTAH BANCORPORATION

Quar Mar 31:	1970	1969
aShr earns ..	$.26	$.28
Income	272,670	284,922
Sec loss	1,656	9,369
bNet inco	271,014	275,553

a-Based on income before results of securities transactions. b-Equal to 26 cents a share in 1970 and 28 cents a share in 1969.

FIGURE 28: STANDARD OIL OF CALIFORNIA QUARTERLY EARNINGS.
Report from *The Wall Street Journal* (April 30, 1970)

Note that the quarterly earnings per share are already *calculated* and *compared* for you. You are shown both the 1970 first quarter figure of $1.22 and the corresponding 1969 figure of $1.34.

The Investor's Need to Examine the Quarterly Earnings Reports

It is important that you do your homework and examine the quarterly earnings reports for the companies in which you are interested *as the reports are published.* The reason is to quickly spot whether your company is having profit problems that could result in a dividend cut. Refer to Figure 28. Compare SD's quarterly earnings for January, February, March of 1970 with those for January, February, March of 1969.

In the first quarter of 1970 SD reported quarterly earnings of $1.22. Compare this report with that for the first quarter of 1969, when SD reported $1.34. SD reported *lower* quarterly earnings. An alarm bell should go off in your mind. (More about this later when line 21 of the Profit Estimate Sheet is examined.)

How To Find Quarterly Earnings for Previous Years

To fill in Section Two properly it is necessary to know the quarterly earnings for the past three years. As you can see from Figures 27 and 28, only the specific quarterly or annual figures being reported are shown. Refer to Figure 23A. The quarterly earnings are usually listed under "Common Share Earnings" (pointed out by Arrow 1 in Figure 23A for your convenience).

Section Two: Historical Earnings and Stock Data; How to Fill It Out

You can now start to fill out Section Two. It is easy to do. You simply transfer specific numbers from the different parts of the Stock Report in Figures 23A and 23B to the box structure in the Profit-Estimate Sheet.

At the outset, filling in lines 11, 12, 13, 14 and 15 may seem difficult. But such is not the case.

LINE 11: Refer to circle 11A in Figure 23B. SD's fiscal year ends in December. Enter "Dec." in box 11A in Figure 26. There is also a second way of determining the fiscal year. Refer to circle E in Figure 23A, which points to "Dec." under "Common Share Earnings." The last quarter so noted usually indicates the month that ends the company's fiscal year.

To complete line 11, fill in boxes 11B through E. Refer to circles B, C, D and E in Figure 23A. In box 11B of Figure 26 enter "March," in 11C "June," in 11D "September," and in 11E "December." These are quarterly reporting periods for SD.

Some Strategy for Lines 12, 13 and 14   The fiscal years you use for lines 12, 13 and 14 will change each year. For example, if you are analyzing a stock in early 1973, you should logically enter 1973 on line 15, as that is the year you are *estimating*. You would then select the historical investment data for 1972 on line 14, for 1971 on line 13 and for 1970 on line 12.

When the Profit-Estimate Sheet illustrated in Figure 20 was completed, it was March 1970. Hence 1970 was entered on line 18 (now 15 in revised and updated Profit-Estimate Sheet.)

LINE 12: In Box 12A insert "Dec. 1967." This notes the fiscal period for which you are extracting data from the Stock Report. Refer to circles 12, 13 and 14 in Figure 23A. In box 12B enter $1.18; in box 12C, $1.27; in box 12D, $1.16; in box 12E, $1.22. These are SD's quarterly earnings per share for 1967.

Now turn to Figure 23B. At the top is a section entitled "Income Statistics (Million $) and Per Share ($) Data." Circle F points to a column, headed "Earns." (earnings per share), that gives a ten-year history of SD's earnings. For 1967 SD's earnings per share amounted to $4.83. Enter $4.83 in box 12F. The sum of the quarterly earnings ($1.18 + $1.27 + $1.16 + $1.22) is $4.83.

Circle G points to a column, with the heading "Divs. Paid" (dividends paid), that gives a ten-year history of the cash dividends paid each year by SD. For 1967 SD paid out $2.38 in dividends. Enter that amount in box 12G.

Circle H points to a column with the heading "Price Range" that gives the high and low at which SD's stock traded each year since 1960. For 1967 SD traded at a high of 61⅜ and at a low of 51⅝. Enter these figures in box 12H.

Circle J points to a column, with the heading "Price-Earns. Ratio; HI LO," that is quite important to this stock-selection method and will be more fully discussed when the criteria for line 22 are developed. It gives the high (HI) and low (LO) price/earnings ratios (P/Es) that SD's stock commanded every year since 1960. In 1967 SD's stock was valued at a high P/E of 12 and a low P/E of 10. Enter these figures in box 12J.

Circle K points to a column, headed "Gross Oper. INC." (gross operating income), that notes the gross sales for SD. SD's ten-year sales history is tabulated. For 1967 the sales figure is 3,298.6 in millions of dollars, or $3,298,600,000). Enter this figure in box 12K. There are two ways that it can be entered: "$3,298 MIL" or "$3.2 BIL." We elect to use the latter for clarity. In examining other Stock Reports you will find other nomenclature for gross sales. Some of these are "Oper. Revs." (operating revenues), "Net Sales," "Sales and Rentals," "Gross Revenues," "Sales," "Gross Income," "Total Oper. Rev." etc. They all mean much the same thing.

LINE 13: Fill in the pertinent data for SD for its 1968 fiscal year using the instructions for line 12.

LINE 14: Fill in the data for 1969.

LINE 15: This will contain your projections for the *future* action of the stock. At this point the only box you can fill in is 15A, the current fiscal year, for which you are making estimates. Here is an important point: as the *actual* quarterly earnings are reported you should enter this data. Refer to Figure 28. When the first quarter 1970 earnings were published you should have entered "$1.22" in box 15B. Also you should have crossed out the E, since you are now cognizant of the true quarterly figure. As the year unfolds and the actual investment reports become available, follow the same updating procedure for boxes 15C, D and E.

15

The Profit-Estimate Sheet in Action—
Section Three: Current Data

The purpose of this chapter is to show you how to become acquainted with your stock's current characteristics. You should examine your stock *today*. When you have completely filled out "Section Three: Current Data" you will know the following about the stock you're interested in:

- The current stock price.
- The indicated current cash dividend.
- The current percent yield.
- The latest 12-month earnings per share.
- Whether the cash dividend is adequately protected.
- The current price/earnings ratio.
- Whether the stock is currently "overvalued" or "undervalued."

In Figure 29, as an example, you will find "Section Three—Current Data" of the Profit-Estimate Sheet completely filled out for SD for early March 1970.

LINE 16: Today's stock price: $45.

Refer to the daily newspaper to get the current price on SD. On March 9, 1970, SD traded at a high price of 46¾, a low price of

SECTION THREE - CURRENT DATA

16) Today's stock price: . . . . $ _____ 45 _____

17) Indicated current cash dividend per share: . . . . $ _____ 2.80 _____

(18) Current Yield: (line 17 $ 2.80 divided by line 16 $ 45 ;
Caution if under 4.5%): . . . . | 6.2 % | (OK) CAUTION

19) Most recent quarterly earnings report: Qtr 4th Month December
Fiscal Year _____ 1969 _____

20) Latest 12 months earnings (Addition of 4 most recent quarters) . . . . . $ 5.35

(21) Current dividend protection ratio (line 20 $ 5.35 divided by
line 17 $ 2.80 ; Caution if protection ratio less than 1.4): . . . . | 1.9 | (OK) CAUTION

(22) Current (P/E) Price/Earnings Ratio (line 16 $ 45 divided by
line 20 $ 5.35 ; Caution if P/E is more than 15 to 1): . . . . . . | 8 P/E | (OK) CAUTION

FIGURE 29

45½ and closed at 45⅞. It is generally cumbersome to work with fractions, so the price has been rounded off to 45 per share. Enter that figure on line 16.

LINE 17: Indicated current cash dividend per share: $2.80.

Refer to the *two* circled 17s in Figure 23A, one at the top ("Dividend") and one at the bottom ("Dividend Data").

We will discuss first the upper circle 17, pointing to "Dividend" and the figure $2.80. Enter that figure on line 17. Notice that directly in front of the $2.80 is a superior "2" which directs your attention to a footnote at the bottom of the Stock Report that reads "Indicated Rate." The Indicated Rate tells you what dividends you should expect for the next 12 months.

Refer to the bottom circle 17 in Figure 23A. There are some investment terms that may be unfamiliar to you. Here is a brief explanation of these terms:

Amt. of Divd. $: The cash amount of the dividend paid for one share of stock. The cash payments for the last four quarters are usually shown, as normally cash dividends are paid four times a year.

Date Decl.: The date that the board of directors declared the dividend.

Ex-divd. Date: This date should be of major importance to you.

If you *sell* a stock on "Ex-divd. Date," you should expect to receive the most recently declared dividend. If you *buy* a stock on "Ex-divd. Date," you *do not* receive the most recently declared dividend; you are buying the stock "ex-dividend"—without the dividend. To receive any dividend, you must have bought the stock on the trading day before the ex-dividend date.

Stock of Record: This denotes the fifth business day after the ex-dividend date. This date is primarily an internal bookkeeping date for brokerage firms.

Payment Date: A happy day—your dividend check should be in your mailbox or credited to your account at your brokerage firm.

LINE 18: Current Yield: (line 17: $2.80 divided by line 16: $45; Caution if under 4.5%). The answer is 6.2%, OK.

Line 18 is the first of the eight important characteristics. If you mark it "Caution," you would have reason to stop analyzing this stock and to start analyzing other stocks.

Line 18 requires you to calculate the current percent yield. Use only cash dividends. Take the amount of the indicated cash dividend from line 17 ($2.80) and divide it by the current stock price from line 16 ($45). The answer is 6.2 percent current yield. Enter that figure in the answer box.

Line 18 states, "Caution if under 4.5%." The figure of 6.2 percent is above 4.5 percent. Circle "OK" and cross out "Caution." SD has passed its first test.

Special Discussion: High-Percentage Yield Tends to Put a "Floor" Under a Stock's Price The reasoning behind demanding a potentially undervalued stock to have a high-percentage yield is a superior yield may place an "invisible investment floor" under the stock's current price. Stock market history indicates that a well-secured, high-percent yield frequently acts to aid a stock to hold its price and to resist selling pressures. Such a "floor" should help you to reduce your investment risks in the event of a market sell-off.

This "invisible floor" principle is rather clearly shown in Tables C, D, and E. In these tables selected data on the thirty stocks in the Dow-Jones Industrial Average are presented. Table C shows the

TABLE C

Selected Data on Stocks
in the Dow-Jones Industrial Average for 1962

STOCK	1962 LOW PRICE	$ DIV.	HIGHEST % YIELD	$ SHARE EARNINGS	LOWEST P/E
1. Allied Chemical	34¼	1.80	5.2	2.19	16
2. Aluminum Co.	45	1.20	2.6	2.53	18
3. American Can	38⅛	2.00	5.2	2.81	14
4. American Tel & Tel	49	1.80	3.6	2.90	17
5. American Brands	25⅛	1.50	5.9	2.53	10
6. Anaconda	17½	1.25	7.1	2.28	8
7. Bethlehem Steel	27⅛	2.17	8.0	1.80	15
8. Chrysler	9¼	.24	2.6	1.74	5
9. Du Pont	164½	7.50	4.5	9.60	17
10. Eastman Kodak	20¼	.58	2.8	.86	23
11. General Electric	27⅛	1.00	3.6	2.97	18
12. General Foods	57¾	1.80	3.1	1.57	18
13. General Motors	44¼	3.00	6.7	5.10	9
14. Goodyear	12⅜	.47	3.8	1.02	12
15. Intl. Harvester	21¾	1.20	5.5	1.93	11
16. Intl. Nickel	20¾	.76	3.6	1.28	16
17. Intl. Paper	22⅝	1.05	4.6	1.56	15
18. Johns-Manville	19⅜	1.00	5.1	1.41	14
19. Owens-Illinois	32	1.25	3.9	2.05	16
20. Proctor & Gamble	28⅛	.72	2.5	1.30	22
21. Sears	29½	.82	2.9	1.55	19
22. Std. Oil of Calif.	41	1.65	4.0	3.78	11
23. Std. Oil of N.J.	45⅜	2.50	5.5	3.88	12
24. Swift	15½	.80	5.1	1.36	11
25. Texaco	21⅜	.88	4.1	1.80	12
26. Union Carbide	41½	1.80	4.3	2.66	16
27. United Aircraft	25½	1.33	5.2	1.73	15
28. U.S. Steel	37¾	2.75	7.2	2.56	15
29. Westinghouse	25	1.20	4.8	1.56	16
30. Woolworth	18¼	.83	4.5	1.67	11

lowest price that each Dow stock registered in the 1962 sell-off. The cash dividend paid that year is also noted, as well as the highest percent yield that could have been available to you, assuming that you were fortunate enough to have bought each of the stocks when it was at its lowest price of the year. Table D shows

TABLE D

Selected Data on Stocks
in the Dow-Jones Industrial Average for 1966

| | 1966 LOW | $ | HIGHEST % | $ SHARE | LOWEST |
STOCK	PRICE	DIV.	YIELD	EARNINGS	P/E
1. Allied Chemical	32	1.90	5.9	3.25	10
2. Aluminum Co.	66½	1.55	2.3	4.83	14
3. American Can	44¾	2.20	4.9	4.12	11
4. American Tel & Tel	49¾	2.20	4.4	3.69	13
5. American Brands	29⅝	1.80	6.0	3.01	10
6. Anaconda	32½	2.50	7.6	5.99	5
7. Bethlehem Steel	26	1.80	6.9	3.72	7
8. Chrysler	29¾	2.00	6.7	4.16	7
9. Du Pont	143¼	5.75	4.0	8.23	17
10. Eastman Kodak	52½	1.02	1.9	2.15	24
11. General Electric	40	1.30	3.2	3.75	21
12. General Foods	62¾	2.20	3.5	1.97	16
13. General Motors	65⅝	4.55	6.9	6.24	11
14. Goodyear	20⅛	.65	3.2	1.65	12
15. Intl. Harvester	32	1.72	5.3	3.86	8
16. Intl. Nickel	29¼	1.12	3.8	1.59	18
17. Intl. Paper	23¾	1.23	3.1	2.40	10
18. Johns-Manville	22⅜	1.10	4.9	2.25	10
19. Owens-Illinois	52½	1.35	2.5	3.51	15
20. Proctor & Gamble	30⅛	.96	3.1	1.73	17
21. Sears	45¾	1.20	2.6	2.38	19
22. Std. Oil of Calif.	50	2.26	4.5	4.73	11
23. Std. Oil of N.J.	59¾	3.30	5.5	5.06	12
24. Swift	17¾	1.00	5.6	1.60	11
25. Texaco	30⅝	1.25	4.0	2.56	12
26. Union Carbide	45⅝	2.00	4.3	3.97	12
27. United Aircraft	61¼	1.60	2.6	4.01	16
28. U.S. Steel	35	2.10	6.0	4.60	8
29. Westinghouse	40	1.40	3.5	3.16	13
30. Woolworth	19½	1.00	5.1	2.34	8

the same data on the Dow stocks for the 1966 sell-off, and Table E for the 1970 decline.

Look carefully at the highest percent yield columns in these tables. In the 1962 decline only fourteen of the Dow stocks dipped low enough in price to produce yields exceeding 4.5 percent. In the

TABLE E

Selected Data on Stocks
in the Dow-Jones Industrial Average for 1970

STOCK	1970 LOW PRICE	$ DIV.	HIGHEST % YIELD	$ SHARE EARNINGS	LOWEST P/E
1. Allied Chemical	16⅛	1.20	7.4	1.56	10
2. Aluminum Co.	47	1.80	3.8	5.20	9
3. American Can	34	2.20	6.4	3.55	10
4. American Tel & Tel	40⅜	2.60	6.4	3.62	10
5. American Brands	29½	2.10	7.1	4.03	7
6. Anaconda	19⅛	1.90	9.9	3.11	6
7. Bethlehem Steel	19½	1.80	9.2	2.05	10
8. Chrysler	16⅛	2.60	16.1	(.16)	0
9. Du Pont	92½	5.00	5.4	6.76	14
10. Eastman Kodak	57⅝	1.32	2.2	2.50	23
11. General Electric	30⅛	1.30	4.3	3.63	17
12. General Foods	66½	2.60	3.9	2.38	14
13. General Motors	59½	3.40	5.7	2.09	28
14. Goodyear	21	.85	4.0	1.78	12
15. Intl. Harvester	22	1.80	8.1	1.92	11
16. Intl. Nickel	33⅝	1.40	4.1	2.80	12
17. Intl. Paper	28⅜	1.50	5.3	1.85	15
18. Johns-Manville	26½	1.20	4.5	2.02	13
19. Owens-Illinois	38	1.35	3.5	3.90	10
20. Proctor & Gamble	40⅛	1.32	3.2	2.60	15
21. Sears	51	1.35	2.6	3.01	17
22. Std. Oil of Calif.	38	2.80	7.3	5.35	7
23. Std. Oil of N.J.	49⅞	3.75	7.5	5.90	8
24. Swift	22	.60	2.7	2.24	10
25. Texaco	24	1.60	6.6	3.02	8
26. Union Carbide	29½	2.00	6.7	2.60	11
27. United Aircraft	23⅝	1.80	7.6	3.74	6
28. U.S. Steel	28⅛	2.40	8.5	2.72	10
29. Westinghouse	53¼	1.80	3.3	3.06	17
30. Woolworth	25⅜	1.20	4.7	2.52	10

1966 sell-off fifteen stocks had yields of 4.5 percent or more. In the 1970 market debacle nineteen Dow stocks came down low enough in price to return 4.5 percent or more.

Further analysis of the highest percent yield figures reveals another investment feature. In 1962 only one of the Dow stocks dropped low enough in price to yield 8 percent or higher. In 1966 none of the Dow stocks declined low enough to yield 8 percent. And in 1970 only five stocks ultimately yielded over 8 percent. This stock selection method takes advantage of this general investment characteristic.

Stated as an investment principle, *dividend-paying common stocks tend to resist declining when their yields enter the 4.5 percent to 8 percent range!*

One of the many explanations for the possible existence of this "floor" is shown in Table F. The potential decline-resistance of a

TABLE F

Conservative Stock versus Growth Stock

TYPICAL GROWTH STOCK			TYPICAL CONSERVATIVE STOCK		
PRICE	DIVIDEND	YIELD	PRICE	DIVIDEND	YIELD
$100	none	none	$100	$4.50	4.5%
90	none	none	90	4.50	5.0
80	none	none	80	4.50	5.6
70	none	none	70	4.50	6.4
60	none	none	60	4.50	7.5
50	none	none	50	4.50	9.0
40	none	none	40	4.50	11.2
30	none	none	30	4.50	15.0
20	none	none	20	4.50	22.5
10	none	none	10	4.50	45.0

"conservative" stock yielding 4.5 percent is compared to a "growth" stock that does not pay any cash dividend. If you owned the conservative stock, you would find that the percent yield would *increase* markedly as the stock's price dropped. As you can see in Table F, if the conservative stock's price fell to 80, your percent yield, if you bought it at that price, would be 5.6 percent. At the lower price of 60 your yield would be 7.5 percent. We are assuming that the cash dividend of this conservative stock is well protected.

On the other hand, non-dividend paying "growth" stocks tend not to have the protection of any "floor." In the sharp market sell-offs of 1962, 1966 and 1969–70 many of the "glamour growth" stocks declined 60 percent and 70 percent and more, particularly during the fear and panic phases of those declines.

LINE 19: Most recent quarterly earnings report: Qtr: 4th; Month: December; Fiscal Year: 1969.

As of March 1970, SD's most recently published earnings report was the fourth quarter of 1969. Enter this data in line 19.

Line 19 serves an important function. It helps you periodically to *update* and to *monitor* the status of your investment. With each quarterly earnings report, you are given the opportunity and the investment data to update your information about any stock. You should recalculate the Profit-Estimate Sheet with the appearance of each new quarterly earnings report. The newly developed information should help you to reevaluate your position. You may decide to buy more of your stock or to continue holding it or to sell it.

LINE 20: Latest 12 months earnings (addition of 4 most recent quarters): $5.35.

Start with the $1.34 in box 14E. Add $1.34 (box 14E), $1.31 (box 14D), $1.36 (box 14C) and $1.34 (box 14B) for a total of $5.35. Enter that amount on line 20.

To update the latest twelve-month earnings information, refer to Figure 28, which illustrates SD's first quarterly (March 1970) earnings published in April 1970. You already know from Chapter Fourteen that you should enter the $1.22 in box 15B and cross out the "E." When the 1970 March report of $1.22 is published, you add $1.22 (box 15B), $1.34 (box 14E), $1.31 (box 14D) and $1.36 (box 14C) for a total of $5.23 (down slightly from $5.35).

This is crucial investment information as you will find out as the important data for line 21 are developed. The criteria arrived at in line 21 should help you protect already invested money.

LINE 21: Current dividend protection ratio: (line 20: $5.35 divided by line 17: $2.80; Caution if protection ratio less than 1.4). The answer is 1.9, OK.

Line 21 is the second of the eight important characteristics. If you mark it "Caution," you should stop analyzing the stock and look elsewhere.

Dividend Protection Ratio   The investment principle in line 21 is borrowed from another branch of security analysis, namely, bond analysis. Bond analysis is concerned with the degree of safety of bond issues. Bonds pay interest and this interest money comes from the company's income. The primary measurement used to judge the "certainty" of any company's ability to pay the interest on its bonds is the number of times the total interest charges have been covered by the company's available earnings for some years back.

As you can see from line 21, the protection afforded to the cash-dividend payout for stocks is treated in a more cavalier manner. A dividend-protection ratio of 1.4 or higher rates an OK. Ratios under 1.4 are viewed with suspicion and should trigger a "Caution" warning in that you have reason to believe the cash dividend may be in danger of being reduced.

The cash amount of any dividend is decided only by the company's board of directors. It is quite important that you realize that any cash dividend can vary with either the fortunes of the company; the amount of cash in the company's treasury; or the inclinations of the board of directors; or with a combination of these factors. The dividend may be reduced or omitted if business is poor, or if the directors elect to modernize or update the company by investing in plant and equipment. On the other hand, sometimes the directors will decide to pay a dividend out of past earnings even though the company is not currently operating at a profit.

Standard & Poor's Corporation, in the *Stock Guide, Dividend Record, Stock Report* and elsewhere records the dividend payments on virtually every American and Canadian preferred and common stock. In the 30-month period from January 1969 to June 1971 almost 1,000 corporations cut or omitted dividends. During the same period over 5,000 concerns increased or resumed dividend payments, or declared an extra dividend. In the 30-month period just mentioned there were almost 80,000 "dividend declarations" in all by the many boards of directors that Standard & Poor's tabulates.

Dividend cuts, threatened or actual, often cause a stock's price to decline. Figure 30 should help illustrate why a Caution signal is

Indicated Cash Dividend	Latest 12-Months Earnings per Share	Dividend Protection Ratio	% of Earnings Paid Out
$1.00	$2.00	2.0	50%
1.00	1.90	1.9	53
1.00	1.80	1.8	55
1.00	1.70	1.7	58
1.00	1.60	1.6	62
1.00	1.50	1.5	66
1.00	1.40	1.4	71
1.00	1.30	1.3	78
1.00	1.20	1.2	83
1.00	1.10	1.1	91
1.00	1.00	1.0	100
1.00	.90	.9	110
1.00	.80	.8	125
1.00	.70	.7	141

FIGURE 30: DIVIDEND PROTECTION RATIO DATA.

triggered when the dividend-protection ratio is under 1.4. As you can see, a dividend-protection ratio of 1.4 means that a $1.40 in current earnings exists to cover each $1.00 in dividends. Yet this ratio of 1.4 is borderline. It means that the company is paying out 71 percent of its earnings in cash dividends. Such a payout is considered to be abnormally high when compared to the average payout of all stocks on the New York Stock Exchange. In the six-year period 1964 through 1969 the average dividend payout of stocks listed on the New York Stock Exchange amounted to approximately 52 percent of earnings (an average dividend-protection ratio of 1.93). Research indicates that over the past twenty years, dividends have tended to be increased at an average rate of about 5 percent annually. In 1969, millions of Americans collected billions of dollars in cash dividends.

It should be obvious that the higher the "protection ratio," the more net earnings are available to maintain (and possibly increase) the current dividend. SD's protection ratio of 1.9 means that the company is currently earning $1.90 for each $1.00 in cash dividends it pays out. SD's ratio is average.

As we have already suggested, dividend cuts occur more frequently than most investors realize. The 30 Dow stocks have experienced 31 cuts in dividend payouts in the 11-year period from 1960 to August 1971.

Table G tabulates each of the Dow stocks that recorded a

TABLE G

The Years in Which Dividends Were Reduced or Omitted in Any of the 30 Dow Stocks

Period: 1960 through August 1971

Allied Chemical	1968
Anaconda	1967, 1968, 1969, 1971 (twice)
Bethlehem Steel	1962, 1967, 1971
Chrysler	1961, 1970
Du Pont	1960, 1964, 1965, 1966, 1967, 1969, 1970
General Motors	1966, 1967, 1970
International Harvester	1971
International Nickel	1966, 1969, 1971
International Paper	1966
Swift	1962, 1968
United Aircraft	1960
U.S. Steel	1962, 1970

dividend cut. After each stock is listed the individual year in which a dividend reduction or omission was decided by the company's directors.

Below you will find the recent dividend record of three stocks, Penn-Central, General Motors and International Nickel, that should illustrate the varying inclinations that boards of directors have toward dividends.

Penn-Central Tabulated below you will find the quarterly earnings reports, yearly earnings and dividends for Penn-Central.

YEAR	QUARTERLY EARNINGS ($)				$ SHARE EARNINGS	$ YEARLY DIVIDENDS
	Mar.	*June*	*Sept.*	*Dec.*		
1968	.58	1.03	.66	1.48	3.75	2.40
1969	.19	.91	(.37)	(.55)	.18	1.80

At the end of December 1968 Penn-Central's annual earnings amounted to $3.75. The cash dividend was $2.40 (60¢ quarterly). The dividend-protection ratio works out to 1.57 ($3.75 divided by $2.40). On April 24, 1969, Penn-Central reported first quarter earnings of $.19, down sharply from the $.58 for the same period a year earlier. The latest twelve-month earnings totaled $3.36 (.19 plus $1.48 plus .66 plus 1.03). The dividend-protection ratio works out to 1.4 ($3.36 divided by $2.40). On April 24, 1969, Penn-Central's stock price closed at 52¼. As you can readily see, the dividend was just barely protected.

On July 29, 1969, Penn-Central reported second quarter earnings of $.91, down from $1.03 for the same period a year earlier. The latest twelve-month earnings totaled $3.24 (.91 plus .19 plus 1.48 plus .66). The dividend-protection ratio works out to 1.35. On July 29, 1969, the stock price closed at 41⅛. By the "cut-off" numbers used in this stock-selection technique, a Caution warning was indicated.

On October 21, 1969, Penn-Central reported a loss for the third quarter of ($.37), a major negative change from the profit of $.66 for the same period one year earlier. A loss is noted by the number's being enclosed in parentheses. The latest twelve-month earnings amounted to $2.21 [(.37) plus .91 plus .19 plus 1.48]. The dividend-protection ratio was negative, showing that the $2.40 cash dividend was not covered by earnings. On October 21, 1969, the stock price closed at 34¾.

On November 28, 1969, the Penn-Central board of directors omitted the payment of the quarterly cash dividend of 60¢ "to conserve cash." Seven months later, in late June 1970, Penn-Central declared bankruptcy. The stock price ultimately hit a low of 4⅛.

General Motors　General Motors is an example of a stock in which the dividend-protection ratio also fell under 1.4. Only part of the dividend was cut. This occurred in 1970, when GM experienced its first strike in a number of years. Following are the quarterly earnings reports, yearly earnings and dividends for GM for the years under discussion:

YEAR	QUARTERLY EARNINGS ($)				$ SHARE EARNINGS	$ YEARLY DIVIDENDS
	Mar.	*June*	*Sept.*	*Dec.*		
1969	1.82	1.56	.79	1.77	5.94	4.30
1970	1.21	1.64	(.28)	(.49)	2.08	3.40

It had been GM's policy to pay a "base" dividend and a varying "extra" dividend depending on the company's fortunes. The extra was usually paid in the second and fourth quarters. In anticipation of the pending strike, GM's board of directors paid the regular dividend of 85¢ per share for the second quarter of 1970, but omitted the extra. For the third quarter of 1970 GM reported a strike-inflicted loss of ($.28), a sharp drop from the profit of $.79 for the same period one year earlier. The latest 12-month earnings amounted to $4.34. The dividend-protection ratio works out to 1.27. A Caution signal was indicated. However, GM's directors elected to pay the regular 85¢ base dividend out of past earnings, despite the loss. Due to the strike, GM again reported a loss in the fourth quarter. The full year's earnings per share for 1970 amounted to $2.08. The base dividend of $3.40 was not covered. However, GM's board of directors chose to continue paying the base dividend of 85¢ a share. GM's stock hovered around the 70 to 80 range during this period.

International Nickel International Nickel is an example of a stock in which the dividend-protection ratio did not go under 1.4, yet the company's board of directors elected to reduce the dividend.

YEAR	QUARTERLY EARNINGS ($)				$ SHARE EARNINGS	$ YEARLY DIVIDENDS
	Mar.	*June*	*Sept.*	*Dec.*		
1970	.59	.78	.79	.64	2.80	1.40
1971	.49	.35				

On August 3, 1971, International Nickel announced simultaneously a cut in its quarterly dividend to 25¢ a share from 40¢ and that second quarter earnings had skidded 55 percent, to $.35 a share. This was a marked decline in profit from the $.78 in the same 1970 period. The company stated that it was reducing its dividend because of the current low level of earnings. The latest 12-

month earnings amounted to $2.27. The dividend-protection ratio works out to 1.41. Because of the timing of the company's report of lower earnings and dividend cut, you had no warning. The stock dropped about 10 percent from 33 down to 30 and thereafter drifted down to 25 in early November.

LINE 22: Current (P/E) Price/Earnings Ratio: (line 16: $45 divided by line 20: $5.35; Caution if P/E is more than 15 to 1). The answer is 8 P/E, OK.

Line 22 is the third of the eight important characteristics. If you mark it "Caution" you have reason to believe that the stock may be overpriced. You might be best rewarded to pass it and to search elsewhere.

Line 22 requires you to calculate the current price/earnings ratio. Take the current stock price from line 16 ($45) and divide it by the latest twelve-month earnings from line 20 ($5.35). The answer is 8. Enter that figure in the answer box.

Line 22 states "Caution if P/E is more than 15 to 1." As your answer is less than 15, circle "OK." SD has passed its third test for you.

A Brief Explanation of Price/Earnings Ratio   When you know a stock's price/earnings ratio, you are better able to judge if the stock's *current price* is "overvalued" or "undervalued." It is your personal judgment. As a general rule, the greater your acumen in this critical area, the greater your potential of stock market success. Yet stocks do not behave like trained seals. It is stock market history that many stocks considered overpriced as measured by high P/Es have continued to rise. On the other hand, stocks believed underpriced because of low P/Es have disconcertingly continued their price declines. But these events tend to be exceptions.

Extensive stock market research has consistently revealed that stocks with low P/Es usually outperform stocks with high P/Es. This investment concept is quite clearly seen in Figure 31, which illustrates the Standard & Poor's 425-Industrial Stock Average for nineteen years, from 1953 to 1971. Each line covers a month's activity. The point of interest to you is the price/earnings ratios shown at the peaks and valleys of the price action on the chart. The highest P/E recorded in the last nineteen years was in late

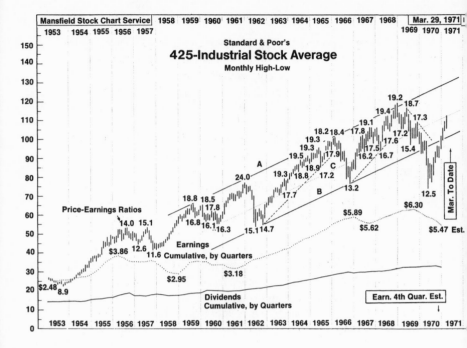

FIGURE 31

Courtesy R. W. Mansfield Company

1961, with a reading of 24.0. The lowest P/E was the 8.9 of 1953.

The reasoning behind requiring the stock to have a low P/E is similar to that for requiring the stock to have a high percent yield. You are hopeful that a low P/E may put an "invisible investment floor" under the stock's current price so as potentially to reduce investment risks in the event of a market sell-off.

This is graphically illustrated in Tables C, D and E describing the Dow-Jones Average. Look closely at the LOWEST P/E columns in those tables. In the 1962 decline, 17 stocks registered P/Es of 15 or lower and only three went under 10 to 1. In the 1966 sell-off, 22 stocks had P/Es of 15 or lower with only six dipping below 10 to 1. In the 1970 market crisis, 24 stocks recorded P/Es of 15 to 1 or lower, with seven of these sinking under 10 to 1.

It may be stated as an investment principle that *common stocks tend to resist declining when their P/Es fall below 15 to 1*.

The authors' have consistently found that it is frequently a major source of confusion to new investors that different priced stocks may have similar P/Es. On the other hand, similarly priced stocks often have different P/Es. This is best illustrated by Table H below, in which all of the stocks shown have the *same* P/E of 10 to 1. The Table I shows stocks in the same price area that have varying P/Es. The P/E is more important than the price of the stock.

TABLE H

All of the Stocks Below Have the Same P/E of 10-to-1

STOCK	PRICE	EARNINGS PER SHARE	P/E
A	$100	$10.00	10 to 1
B	90	9.00	10 to 1
C	80	8.00	10 to 1
D	70	7.00	10 to 1
E	60	6.00	10 to 1
F	50	5.00	10 to 1
G	40	4.00	10 to 1
H	30	3.00	10 to 1
I	20	2.00	10 to 1
J	10	1.00	10 to 1
K	5	.50	10 to 1

TABLE I

All of the Stocks Below Have Different P/Es, Even Though All of the Stocks are Similarly Priced

STOCK	PRICE	EARNINGS PER SHARE	P/E
L	$100	$10.00	10 to 1
M	100	9.00	11 to 1
N	100	8.00	12 to 1
O	100	7.00	14 to 1
P	100	6.00	16 to 1
Q	100	5.00	20 to 1
R	100	4.00	25 to 1
S	100	3.00	33 to 1
T	100	2.00	50 to 1
U	100	1.00	100 to 1
V	100	.50	200 to 1
W	100	Loss	None

16

The Profit-Estimate Sheet in Action— Section Four: Criteria for Future Estimates

Now you are ready to try to look into the future. Up to this point in the Profit-Estimate Sheet you have researched both your stocks' recent history and its current position. The key principle that *history tends to repeat itself* underlies the criteria for this section. When you have completely filled out Section Four you should be pleasantly surprised that you have come up with some answers to these crucial questions concerning your stock:

- What *low* price/earnings ratio might be expected this year?
- What *high* price/earnings ratio should be logically used?
- What are the *estimated* earnings per share for the coming year?
- What are the *estimated* dividends?

These are indeed pertinent questions. Your precise, astute answers should help you pinpoint stocks you might consider as being currently undervalued. In Figure 32, as an example, you will find Section Four of the Profit-Estimate Sheet completely filled out for SD for early March 1970.

LINE 23: (A): Average LOW Price/Earnings Ratio (P/E) last 2 years (13J LO: 10 plus 14J LO:9 divided by 2 equals 9½; (B): *JUDGMENT*—use actual LOW P/E, which is 8 P/E.

Line 23 is divided into two parts. (A) gives you the "cold

SECTION FOUR – CRITERIA FOR FUTURE ESTIMATES

23) (A): Average LOW Price/Earnings Ratio (P/E) last 2 years
(13J LO __10__ plus 14J LO __9__ divided by 2 equals _9 1/2_);
(B): JUDGMENT – use LOW P/E of . . . . __8__ P/E

24) (A): Average HIGH Price/Earnings Ratio (P/E) last 2 years
(13J HI __14__ plus 14J HI __14__ divided by 2 equals __14__);
(B): JUDGMENT – use HIGH P/E of (but not more than 1-1/2 times
P/E of 23B): . . . . __12__ P/E

25) Enter estimated HIGH (HI) and LOW (LO) Price/Earnings Ratio in box 15J

26) Estimated earnings per share for fiscal year ending 19 __70__ ;
(Caution if less than line 20; Enter in box 15F) . . . . $ 5.40 (OK) CAUTION

27) Source of estimate ____Standard & Poor's Forecaster 2-20-70____

28) Estimated quarterly earnings (fill in boxes 15B, 15C, 15D and 15E)

29) Estimated dividends per share for fiscal 19 __70__ ; (Enter in box 15G) . $ __2.80__

30) Estimated dividend protection ratio (line 26 $ _5.40_ divided by
line 29 $ _2.80_ ; Caution if less than 1.4): . . . . 1.9 (OK) CAUTION

FIGURE 32

statistics" of the average low P/E that the stock market has, via its free auction system, valued SD for the last two years. (B) requires you to use judgment and is the more important part. You need to put your own knowledge and stock market savvy to work to decide what low P/E figure you might use for SD. You will find some guidelines below to aid you in arriving at a reasonably sound decision.

First, fill in line 23(A). Refer to box 13J in Section Two (Chapter 14). Look for the 1968 Low P/E for SD of 10. In line 23 enter 10 in the blank space after 13J LO. Refer to box 14J and look for SD's Low P/E for 1969 of 9. Enter 9 after 14J LO. Add both numbers. You get 19. Divide by 2. Your answer is 9½, SD's *average* low P/E for the last two years.

So much for cold statistics. Now it is necessary to use your judgment. You know from line 22 in Section Three (Chapter 15) that SD's current P/E is 8. The authors believe that an eleventh commandment exists in the stock market: *"Thou shalt not kid thyself."* You know that the cold statistics calculate out to a 9½ low P/E for SD. Yet the irrefutable fact of your calculation for line 22 is that SD is currently selling at the lower P/E of 8. The authors believe that you should use this lower P/E of 8 and not 9½. You can be accused of kidding yourself if you use the 9½ figure since you know that SD has sold down to the lower P/E of 8. Hence, in (B) your judgment should cause you to use the low P/E of 8 (which is what the authors used). Enter 8 in line 23 (B).

LINE 24: (A) Average HIGH Price/Earnings Ratio (P/E) last two years (13J HI: 14, plus 14J HI: 14, divided by 2 equals 14); (B): *JUDGMENT*—Use HIGH P/E of (but not more than 1½ times P/E of 23B): 12 P/E.

Line 24 is also divided into two parts. (A) gives you the average high P/E for SD for the last two years; (B) is where you'll use your judgment.

Refer to box 13J in Section Three (Chapter 15). Look for the 1968 High P/E for SD of 14. Enter that figure after 13J HI in line 24. Refer to box 14J. Find SD's High P/E for 1969 of 14. Enter that figure after 14J HI in line 24. Add both numbers. You get 28. Divide by 2. Your answer is 14.

You have developed additional, important facts. SD sold at a high P/E of 14 in both 1968 and 1969. Also SD's average high P/E for the last two years has been 14.

Now it is necessary to put on your thinking cap. Should you use that high P/E of 14? Would it be wiser for you to use a higher or a lower number? A hint is given to you in line 24 (B). It reads, "but not more than 1½ times P/E of 23B." Multiply 8 times 1½ to get 12. By the cutoff numbers in this stock-selection method you should avoid using a P/E higher than 12 for line 24(B) for SD.

Here is the reasoning. You may be asking for too great a swing between the high and low prices for this stock. A low P/E of 8 and a high P/E of 12 produces a 50 percent rise in the stock's price. Assume that the earnings per share are $5.00. Multiply the low P/E of eight times $5.00. The answer is 40. Then multiply the high P/E of twelve times $5.00. Your answer is 60. A move from 40 to 60 is a 50 percent upswing. The authors believe that such a percentage move is quite attractive for a conservative stock. You should not ask your stock to perform any greater price gymnastics.

Enter 12 in line 24(B).

There will be times when your judgment will caution against using the maximum move of 50 percent. Each conservative stock produces its own set of pertinent numbers.

LINE 25: Enter estimated HIGH (HI) and LOW (LO) Price/Earnings Ratio in box 15J.

Enter the estimated HI P/E of 12 and the LO P/E of 8 in box 15J. The purpose of your entering these figures is to be able to "eyeball" them so that your "sense of feel" can tell you that they look right in relationship to the historical perspective of the previous numbers. Here is what you should see:

Excerpt From Section Two

	(A)	(J) PRICE/EARN. RATIO (P/E)	
	FISCAL YEAR ENDING—MONTH	HI	LO
(Line 12)	Dec. 1967	12	10
(Line 13)	Dec. 1968	14	10
(Line 14)	Dec. 1969	14	9
(Line 15)	Dec. 1970	12E	8E

The authors believe that the estimated P/Es for 1970 look right. But your judgment may cause you to believe otherwise. It is fine for you to think independently. With time and practice your thinking, if sufficiently astute and perceptive, should increase your rewards from stock investments.

LINE 26: Estimated earnings per share for fiscal year ending 1970; (Caution if less than line 20; Enter in box 15F): $5.40, OK.

LINE 27: Source of estimate: *Standard & Poor's Earning Forecaster* dated February 20, 1970.

Lines 26 and 27 will be explained together.

Line 26 shows the fourth of the eight important characteristics. As with the other key lines, if you are required to mark this line "Caution," you would have adequate reason to cease analyzing this stock.

Line 26 requires you to zero in on the particular fiscal year you are analyzing. You are making this theoretical analysis in March 1970 for the fiscal year ending December 1970. Enter "70" to identify the year being estimated in line 26.

We now move to line 27.

What are your sources of information for obtaining estimated earnings? They are (1) the research departments of various New York Stock Exchange firms, and (2) investment advisory services.

In this analysis you will make use of an investment advisory service, published weekly by Standard & Poor's Corporation called the *Standard & Poor's Earnings Forecaster.* (See Selected Readings for more data on this service.)

See Figure 33, which illustrates how, in early 1970, different investment organizations estimated the 1970 earnings per share for Standard Oil of California. The estimates ranged from a low of $5.25 (United Business Service) to a high of $5.80 (Blair & Co.). Which one should you use? The authors lean toward a conservative middle-of-the-road approach and selected $5.40. Enter that figure in line 26 and in box 15F.

Line 26 states, "Caution if less than line 20." Line 20, from Section Three (Chapter Fifteen), reads $5.35. Your answer of $5.40 is greater so circle "OK" and cross out "Caution." SD has passed the fourth test.

Enter your data source in line 27: *Standard & Poor's Earnings Forecaster,* dated February 20, 1970.

Estimated Earnings per Share   From the authors' point of view, the overwhelming value of the *Earnings Forecaster* is that it gives a composite analysis for a company. You do not have all of your eggs in the single basket of one analyst. You are able quickly to see how different analysts view the company in which you are interested.

Quoting an excerpt from "Use of the Earnings Forecaster":

Recognizing that estimated future earnings play an increasingly important role in investment decisions, Standard & Poor's in this bulletin endeavors to bring together the best projections by Wall Street researchers on prospective results of well over 1,000 leading corporations. These estimates will often be far from the actual results finally reported, but that does not lessen their worth as an analytical tool. They represent the best estimates of leading analysts at the moment and therefore have a significant bearing on current stock values.

STANDARD & POOR'S EARNINGS FORECASTER

COMPANY & FISCAL YEAR END ESTIMATOR	DATE OF ESTIMATE OR REVIEW	—EARNINGS PER SHARE ($)— A-1968	E-1969	E-1970
●SQUIBB BEECH-NUT(Dec)		j2.06	A2.31	
Alex Brown & Sons, Inc.	Feb 25			2.60
Drysdale & Co.	Feb 24			2.70
Goodbody & Co.	Dec			2.70
United Business Service	**			2.70
S&P	★			2.70
STA-RITE INDS.(Dec)		Rpz1.15 RQpz1.00	RpzA1.14 RQpzA1.00	
Robert W. Baird & Co.	Mar 26			R1.25
●STALEY (A. E.) MFG.(Sep)		2.50	A3.12	
S&P	★			2.75
●STANDARD BRANDS INC.(Dec)		2.48	A2.65	
Shearson, Hammill & Co.	Feb 10			†1.25
S&P	★			2.90
●STANDARD BRANDS PAINT(Sep)		0.93	A1.13	
Shearson, Hammill & Co.	Apr 6			†1.30
United Business Service	**			1.40
S&P	★			1.30
†-1971 estimate 1.45.				
●STANDARD INTL.(Jun)		z1.15 RQz0.95	jzA1.28 RQjzA1.07	
S&P	★			R1.30
●STANDARD KOLLSMAN(Dec)		d0.15	A0.35	
S&P	★			0.55
●STANDARD OIL CALIF.(Dec)		z5.33	zA5.35	
Bache & Co.	●●			5.50
Blair & Co.	Feb --			5.80
Harris, Upham & Co.	Jan 26			5.56
E. F. Hutton & Co.	Feb 25			5.60
Sutro & Co.	≠			5.45
Thomson & McKinnon, Auchincloss	Feb 11			5.50
United Business Service	**			5.25
S&P	★			5.45
●STANDARD OIL IND.(Dec)		4.37	P4.54	
Bache & Co.	●●			4.30
Goodbody & Co.	Feb 16			4.80
W. E. Hutton & Co.	Jan 5			5.00
Shearson, Hammill & Co.	Feb 10			4.95
S&P	★			4.50

EXPLANATION OF SYMBOLS—● Listed NYSE, ▲ Listed AMEX,
A-ACTUAL, E-ESTIMATE, P-PRELIMINARY, R-PRIMARY EARNINGS PER
SHARE, RQ-FULLY DILUTED EARNINGS PER SHARE.

Information has been obtained from sources believed to be reliable,
but its accuracy and completeness, and that of the opinions
based thereon, are not guaranteed.

**FIGURE 33: STANDARD OIL OF CALIFORNIA EXCERPT
FROM EARNINGS FORECASTER.**
Courtesy Standard and Poor's Corporation

Published estimates are intended to reflect the current thinking of the participating brokers and every effort is made to achieve these aims. With respect to Standard & Poor's, our own analysts endeavor to keep their estimates reasonably up-to-date at all times. They provide the *Earnings Forecaster* publication with a complete updating, once a month, and supplement it with interim revisions. In much the same manner, all contributors are provided with a print-out of their estimates on a regular basis for purposes of review. They are encouraged to notify us promptly of any resulting changes and, in addition, keep us supplied with all interim analyses and reports.

Figure 34 illustrates a random weekly update to the *Earnings Forecaster* for September 1971. You see the columns headed "Revised Upward" and "Revised Downward."

There are other usually reliable sources for estimated earnings. Your primary source should be the research department of the brokerage firm handling your account. Your registered representative can get the information you want.

There are a number of investment services to which you can subscribe to receive estimated earnings. These are national services such as *Value Line* and others. (See Selected Readings.) Obviously the more sources of information you have, the more accurate your work should be, and hopefully, the greater your potential profits.

It is the authors' opinion that it is quite important to abide by the caution conditions detailed in line 26. If the consensus of estimated earnings is lower than the latest 12-month earnings from line 20, you are exposing your investment funds to unnecessary risks. If there is one general theme to the stock market and to stocks, it is that *higher earnings usually make for higher stock prices.* The opposite also holds true.

It is generally not wise to go against the best of professional analysts when they cannot project an increase in earnings for the stock in which you are interested. It is not wise to decide arbitrarily that your stock is going to hold at your predetermined price level, resist selling pressures, and even rise. You would truly be bucking the odds and flying in the face of logic with such a point of view. It is far better if the estimated earnings of your stock are higher than its current actual earnings. This suggests growth.

How do analysts estimate, review and revise the estimated earnings for a company? By the hard work of analyzing the company,

STANDARD & POOR'S EARNINGS FORECASTER

THIS WEEK'S CHANGES (1971 Estimates)

Company	From ($)	To ($)	Contributor	Company	From ($)	To ($)	Contributor
REVISED UPWARD				**REVISED DOWNWARD**			
Amer. Hospital Supply	0.75/0.80	0.80/0.85	S & P	Amer. Bakeries	1.25	0.75	S & P
Amer. Sterilizer	1.20	1.20/1.25	S & P	Ampex Corp.	0.25/0.50	0.25	S & P
Belding Hemenway	1.80	2.00	S & P	Amsted Industs.	3.25	3.15	S & P
Gerro Corp.	1.00	1.50	S & P	Assoc. Transport.	0.85	0.80	S & P
Cooper-Jarrett	1.00	1.15	S & P	Big Three Industries	R1.75	R1.55	S & P
Crompton Co.	2.38	2.60	H. Hentz & Co.	Boeing Co.	1.30	1.25	S & P
Cummins Engine	R3.20	R3.25	S & P	Boise Cascade	R1.05	R0.80	S & P
DeLuxe Check Printers	1.75	1.80	United Business Service	Brown Shoe Co.	2.85	2.70	S & P
Dennison Mfg.	R2.00	R2.20	H. Hentz & Co.	Bunker-Ramo Corp.	R0.30	R0.25	Abraham & Co.
Elixer Industries	†1.05	†1.10	Bateman Eichler, Hill Richards		R0.25	R0.10	S & P
Helmerich & Payne	R1.90	R2.10	H. Hentz & Co.	Chesapeake & Ohio Ry.	6.75	6.50	S & P
Honeywell Inc.	2.50	2.60	S & P	Chic. Milw. St. Paul & Pac.	0.25	def.	S & P
Houston Lighting & Power	2.75	2.85	S & P	Consol. Freightways	R2.90	R2.75	S & P
Imperial Oil Ltd.	1.00	1.05	S & P	Cont. Can	2.75	2.50	S & P
Intl. Chem. & Nuclear	R1.20	R1.25	S & P	Cooper Industries	R2.60	R2.00	S & P
Kansas Power & Light	2.50	2.60/2.70	Abraham & Co.	Curtis-Wright	d0.25	d0.35	S & P
Kendall Co.	1.55	1.60	S & P	Del Monte Corp.	R2.05	R1.95	Abraham & Co.
Leaseway Transportation	2.40	2.50	S & P	Desert Pharm. Co.	1.00	0.90	Bateman Eichler, Hill Richards
MSL Industries	R0.70	R1.00	Research Institute	Diamond Intl.	3.30	3.20	H. Hentz & Co.
McNeil Corp.	1.40	1.65	S & P	Fairmont Foods	†R1.35	†R1.20	S & P
Munsingwear Inc.	1.65	2.60	S & P	Farr Co.	0.65/0.70	0.65	Bateman Eichler, Hill Richards
PPG Industries	2.50	2.95	S & P	GCA Corp.	0.80	0.75	S & P
Riegel Paper Corp.	0.75	0.80	S & P	Gould, Inc.	R3.50	R3.40	S & P
Rohr Corp.	†R1.80/2.10	†R2.00/2.35	Harris, Upham & Co.	Grace (W.R.) & Co.	R2.15	R2.10	S & P
Royal Industries	R0.70	R0.80	S & P	Grand Union	†2.65	†2.55	S & P
Seaboard Coast Line Indus.	5.00	5.25	S & P	Graniteville Co.	2.60	2.50	H. Hentz & Co.
Skil Corp.	R1.25	R1.30/1.40	S & P	Greenman Bros.	†1.20/1.30	†1.20	Shearson, Hammill & Co.
TI Corp.	2.00	2.05	S & P	Growth Intl., Inc.	1.10	1.00	J. N. Russell, Inc.
Western Air Lines	d0.10	0.25	S & P	Hammermill Paper	R1.40	R1.00	S & P
Yellow Freight System	3.00	3.25/3.50	S & P	Intl. Aluminum Corp.	†1.75/2.00	†1.75	Bateman Eichler, Hill Richards

R—PRIMARY EARNINGS PER SHARE, RQ—FULLY DILUTED EARNINGS PER SHARE, †—1972 ESTIMATE.
October 1, 1971

Information has been obtained from sources believed to be reliable, but its accuracy and completeness, and that of the opinions based thereon, are not guaranteed.

FIGURE 34: EXCERPT OF WEEKLY UPDATE EARNINGS FORECASTER.

Courtesy Standard and Poor's Corporation

contacting its officials, analyzing the company's competitors, industry trends and overall government policy, and periodically checking, reviewing and updating. Normally, an analyst finds a niche. He specializes in certain industries and companies and learns to spot the trends.

LINE 28: Estimated quarterly earnings (fill in boxes 15B, 15C, 15D and 15E).

The purpose of this line is to give some idea of what to expect from the yet to be reported quarterly earnings. You should want to avoid any sudden surprises. In this example, the $5.40 estimated for SD for 1970 is quite close to the actual $5.35 for 1969. Hence, you should logically expect the quarterly earnings for 1970 to be quite similar to the quarterly earnings reported for 1969.

The authors used these estimated quarterly figures: $1.33 for box 15B; $1.36 for box 15C; $1.32 for box 15D; and $1.39 for box 15E. Enter these figures in the appropriate boxes in line 15.

These quarterly figures are *guidelines*. If the actual quarterly earnings exceed these figures, then you may expect higher annual earnings. On the other hand, if the figures reported are substantially below the estimates, it would behoove you to reevaluate your position and, even more important, to update the estimated earnings for the year.

In April 1970 SD reported $1.22 for the first quarter, ending March 1970. This was below the estimated figure of $1.33. The authors found it necessary to reexamine their position toward SD.

LINE 29: Estimated dividends per share for fiscal year 1970; (Enter in box 15G): $2.80.

Line 29 requires you to estimate the cash dividends for the fiscal year you are analyzing. Enter "70" to complete line 29.

From the examples of Penn-Central, General Motors and International Nickel discussed in the preceding chapter, you should be aware that it is immensely difficult to prejudge what any board of directors is going to do as far as dividends are concerned. Yet all is not lost. You have some clues so as to fill in line 29.

Two clues are noted in Figure 23B, the back of the Standard & Poor's Stock Report for SD. The first important clue is that SD's cash dividend has been raised every year for the past ten years.

Hence a dividend cut may be considered remote. The second clue is that SD paid out, on average, 50 percent of its earnings as dividends. Do some quick multiplying: 50 percent of your estimated $5.40 amounts to $2.70. This figure is less than the current indicated rate of $2.80. An increase in the cash dividend seems unlikely. So the same cash dividend rate of $2.80 for 1970 appears most probable.

Enter $2.80 in line 29 and in box 15G.

LINE 30: Estimated dividend protection ratio (line 26: $5.40 divided by line 29: $2.80; Caution if less than 1.4) works out to 1.9, OK.

Line 30 is the fifth of the eight important characteristics. This line is not important when a stock is originally selected. By the makeup of the cutoff numbers, you will find that this line is almost invariably marked "OK" if line 26 is marked "OK." The logic is that an increase in estimated earnings should provide even greater protection for the cash dividend.

Line 30 assumes importance when reduced estimated earnings for line 26 trigger a Caution signal. This occurs when you are monitoring an existing position. Line 30 will then alert you as to whether or not your current cash dividend is adequately protected by the lower estimated earnings. In short, line 30 is most often used when you are updating your information on a stock in the light of new earnings reports or revised earnings estimates.

Take the estimated earnings from line 26 ($5.40) and divide it by the estimated dividends from line 29 ($2.80). The resulting figure, 1.9, is above the caution point of 1.4. Circle "OK." SD has passed its fifth test for you.

17

The Profit-Estimate Sheet in Action—
Section Five: Estimated Loss Versus Gain

The purpose of this chapter is to show you how you can assess
your risks, assuming that you elect to make a theoretical investment in SD. In this chapter you'll be comparing your potential gain
versus your potential loss. The first four sections of the Profit-
Estimate Sheet have given you an adequate data basis to answer
these questions:

- What *low* stock price may be expected this year?
- What *high* stock price may be expected?
- What is the potential *downside risk?*
- What is the potential *upside gain?*

The answers developed in this section should help you determine whether the potential gain is worth the inherent risk. You
should want the odds to be very much in your favor as a condition
of investing in the stock. In Figure 35, for example, you will find
Section Five of the Profit-Estimate Sheet filled out for SD for
March 1970.

LINE 31: Estimated 1970 LOW stock price AREA (line 23B: 8
LOW P/E × line 26: $5.40): $43 LOW. Use Actual Low of
42¼.
  Enter the year for which you are making the estimate, 1970 in
the profit sheet. Then refer to line 23B in Section Four (Chapter

SECTION FIVE - ESTIMATED LOSS VERSUS GAIN

USE ACTUAL
LOW OF 42 1/4

31) Estimated 19 <u>70</u> LOW stock price AREA
(line 23B <u>8</u> LOW P/E x line 26 $ <u>5.40</u>) . . . . $ <u>43</u>   LOW

32) Estimated 19 <u>70</u> HIGH stock price AREA
(line 24B <u>12</u> HIGH P/E x line 26 $ <u>5.40</u>) . . . . $ <u>64</u>   HIGH

33) Enter estimated HIGH (HI) and LOW (LO) stock prices in box 15H

34) Estimated loss per share (line 16 $ <u>45</u> minus line 31 $ <u>42 1/4</u>) . $ <u>2-3/4</u>

35) % Potential Downside Risk (line 34 $ <u>2 3/4</u> divided by
line 16 $ <u>45</u> ; Caution if more than 20%) . . . .   <u>6</u> % ⓄⓀ CAUTION

36) Estimated profit per share (line 32 $ <u>64</u> minus line 16 $ <u>45</u>) $ <u>19</u>

37) % Potential Upside Gain (line 36 $ <u>64</u> divided by line 16 $ <u>45</u>)   <u>42</u> %

38) Gain to Loss Ratio (line 36 $ <u>19</u> divided by line 34 $ <u>2 3/4</u> ;
Caution if less than 2 to 1) . . . .   6-to-1 ⓄⓀ CAUTION

FIGURE 35

16) to obtain the low P/E you have already decided upon. Enter 8 in the space provided for this low P/E figure. From line 26 you get the estimated earnings of $5.40. Multiply 8 times $5.40. The answer is an estimated 1970 low stock price area for SD of 43. But this price is tentative. When this calculation was made, SD had already traded at the lower figure of 42¼, which is the figure this Profit-Estimate Sheet will actually use.

LINE 32: Estimated 1970 HIGH stock price AREA (line 24B: 12 HIGH P/E × line 26: $5.40): $64 HIGH.

Line 32 is filled out in much the same manner as line 31. The difference is that you refer to line 24B for the estimated High P/E. Enter 12 in the space provided for the High P/E figure. Having already estimated earnings of $5.40, multiply 12 times $5.40. The answer is an estimated high SD stock price area of 64.

Special Discussion: Lines 31 and 32 You have no assurances that the specific low and high prices that you are estimating in lines 31 and 32 will be the exact bottom and top prices. The history of SD's price action is that it ultimately traded at the lower price of 38 *two months later,* in May 1970. On the other hand, the highest price SD reached in 1970 was 54⅞, in December 1970. SD traded at the higher price of 63⅜ in April 1971.

You should think of line 31 as pointing out the general bottom area and of line 32 as indicating the approximate top area. You'll be misled and unnecessarily disappointed if you believe that lines 31 and 32 will pinpoint the exact bottom and top prices for you. You should train yourself to think in terms of areas or price ranges.

LINE 33: Enter estimated HIGH (HI) and LOW (LO) stock prices in box 15H.

Enter the estimated stocks prices of 42¼ low and 64 high in box 15H. This gives you a chance to see if they "look right" when compared to the previous year's price ranges.

The figures for SD should look like this:

Excerpt From Section Two

	(A)	(H) STOCK PRICE	
	FISCAL YEAR ENDING—MONTH	HI	LO
(Line 12)	Dec. 1967	61	51
(Line 13)	Dec. 1968	73¼	54
(Line 14)	Dec. 1969	75	48¼
(Line 15)	Dec. 1970	64E	42¼E

Your price projections look plausible.

LINE 34: Estimated loss per share (line 16: $45 minus line 31: $42¼): $2¾.

Enter the current price of 45 from line 16 of Section Three (Chapter 15). Use the actual low of 42¼ from line 31. Subtract the actual low price from the current price (45). The answer is an estimated loss of 2¾. The figure developed in line 34 is not—at this point—very significant. The reason is that we believe you'll find you are more in touch with the realities of profit and loss when you deal in percentage movement (covered in the next line) rather than price movement.

LINE 35: % Potential Downside Risk (line 34: $2¾ divided by line 16: $45; Caution if more than 20%): 6%, OK.

Line 35 is the sixth of the eight important characteristics. As noted with the other key lines, if you find it necessary to mark this line "Caution," you should terminate your analysis of this stock.

Line 35 states, "Caution if more than 20%." Your answer of 6 percent allows you to circle "OK" and cross out "Caution." SD has passed your sixth test.

Bear in mind that the risk factor described here is only a guideline. It is generally unwise to enter into a stock market transaction when you *know in advance* that your risk exceeds 20 percent. The reason is that the fluctuations of the stock's price frequently will cause your investment to be exposed to a percentage risk greater than that which you calculated and anticipated. As mentioned earlier, SD ultimately hit a low of 38, a drop of 7 points from the current price of 45. This decline amounted to an actual "paper loss" of over 14 percent, more than double your estimate.

Another reason to avoid exposing yourself to no more than a 20 percent downside risk is that the stock may not be sufficiently undervalued to merit consideration and purchase. You can probably find better buying opportunities elsewhere in the market.

LINE 36: Estimated profit per share (line 32: $64 minus line 16: $45): $19.

Enter the estimated high stock price of 64 from line 32 and the current price of 45 from line 16. Subtract the current price from the estimated high price to get 19. You are estimating that SD—if history repeats itself—should "normally" move up approximately 19 points from its current price of 45.

LINE 37: % Potential Upside Gain (line 36: $19 divided by line 16: $45): 42%.

It's good to know the potential upside percent gain that you are estimating.

Enter the projected 19 point rise from line 36 and the current stock price of 45. Divide 19 by 45. Your answer should be 42 percent.

LINE 38: Gain to Loss Ratio (line 36: $19 divided by line 34: $2¾; Caution if less than 2 to 1). The answer is 6 to 1, OK.

Line 38 is the seventh of the eight important characteristics. If you find it necessary to tag it with a Caution sign, you should move on to analyzing other stocks.

Enter the 19-point estimated price rise from line 36 and the estimated loss per share of 2¾ from line 34. Divide 19 by 2¾ (use 2.75). The answer should be expressed as a ratio. The answer here is 6 to 1.

Line 38 states, "Caution if less than 2 to 1." Your answer of 6 to 1 is substantially greater than your caution cutoff point of 2 to 1. Circle "OK" and cross out "Caution." SD has passed the seventh test.

Gain to Loss Ratio The purpose of line 38 is to find out whether the odds are in your favor. Assuming that history will be

SD'S Estimated Price Range	Potential Gain to 64	Potential Loss to 42	Gain to Loss Ratio	
43	21	1	21 to 1	
44	20	2	10 to 1	
45	19	3	6.3 to 1	Buy
46	18	4	4.5 to 1	Area
47	17	5	3.4 to 1	
48	16	6	2.6 to 1	
49	15	7	2.1 to 1	
50	14	8	1.7 to 1	
51	13	9	1.4 to 1	Neutral
52	12	10	1.2 to 1	Area
53	11	11	1 to 1	
54	10	12	Under 1 to 1	
55	9	13	Under 1 to 1	
56	8	14	Under 1 to 1	
57	7	15	Under 1 to 1	
58	6	16	Under 1 to 1	Sell
59	5	17	Under 1 to 1	Area
60	4	18	Under 1 to 1	
61	3	19	Under 1 to 1	
62	2	20	Under 1 to 1	
63	1	21	Under 1 to 1	
64	0	22	Under 1 to 1	

FIGURE 36: GAIN-TO-LOSS RATIO.

so kind as to repeat itself, you have strategically selected an investment vehicle with an upside profit potential six times greater than your estimated potential loss.

The Caution flag flies if your gain-to-loss ratio is less than 2 to 1. You should avoid investing unless you can calculate odds of at least 2 to 1 in your favor. This principle is illustrated in Figure 36, which tabulates the different gain-to-loss ratios for SD for the prices between 43 and 64. SD may be considered to be a buy candidate when its price is 49 or less (assuming all eight tests are passed).

Investment vs. Speculation vs. Gambling   The gain-to-loss ratio gives you specific information to determine if your potential stock purchase has the characteristics of an investment, or a speculation, or of a gamble. The authors hold these opinions. An *investment* may be defined as where you assign first priority to the safety of your capital (money). Lower priorities are assigned to capital gain possibilities. In *speculation* these conditions are reversed. The potential of capital gains has first priority. The safety of your money has second priority. *Gambling* exists where you knowingly create risks by going against the odds.

The investment principle of importance to you is: *the same good, quality stock may be a sound, fundamental investment in one price range, a speculation at a slightly higher price level, and a gamble at a third, higher level.*

Specifically, in this example, the authors believe, from a fundamental viewpoint, SD is an investment at 49 or lower. At 49 or lower, the "odds" are 2 to 1 in your favor. SD possesses a low P/E, a generous yield and a low fundamental risk. Moving up, SD could be a speculation between 50 and 53. The odds are now even in that SD's price—fundamentally—has the same chance to advance or decline. Also, the yield is less and the P/E is higher. Moving up even higher, SD may be a gamble above 54. From a fundamental viewpoint, a buyer would be asking SD to exhibit upward price performance, that it has not demonstrated in the past two years.

When the criteria in Section Four changes, a new gain-to-loss range will usually be established by means of the easy calculations in Section Five.

18

The Profit-Estimate Sheet in Action— Section Six: Profit Estimate for Stock (100 Percent Cash)

Here you'll be estimating your profit potential in dollars and cents from an assumed investment. From Section Five you have already projected a possible high stock price of 64 for SD. You are now faced with the following questions:

- What is the number of shares you can buy with the particular amount of money you plan to invest?
- What are the buy and sell commissions and other expenses?
- What is the estimated net capital gains profit?
- What is the amount of dividends you should expect to receive?
- What is the estimated percent gain on your investment?

In this section you will be translating SD's projected price rise into understandable money figures. In Figure 37, for example, you will find Section Six filled out as though you had bought 100 shares of SD at 45 in March 1970. For illustrative purposes, we have assumed you'll be making an investment of approximately $4,500. In any analysis it is much more meaningful if you think in terms of making such an investment, either actual or imagined, so that you can watch the developments with keener interest.

SECTION SIX - PROFIT ESTIMATE FOR STOCK (100% CASH)

39) Assume a cash investment of . . . . $ 4,500

40) Number of shares purchaseable (line 39 $ 4,500 divided by
line 16 $ 45): . . . . 100 SH.

41) Estimated gross profit (line 36 $ 19 x line 40 100 SH) . . . . $ 1,900

42) Commissions: a) Buy $ 62.50 b) Sell $ 65.00 c) SUM of a + b . . $ 128

43) Estimated net CAPITAL GAINS profit (line 41 $ 1,900 minus
line 42c $ 128). . . . . $ 1,772

44) Dividends received per year (line 29 $ 2.80 x line 40 100 SH) . . $ 280

45) Total dividends received (line 44 $ 280 x 1 years). . . . . $ 280

46) Total estimated return from capital gains and dividends
(line 43 $ 1,772 + line 45 $ 280). . . . . $ 2,052

47) ESTIMATED ANNUAL % NET GAIN (line 46 $ 2,052 divided by
line 39 $ 4,500 ; Caution if less than 25%). . . . . | 45 % | (OK) CAUTION

FIGURE 37

LINE 39: Assume a cash investment of $4,500.

Enter $4,500, which is the cost of 100 shares of SD. The additional costs of commissions, taxes, etc., will be covered in other lines. Line 39 is specifically set up so that you can work with any sum of money. However, if you ever actually do invest, it is important that you invest only that money you feel you can afford.

LINE 40: Number of shares purchasable (line 39: $4,500 divided by line 16: $45): 100 SH.

Enter $4,500 from line 39 and the current stock price of 45 from line 16. Divide $4,500 by 45. You can buy 100 shares. Line 40 tells you the specific number of shares that you can purchase.

LINE 41: Estimated gross profit (line 36: $19 × line 40: 100 SH): $1,900.

Enter your projected 19-point gain figure from line 36 and from line 40, the 100 shares you are buying. Multiplying 19 times 100 equals $1,900, your estimated gross profit. But you know that your profit is going to be reduced by commissions. What are the commissions?

LINE 42: Commissions: *a*) Buy: $62.50 *b*) Sell: $65.00 *c*) SUM of *a* + *b*: $128

Now you determine your costs of handling this transaction. See Figure 38, which is the new minimum buy and sell commission schedule used by member brokerage firms for transactions on the New York and American Stock Exchanges and other exchanges. This commission schedule became effective March 24, 1972. The commission rates noted in Figure 38 are for 100-share lots only. An advantage of the new commission schedule is that it affords reduced commissions for larger share lot purchases. Ask your local broker for a free copy of this new schedule.

The Buy commissions for 100 shares of any stock priced at 45 is $62.50. Enter $62.50 in part A. The Sell commissions for 100 shares of any stock transacted at 64 is $65.00. Enter $65.00 in part B. Part C requires that you add up your buy and sell commissions. The answer is $127.50 ($62.50 plus $65.00). This is the amount of your round-trip costs. Round off $127.50 to $128.00. Enter $128.00 in part C.

If you buy SD, the actual amount of money you need is $4,562.50 ($4,500.00 plus $62.50). Normally you do not pay the sell commissions until you actually sell.

LINE 43: Estimated net CAPITAL GAINS profit (line 41: $1,900 minus line 42*c*: $128): $1,772.

Line 43 gives your estimated net capital gains. Enter $1,900 from line 41 and your commission costs of $128 from line 42*c*. Subtract the commission costs from the estimated gross profit. The answer is $1,772. Naturally it is subject to income tax.

LINE 44: Dividends received per year (line 29: $2.80 × line 40: 100 SH): $280.

If you held SD for one year, you would expect to receive the cash dividends. How much? Enter the estimated cash dividend per share of $2.80 from line 29 and the number of shares you are buying from line 40. Multiply $2.80 times 100 shares: $280.

LINE 45: Total dividends received (line 44: $280 × 1 year): $280.

NEW YORK AND AMERICAN STOCK EXCHANGE COMMISSION RATES
(Effective March 24, 1972)

Partial Schedule—100 Share Lots Only

SHARES Selling at $	Even	1/8	1/4	3/8	1/2	5/8	3/4	7/8
1	$ 8.40	8.65	8.90	9.15	9.40	9.65	9.90	10.15
2	10.40	10.65	10.90	11.15	11.40	11.65	11.90	12.15
3	12.40	12.65	12.90	13.15	13.40	13.65	13.90	14.15
4	14.40	14.65	14.90	15.15	15.40	15.65	15.90	16.15
5	16.40	16.65	16.90	17.15	17.40	17.65	17.90	18.15
6	18.40	18.65	18.90	19.15	19.40	19.65	19.90	20.15
7	20.40	20.65	20.90	21.15	21.40	21.65	21.90	22.15
8	22.40	22.56	22.73	22.89	23.05	23.21	23.28	23.54
9	23.70	23.86	24.03	24.19	24.35	24.51	24.68	24.84
10	25.00	25.16	25.33	25.49	25.65	25.81	25.98	26.14
11	26.30	26.46	26.63	26.79	26.95	27.11	27.28	27.44
12	27.60	27.76	27.93	28.09	28.25	28.41	28.58	28.74
13	28.90	29.06	29.23	29.39	29.55	29.71	29.88	30.04
14	30.20	30.36	30.53	30.69	30.85	31.01	31.18	31.34
15	31.50	31.66	31.83	31.99	32.15	32.31	32.48	32.64
16	32.80	32.96	33.13	33.29	33.45	33.61	33.78	33.94
17	34.10	34.26	34.43	34.59	34.75	34.91	35.08	35.24
18	36.70	35.56	35.73	35.89	36.05	36.21	36.38	36.54
19	35.40	36.86	37.03	37.19	37.35	37.51	37.68	37.84
20	38.00	38.16	38.33	38.49	38.65	38.81	38.98	39.14
21	39.30	39.46	39.63	39.79	39.95	40.11	40.28	40.44
22	40.60	40.76	40.93	41.09	41.25	41.41	41.58	41.74
23	41.90	42.06	42.23	42.39	42.55	42.71	42.88	43.04
24	43.20	43.36	43.53	43.69	43.85	44.01	44.18	44.34
25	44.50	44.61	44.73	44.84	44.95	45.06	45.18	45.29
26	45.40	45.51	45.63	45.74	45.85	45.96	46.08	46.19
27	46.30	46.41	46.53	46.64	46.75	46.86	46.98	47.09
28	47.20	47.31	47.43	47.54	47.65	47.76	47.88	47.99
29	48.10	48.21	48.33	48.44	48.55	48.66	48.78	48.89
30	49.00	49.11	49.23	49.34	49.45	49.56	49.68	49.79
31	49.90	50.01	50.13	50.24	50.35	50.46	50.58	50.69
32	50.80	50.91	51.03	51.14	51.25	51.36	51.48	51.59
33	51.70	51.81	51.93	52.04	52.15	52.26	52.38	52.49
34	52.60	52.71	52.83	52.94	53.05	53.16	53.28	53.39
35	53.50	53.61	53.73	53.84	53.95	54.06	54.18	54.29
36	54.40	54.51	54.63	54.74	54.85	54.96	55.08	55.19
37	55.30	55.41	55.53	55.64	55.75	55.86	55.98	56.09
38	56.20	56.31	56.43	56.54	56.65	56.76	56.88	56.99
39	57.10	57.21	57.33	57.44	57.55	57.66	57.78	57.89
40	58.00	58.11	58.23	58.34	58.45	58.56	58.68	58.79
41	58.90	59.01	59.13	59.24	59.35	59.46	59.58	59.69
42	59.80	59.91	60.03	60.14	60.25	60.36	60.48	60.59
43	60.70	60.81	60.93	61.04	61.15	61.26	61.38	61.49
44	61.60	61.71	61.83	61.94	62.05	62.16	62.28	62.39
45	62.50	62.61	62.73	62.84	62.95	63.06	63.18	63.29
46	63.40	63.51	63.63	63.74	63.85	63.96	64.08	64.19
47	64.30	64.41	64.53	64.64	64.75	64.86	64.98	65.00
48	65.00	65.00	65.00	65.00	65.00	65.00	65.00	65.00

The minimum commission on any 100 share transaction (buy or sell) need not be more than $65.00.

FIGURE 38

The purpose of line 45 is to enable you to calculate the total dividends that you should receive if you held SD for a number of years. In this example a holding period of one year was used. Enter $280 from line 44 and the number of years that you are contemplating holding SD in the spaces provided (in this case, for the latter, enter 1). Multiply your estimated cash dividends of $280 per year times the number of years. In this example, the answer is $280.

LINE 46: Total estimated return from capital gains and dividends (line 43: $1,772 + line 45: $280): $2,052.

The total estimated return that you are projecting is the sum of your estimated net capital gains and dividend income. Enter the estimated capital gain of $1,772 from line 43 and your projected dividend income of $280 from line 45. Add these two figures: $2,052.

LINE 47: ESTIMATED ANNUAL % NET GAIN (line 46: $2,052 divided by line 39: $4,500; Caution if less than 25%). The answer is 45%, OK.

Line 47 is the eighth of the eight important characteristics. A "Caution" tag here should throw ice water on your interest in this stock.

You are now starkly face to face with the potential dollars and cents gain measured in *percentages.* Enter your estimated total return of $2,052 from line 46 and the amount of cash—$4,500— that you are investing from line 39. Divide $2,052 by $4,500. Your answer is an *estimated annual percent net gain* of 45 percent.

Line 47 states, "Caution if less than 25%." Your answer is adequately more than 25 percent. Circle "OK" and cross out "Caution." SD has passed its eighth and final test for you.

Estimated Annual Percent Net Gain

The profit-making power of investing your funds in "special situations" that rather clearly demonstrate an estimated percentage gain of 25 percent or more per year should be clear to you from the data covered in Chapter One. Look again at Figure 1 and see the enormous money accumulation if you could compound your money at 25 percent annually.

The reason that a cutoff of 25 percent is used is that, unfortunately, the best-designed plans have been known to go astray. Stock market circumstances could force you to settle for less than you desire. The authors feel that the Profit-Estimate Sheet is adequately designed to *uncover* undervalued stocks. However, it is important to realize that the more stocks you can own, the greater your probabilities of success. Here's why. Sometimes it may take two or more years for a particular stock to work out profitably for you. At other times an investment may turn sour immediately and remain sour for many years. This has happened in the past and will undoubtedly occur in the future. Hence, your best protection is to spread your risk over a number of candidates. Though you naturally hope that *all* of your investments will produce an annual percentage net gain of 25 percent or more, you will probably find that some do better and some do worse. The law of averages, which has yet to be repealed, should ultimately produce results for you.

A concept of considerable importance, already mentioned, is worth repeating. The Profit-Estimate Sheet should direct your attention toward those stocks from which you could be receiving an adequate cash dividend of 4.5 percent or more while waiting for a projected price upswing in a low P/E stock.

19

The Profit-Estimate Sheet in Action— Section Seven: Margin Profit Estimate

The purpose of this chapter is to expand on the margin information given to you in Chapter Eleven, to show you some of the details as to how you may "leverage" your investment through the use of margin. Margin is the use of money borrowed from your broker or a bank. The intent of margin and leverage is to increase the number of shares that you can buy. With more shares, both your potential profit and loss are *increased*. The shares purchased serve as the collateral for the money loaned. In this section you should find the answers to these questions:

- How can you find the current margin requirements for stock?
- How many shares may be purchased?
- What is the amount of the margin loan and the interest rate for the loan?
- At what price would a margin call probably occur?
- What is the estimated percent gain on your invested cash using margin?

As you will see, the use of margin will expose your cash to a higher percent gain. It is your personal decision. Many investors reject its use for stock purchases because of the risk of greater loss and margin calls. Others readily accept it. You should decide for

SECTION SEVEN – MARGIN PROFIT ESTIMATE

48)   Current Stock Margin requirements set by FRB or Exchange . . . . . .   __80__   %

49)   Assume same number of shares as line 40 . . . .   __100__   SH.

50)   Cash required to purchase shares per line 49 (line 39 $ __4,500__ x
line 48 __80__ %) . . . . $ __3,600__

51)   Amount of margin loan (line 39 $ __4,500__ minus line 50 $ __3,600__) . . $ __900__

52)   Margin call when stock price is (1ine 16 $ __45__ x __33__ %) . . . . $ __15__

53)   Approx. cash required for one margin call (line 51 $ __900__ x
__33__ %) . . . . $ __300__

54)   Maximum $ amount of margin calls (same as line 51; amount of loan) . . . $ __900__

55)   Margin interest costs for one year (line 51 $ __900__ x __10__ %) . . . $ __90__

56)   Total estimated return from capital gains and dividends
(line 46 $ __2,052__ minus line 55 $ __90__) . . . . $ __1,962__

57)   ESTIMATED ANNUAL % NET GAIN USING MARGIN (line 56 $ __1,962__
divided by line 50 $ __3,600__) . . . .   __54__   %

IT IS ADVISED THAT A PERSON UNABLE TO KEEP AN ADEQUATE CASH RESERVE, OR UNABLE
TO HONOR ONE OR MORE MARGIN CALLS, NOT PARTICIPATE IN ANY MARGIN PURCHASES.

FIGURE 39

yourself whether you want to use it for your investments. In Figure
39, as an example, you will find Section Seven completed in detail.

We will start with the stock margin requirements in March 1970
as the rules then applied to SD. You will *not* find all of your
answers to margin in this chapter, but you will be given enough
data so that you can make an intelligent decision as to whether or
not margin appeals to you.

LINE 48: Current Stock Margin requirements set by FRB or
Exchange: 80%.

In March 1970 the Federal Reserve Board set margin for stock
purchases at 80 percent. As we have seen, the Federal Reserve
Board has the legal power to set margin requirements for stocks
listed on all the major exchanges and for selected stocks traded
over the counter.

This meant that the buyer (or short-seller) had to put up 80
percent of the cash required. He could borrow the remaining 20
percent from his broker, paying interest on the loaned money.

It is easy to find out just what the current margin requirements are. Ask your broker. He should have this pertinent information on the tip of his tongue.

LINE 49: Assume same number of shares as line 40: 100 SH.

For this analysis it will be assumed that you wish to purchase the same number of shares as available on a 100 percent cash basis in Section Six (Chapter 18). Enter 100 shares.

LINE 50: Cash required to purchase shares per line 49 (line 39: $4,500 × line 48: 80%): $3,600.

Enter the $4,500 figure from line 39, as this is the amount required for 100 shares of SD either as a 100 percent cash purchase or on margin. Enter the current margin requirements of 80 percent from line 48. Multiply $4,500 by 80 percent (use .80). $3,600 is the amount of cash required from the buyer. Add the buy commissions of $62.50, for a total of $3,662.50 cash required.

Cash Required for Margin Purchases At the outset you should understand that the use of margin is essentially a privilege, not a right. This will help you understand the variations in margin rules and requirements that exist in different brokerage firms and exchanges.

Starting at the top, the Federal Reserve Board establishes the margin requirements. At the next level each of the major exchanges may suspend margin privileges on any stock, requiring 100 percent cash for its purchase. This most often occurs when a stock attracts heavy volume and becomes a trading favorite. Next, each brokerage house may establish more restrictive margin requirements than those established by the Fed. Currently the minimum cash required in an account is $2,000 before a stock may be purchased on margin. But some brokerage firms require minimums of up to $5,000 or more.

Next, your registered representative is normally required to ascertain that your use of margin is compatible with your investment objectives.

LINE 51: Amount of margin loan (line 39: $4,500 minus line 50: $3,600): $900.

What is the size of your margin loan? Enter $4,500, which is the total amount required, from line 39. Enter $3,600, the cash that you are required to put up, from line 50. $4,500 minus $3,600 equals $900.

On Wall Street the margin loan is usually called a "debit balance." Periodically you receive a statement from your brokerage firm that updates and fully details your current debit balance, plus interest charges, in accordance with federal regulations.

LINE 52: Margin call when stock price is (line 16: $45 × 33%): $15.

Whenever you purchase stock on margin it is important to be fully aware that you may receive one or more margin calls. You receive a margin call when the stock price *drops* to a certain price. The reason that you receive a margin call is that the price drop reduces your equity. The lender's position may be endangered, and he has the right to send you a margin call, which is a request for more money. If you do not answer the margin call by putting up additional cash (or collateral), the lender (the brokerage firm or bank) has the legal right to sell you out.

An easy way to understand when you may receive a margin call is to think in terms of a single share of any stock priced at $100. For purposes of this illustration, put SD and its price of $45 completely out of your mind.

Let us take as an example stock X, priced at $100. To buy this stock on margin, you must put up $80 (80 percent). You then have a margin loan of $20 (20 percent). New York Stock Exchange rules require a brokerage firm to maintain a 25 percent "cushion" to protect its stock margin loans. Firms attempt to avoid exposing themselves to margin violations by *increasing* the cushion. Here is how the margin call multiplier of 33 percent used above was developed. It is a judgment figure arrived at individually by each brokerage firm. Multiply the $20 loan for stock X by 1.25. The answer is $25. If stock X drops to $25 per share, your margin loan is $20 and your equity is the remainder of $5. And the brokerage firm is in violation of New York Stock Exchange rules.

To find the "violation" price for any stock, with margin set at 80 percent, multiply the stock price by 25 percent. Stock X's price of $100 times 25 percent equals $25.

Arbitrarily, to protect themselves, brokerage firms send out margin calls well in advance of the violation price. Table J (*p. 182*)

TABLE J

Margin Call Multipliers

MARGIN REQUIREMENTS	APPROX. MARGIN CALL MULTIPLIER
100%	None
95%	10%
90%	18%
85%	25%
80%	33%
75%	40%
70%	48%
65%	55%
60%	60%
55%	66%
50%	72%

notes the general *margin call multiplier* for different margin percentages that a number of firms tend to use. You should check the particular requirements of the firm that is handling your account.

To fill out line 52, enter SD's current price of 45 from line 16. From the table above enter the margin call multiplier of 33 percent for margin requirements of 80 percent. Multiply 45 by 33 percent. The answer is 15. If SD drops to 15, and you originally bought it at 45 on 80 percent margin, and you still own it, you should expect to receive a margin call.

You should also know that you generally do *not* get a margin call if you have a number of stocks in your margin account, and only a few of them drop in price. In most firms it is the policy to lump the value of the margined stocks into one account. Thus, your strong stocks tend to protect the weak.

LINE 53: Approx. cash required for one margin call (line 51: $900 × 33%): $300.

If you are unfortunate enough to get a margin call, how much additional cash is usually requested on your first call? Usually the lender asks for about 33 percent of the loan. It could be more or less, depending on the brokerage firm. Enter the amount of your margin loan ($900) from line 51. Multiply $900 by 33 percent. The answer is $300. After you have paid this margin call, your loan has been reduced to $600. The $300 that you paid increases your equity position.

How do you usually receive a margin call? Usually by telegram.

LINE 54: Maximum $ amount of margin calls (same as line 51; amount of loan): $900.

What is the maximum dollar amount of margin calls that you can receive? The answer is the amount of the margin loan, which, in this example, from line 51 is $900. You cannot pay more for the 100 SD shares than if you had bought them for 100 percent cash, which amounts to $4,500. You have already put up $3,600. The most you can be asked for in margin calls is $900, plus margin interest charges.

LINE 55: Margin interest costs for one year (line 51: $900 × 10%): $90.

Your margin interests costs for one year will usually vary with two items. The first is the *prevailing interest rate*. As this changes, so do the interest charges you pay on a margin loan. The second is the *size* of the margin loan; the larger the loan, the lower the interest rate.

The key determinant is the *prime rate* charged by the major banks. In review, the prime rate is usually the lowest interest rate that banks charge their largest and most credit-worthy clients, which includes most brokerage firms.

You are charged by your brokerage firm an interest rate that is larger than the prime rate, depending on the size of your margin loan. Table K, below, lists the typical interest-cost formula that the

TABLE K

Margin Interest

AMOUNT OF MARGIN LOAN; Average Monthly Balance (debit balance)	INTEREST COST ADDED TO PRIME RATE
$ 1 to $ 9,999	+1½ %
$10,000 to $29,999	+1¼ %
$30,000 to $49,999	+1 %
$50,000 and up	+ ½ %

majority of brokerage firms use to determine the interest rates for margin accounts.

To fill out line 55, for our SD transaction, enter the amount of the margin loan ($900) from line 51. You then have to find out the prime rate. In March 1970 the prime rate was 8½ percent. Refer to Table K, Margin Interest, above. Your $900 margin loan fits into the first category of $1 to $9,999. The interest cost that you should add to the prime rate is 1½ percent. Your interest rate should be 10 percent (8½ percent prime rate plus 1½ percent add-on). Enter 10 percent. Multiply $900 by 10 percent. The answer is $90 annual interest costs, which is usually a tax-deductible item.

If your margin loan was $50,000 or more, your interest rate would have then amounted to 9 percent (8½ percent plus ½ percent).

A point you should be aware of is that as the prime rate rises and falls, so does your margin interest rate. In late March 1970 the major banks lowered the prime rate to 8 percent. Your margin interest rate should have been reduced automatically to 9½ percent (8 percent plus 1½ percent). By April 1971 the prime rate had been lowered in steps to 5¼ percent. Your margin interest rate should have been similarly reduced to 6¾ percent (5¼ percent plus 1½ percent).

Normally the margin interest costs are automatically deducted from your brokerage account on a monthly basis.

LINE 56: Total estimated return from capital gains and dividends (line 46: $2,052 minus line 55: $90): $1,962.

The purpose of line 56 is to reduce your total estimated return by the additional costs of your margin interest. Enter your total estimated return of $2,052 from line 46 and one year's interest cost of $90 from line 55. Subtract $90 from $2,052 to get $1,962.

LINE 57: *ESTIMATED ANNUAL % NET GAIN USING MARGIN* (line 56: $1,962 divided by line 50: $3,600): 54%.

What does your estimated annual percent net gain now amount to if you use margin? Line 57 tells you. Enter your total estimated return of $1,962 from line 56 and the actual amount of cash, $3,600, that you put up on 80 percent margin from line 50.

Divide $1,962 by $3,600. The answer is 54 percent, which is 9 percent *greater* than the 45 percent return estimated in line 47 for 100 percent cash.

If the margin requirements were lower, your estimated profit or loss would be larger since you would be controlling more shares of stock. In December 1971, the Federal Reserve Board reduced margin for stock purchases to 55 percent. If this analysis of SD was taking place with margin requirements of 55 percent, rather than 80 percent, your "Estimated Annual % Net Gain Using Margin" would calculate out to 74 percent. This larger figure is more attractive to capital gains oriented investors.

There are a number of sophisticated techniques you can employ using margin. If you wish to pursue the subject further, the authors suggest that you contact your registered representative.

The last lines of the Profit-Estimate Sheet bear repeating: "It is advised that a person unable to keep an adequate cash reserve, or unable to honor one or more margin calls, not participate in any margin purchases."

An Important Word of Caution: It must be pointed out clearly that the particular example of an investment in SD was selected because it showed a profit and demonstrated the use of the Profit-Estimate Sheet. Naturally, the use of the Profit-Estimate Sheet does not guarantee success on every transaction.

20

Some Examples of the Profit-Estimate Sheet at Work

In this chapter you will find some examples of stocks that appeared to qualify as selections using the eight tools employed by the Profit-Estimate Sheet.

You will find here ten examples listed in alphabetical order. Please note that the names of the example stocks all start with the letter "A." The reason is that over the last ten years a number of stocks qualified at different times. Some stocks qualified three or four times as their prices oscillated. In the interest of fairness and accuracy, the decision was made to highlight as examples the first ten stocks that appeared to meet the qualifications. Some of the illustrations performed quite well; others could have done better.

Perhaps the most important concept to grasp as you analyze the examples is that the more attractive buying opportunities in the stock market usually present themselves to you after a stock market sell-off. Therefore, it pays for you to be patient. Don't rush. Hold out for the "bargains." Try to permit everything to be as right as possible for you.

Special Ten-Year Stock Charts

The charts used with the illustrations depict about ten years of stock market action. Each line represents the high and low price range for a month.

Special Markings on Charts You will note that on each of the following charts (Figures 40–44) there is a *dashed line*. This line marks a 4.5 percent yield level. When the stock price was *below* the dashed line, the stock, per its indicated rate, was yielding 4.5 percent or more and may have been a candidate for purchase. On the other hand, when the stock price was above the dashed line, its yield was less than 4.5 percent and was disqualified as a candidate.

Also shown on the chart is an arrowhead (▲). This designation is important. It indicates approximately when the stock appeared to qualify on all eight tests of the Profit-Estimate Sheet as a buy candidate. Please note that some stocks qualified two or three times or more during the ten-year span.

List of Examples

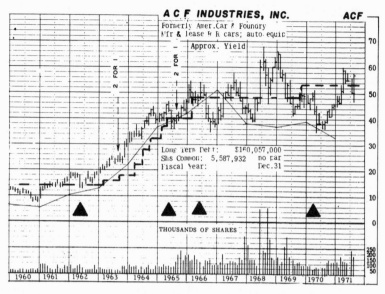

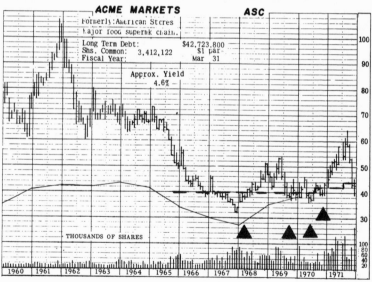

FIGURE 40

Courtesy Graphic Stocks, F. W. Stephens Co.

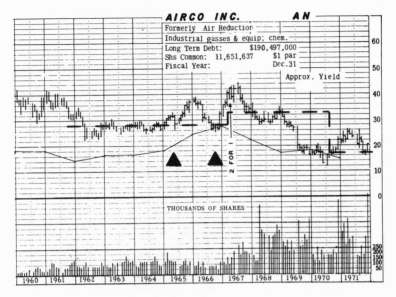

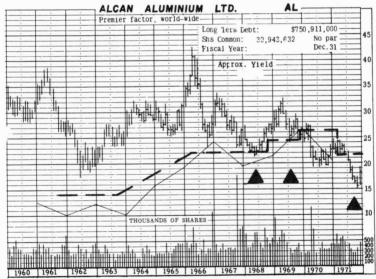

FIGURE 41

Courtesy Graphic Stocks, F. W. Stephens Co.

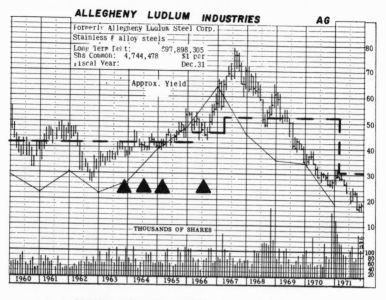

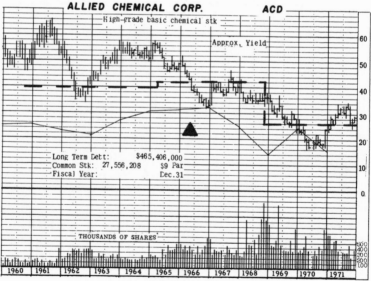

FIGURE 42

Courtesy Graphic Stocks, F. W. Stephens Co.

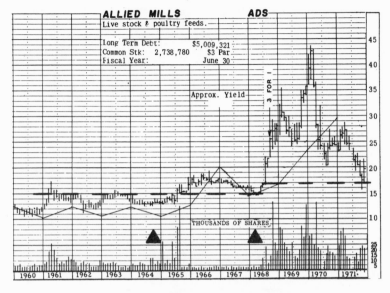

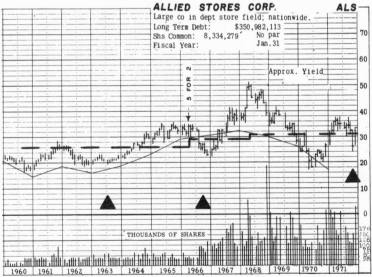

FIGURE 43

Courtesy Graphic Stocks, F. W. Stephens Co.

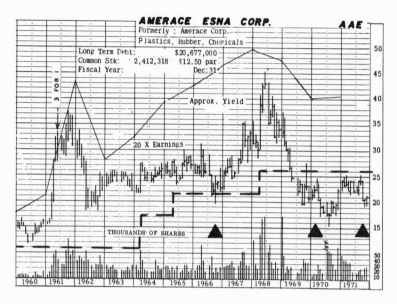

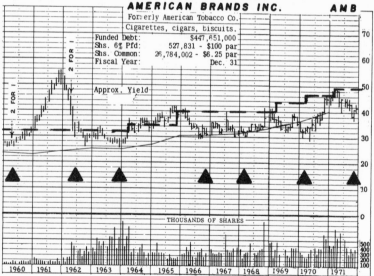

FIGURE 44

Courtesy Graphic Stocks, F. W. Stephens Co.

21

Investment Strategy

*Here are some step-by-step suggestions
on how you might put the eight tests in the Profit-Estimate
Sheet to work for you in today's stock market.*

Step One—Determine Your Investment Objective

Shakespeare wrote a brilliant line on this subject centuries ago: "This above all. To thine own self be true." You must determine for yourself what you want from the investment opportunities offered in the market.

Essentially there are three broad aims in investing:

1. Income.
2. Preservation of capital (high safety factor).
3. Capital gains (profit).

The Profit-Estimate Sheet applies primarily to the second purpose, i.e., investing primarily for preservation of capital. With astute use of the Profit-Estimate Sheet you should also receive the additional investment benefits of the other aims.

As a reminder, if it is essentially stock market profits you are searching for, then the six investment tools outlined in Robert Peisner's previous book, *How To Select Rapid Growth Stocks* (New York, E. P. Dutton & Co., 1966) may help you.

Step Two—Review Your Present Stock Holdings

If you have determined that your investment objective is preservation of capital, your next step is to make a careful review of your *present* stock holdings. Here is what you do:

A. Fill out a Profit-Estimate Sheet for each of your existing stocks.

B. Determine how many OKs or Cautions you assign to each stock.

C. Separate your stock holdings into four main categories:

    1. Stocks you feel qualify as undervalued.

    2. Stocks you judge to be *between* overvalued and undervalued.

    3. Stocks you ascertain are overvalued.

    4. Stocks that momentarily defy classification and about which you are doubtful.

Step Three—Consider Selling Stocks You Classify under C-3 and C-4

Stocks you put in classifications C-3 and C-4 should receive serious consideration as to whether they should be disposed of and the proceeds invested in other stocks. Remember—it is the worst form of wishful thinking to hope for your stocks to rise beyond the point of logical expectations. Yes, it is true that over the years a number of stocks have made major price moves that have bewildered and embarrassed the best of analysts. But you will be kidding yourself if you continually expect conservative stocks to consistently make dramatic price moves.

Step Four—A Guideline for When to Sell

Perhaps the easiest guideline to follow as to when to sell is detailed in Figure 36 (Gain-to-Loss Ratio). As you can see, the estimated price range of the stock under consideration is divided into three areas: Buy Area (2 to 1 or better), Neutral Area (between 2 to 1 and 1 to 1) and Sell Area (under 1 to 1). When the price of your stock is in the Sell Area, it means that your potential loss is greater than your potential gain. In other words, the odds are against you. You should now watch the stock carefully for signs of price erosion or distribution.

Step Five—Review Daily the "Digest of Earnings Reports" Column

Naturally you should at all times be conscious of the forces that help to sustain your stock's price. The best place to start is by reviewing daily the "Digest of Earnings Reports" in *The Wall Street Journal* so as to keep abreast of the most recent earnings data. If you should find, unhappily, that your company has suddenly reported a sharp decline in quarterly earnings, you should promptly recalculate the stock's gain-to-loss ratio, using the Profit-Estimate Sheet. You may thus determine if the stock is currently in the Buy Area, the Neutral Area or the Sell Area.

As you look over this column through the years, you will find certain characteristics that should save you time. Most of the companies use a fiscal year that ends in December. Consequently there will be specific times of the year that hundreds of companies will be reporting their quarterly earnings. At other times only a few companies will be reporting.

Here are the best times of the year to find the largest number of companies reporting their quarterly earnings:

1. April 10 through May 15, to review the fiscal quarter ending March 31.

2. July 10 through August 15, to review the fiscal quarter ending June 30.

3. October 10 through November 15, to review the fiscal quarter ending September 30.

4. January 15 through March 15, to review the fiscal quarter ending December 31.

And you should know when your company publishes its reports.

Step Six—Probable Stocks to Avoid

There are three industry groups into which you can invest: industrial companies, transportation companies and utilities. It is suggested that you avoid the utilities. Most utilities are monopolies within their areas. They do not suffer from the "slings and arrows" of outrageous competition. In exchange for this monopoly, the utility is usually governed by state boards that set rates. Frequently, these state boards drag their feet in granting rate relief. As a result of these and other problems, you will tend to find that most utility stocks pay relatively high yields, sell at low price/earnings ratios and tend to be dull market performers. Hence, investors are frequently offered a better capital gains potential by investing in companies whose profits can oscillate with shifts in the economy.

So we suggest that you concentrate your efforts in industrial and transportation stocks, and avoid utilities.

Step Seven—Invest in Common Stock

There are a number of different kinds of investment vehicles into which you can invest. Common stock, preferred stock, convertible preferred stock and convertible bonds are the primary vehicles available. Straight preferred stock should be avoided since it possesses more of the characteristics of a bond as the dividend is fixed. Convertible preferred stock and convertible bonds have a limited appeal as their prices tend to mirror the price of the common stock because of the conversion feature. However, the majority of convertible preferred stocks and convertible bonds tend to possess a "high premium" at those low levels in which the Profit-Estimate Sheet pinpoints the common stocks as being potentially undervalued. So the authors' preference is to invest primarily in common stocks and to avoid other vehicles except in special situations.

Step Eight—Avoid Stocks in Which the Dividend Has Recently Been Cut or in Which the Dividend Payout Varies from Year to Year

A careful look at the examples will show that they meet this suggested strategy. Once a company's board of directors has cut the dividend, they have "bit the bullet" and can cut it again. Additionally the dividend cut indicates that the company's profit problems may be deeply entrenched. The majority of directors are generally reluctant to cut a company's dividend if they believe the present profit crisis is temporary.

Rule of Thumb: Avoid companies that have cut their base dividend in the last five years.

Another type of company it is suggested that you avoid are those in which the dividend payout varies from year to year directly with the companies' fortunes. With this type of company you oscillate between pleasant surprise and disappointment as the dividend varies. From an analyst's point of view, such companies are difficult to "get a handle on" and you should avoid them in favor of more stable dividend paying companies.

Step Nine—Buy on the Published News of the Earnings Upturn Rather than on Expectations

The purpose of this strategy is to avoid being trapped in companies whose earnings are trending down, but that analysts estimate should improve, but that, unfortunately, *fail* to improve. Below you will find the quarterly earnings per share for the world's largest grocery chain, Great Atlantic & Pacific, a case in point:

GREAT ATLANTIC & PACIFIC

YEAR ENDING	QUARTERLY EARNINGS ($)				FULL YEAR EARNINGS	YEARLY DIVIDENDS
	May	*Aug.*	*Nov.*	*Feb.*		
1970	.49	.46	.50	.70	$2.15	$1.30
1971	.49	.50	.52	.51	2.02	1.30
1972	.46	.24				

In late August 1971, with the stock selling at 24, there were a number of published estimates circulating on Wall Street that Great Atlantic & Pacific was "turning the corner." An estimated earnings per share figure of $2.15 for the year ending February 1972 was being used. The latest twelve-month earnings to the first quarter ending May (published June 1971), amounted to $1.99 (.46 plus .51 plus .52 plus .50). The price/earnings ratio was around 12 to 1. The $1.30 cash dividend provided a yield of 5.3 percent. With the $2.15 earnings estimate, Great Atlantic & Pacific passed all eight tests of the Profit-Estimate Sheet.

Now put on your thinking cap. Notice carefully that the earnings reports for the first quarter, ending in May, was $.46, *down* from the previous year's corresponding report of $.49. For Great Atlantic & Pacific to have met that earnings *estimate* of $2.15, they would have had to close out the remaining three quarters with a strong profit surge.

That is what analysts were anticipating and that is what the company was striving toward. Unfortunately the profit surge did not materialize. Here is what happened. For the second quarter ending in August 1971, Great Atlantic & Pacific reported a major downturn in quarterly earnings. They reported $.24 compared with the previous year's $.50.

With such an earnings report, it appeared that the quarterly dividend payout of $.32½ could be cut as it was not adequately covered. Questions about the company now rose in analysts' minds. The estimated earnings for February 1972 was shaved from $2.15 to, hopefully, $1.70.

Great Atlantic & Pacific stock came under selling pressure as evidenced by its immediately following price decline.

Rule of Thumb: Buy on the published news of the actual earnings upturn rather than on expectations per research reports.

Step Ten—Apply the Eight Investment Characteristics

You should apply the eight investment characteristics with wisdom and logic. Please keep one point firmly in mind—*there is nothing sacred or inviolable about the cutoff points.*

For example, if you elect to be more strict, you can require a yield of five percent or more for line 18. You may wish a higher dividend protection ratio for line 21. You may feel greater comfort with a lower price/earnings ratio than the 15 to 1 suggested for line 22. You may want a larger gain-to-loss ratio of 2 to 1 in line 38.

The purpose of the cutoff points is to bring enough companies to your attention for consideration. If you raise the cutoff points, you will increase the quality of the companies and reduce the number brought to your attention. On the other hand, if you lower the cutoff points, you will find yourself examining more companies with speculative characteristics.

Step Eleven—Buy and Diversify Your Holdings

"Don't put all your eggs in one basket," "Diversify," "Find greater safety in more stocks," "Spread the risk over a number of issues." These are all wise slogans in the stock market. However, the trouble with slogans is that they are too general.

Here are three good rules of thumb you may find useful.

1. If you are going to watch and supervise your own investments, do not invest in more than seven companies at one time.

2. Do *not* invest more than 33 percent of your money in any one industry.

3. If you have considerable holdings, make use of an investment advisor who is registered with the Securities and Exchange

Commission and who will manage your portfolio on a full-time basis. (Advisors normally charge a yearly retainer fee varying between ½-of-1 percent to 2½ percent of the total value of your holdings. Advisors may work independently or be associated with a brokerage firm.)

Step Twelve—Learn to Be Patient

It was suggested that you avoid rushing into any investment decisions and to be patient. Once you have bought, you are asked—and it is definitely to your best advantage—to continue to be patient. It is assumed that before you invested, you verified two things:

1. The money you used to buy the stocks was *surplus* money. By surplus is meant that the money was not required for your everyday living needs. You have a cash reserve in the bank. Your life insurance and mortgage are adequately covered. Your bills are paid up.

2. The stocks fully met *all* the requirements of the Profit-Estimate Sheet (or the requirements as you may have modified them). You did not reduce the qualifications deliberately to invest in a special stock.

All right. You are invested. Now the more difficult time begins. You have nothing to do but wait, hopefully, for the stock's price to rise. You are also waiting for the next quarterly earnings report. Learn to be patient. Meanwhile, the price of your stock may be rising or falling. Recalculate the Profit-Estimate Sheet to check if you are in the Buy, Neutral or Sell area. Finally, the quarterly earnings report is released. Again your need to recalculate the stock. You again ascertain if you are in the Buy, Neutral or Sell area. Now it is waiting time again. Learn to be patient.

Step Thirteen—Cut Your Losses Short

Whenever you are investing in the stock market, you are dealing in the future developments of a company. There is only one thing certain about the future—it is unknown. Consequently it may be to your best advantage to protect your investments from any swift, new developments that may injure you financially. You have the option of using *stop-loss sell orders* or any other techniques that you feel secure with. Ask your broker how such orders work.

In any event, do not lose heart because you have to suffer a loss. But make every effort to determine why it occurred, so that you can more wisely move on to your next stock market investments.

The importance of attempting to cut your losses short is best illustrated by showing you the difficulty of attempting to "break even" after a sell-off. Table L below illustrates a unique statistical

TABLE L

The Difficult Arithmetic of "Breaking Even"

IF A STOCK DROPS THE FOLLOWING % AMOUNT	IT NEEDS TO RISE THIS % AMOUNT FOR YOU TO BECOME EVEN
5% (from 100 down to 95)	5% (from 95 up to 100)
10% (from 100 down to 90)	11% (from 90 up to 100)
15% (from 100 down to 85)	17% (from 85 up to 100)
20% (from 100 down to 80)	25% (from 80 up to 100)
25% (from 100 down to 75)	33% (from 75 up to 100)
30% (from 100 down to 70)	42% (from 70 up to 100)
35% (from 100 down to 65)	53% (from 65 up to 100)
40% (from 100 down to 60)	66% (from 60 up to 100)
45% (from 100 down to 55)	81% (from 55 up to 100)
50% (from 100 down to 50)	100% (from 50 up to 100)
55% (from 100 down to 45)	122% (from 45 up to 100)
60% (from 100 down to 40)	150% (from 40 up to 100)
65% (from 100 down to 35)	185% (from 35 up to 100)
70% (from 100 down to 30)	233% (from 30 up to 100)
75% (from 100 down to 25)	300% (from 25 up to 100)
80% (from 100 down to 20)	400% (from 20 up to 100)
85% (from 100 down to 15)	566% (from 15 up to 100)
90% (from 100 down to 10)	900% (from 10 up to 100)
95% (from 100 down to 5)	1900% (from 5 up to 100)

quirk of which many investors are unaware. A stock needs to rise *100%* to correct a 50% decline to bring you back even. If your stock declines from 100 down to 50, it has dropped 50%. But it needs to double in price (a 100% move) to rise from 50 back up to 100.

14th Step—A Suggested Way to Average Down

The principle of averaging down is to buy additional shares at lower prices so as to reduce your average cost per share. Variations of averaging down are "dollar cost averaging" and "formula investing," both of which are briefly described in the glossary. Most methods of averaging down are based on the stock price. The authors' favorite method of averaging down with conservative stocks is to use the *percentage yield,* as follows.

Refer to Table F in Chapter 15. Let us assume that you buy 100 shares of a typical conservative stock at $100. The dividend is $4.50 per share. Your yield is 4.5 percent. Obviously, the stock should meet all of the requirements of the Profit-Estimate Sheet. But the stock drops further in price. Nevertheless, on recalculating the Profit-Estimate Sheet, you judge that the probabilities are still in your favor.

Should you buy more shares? The authors believe you should. We would suggest buying an additional 100 shares at around $80. At $80, the dividend is still $4.50 per share but your yield is now 5.6 percent. After completing the purchase, you "own" 200 shares at an average cost of $90 per share. More important, from the authors' viewpoint, is the increase in your average yield to around 5.0 percent.

Let us assume that pessimism is rampant and your conservative stock declines further in price to around $60, to yield 7.5 percent. Should you buy additional shares? First recalculate the Profit-Estimate Sheet to see whether you still have 8 OKs. If the answer is yes, you could elect to buy an additional 100 shares. If you do so, your new position will be, per Table M:

TABLE M

Example of Averaging Down

SHARES	SHARE PRICE	COST	DIVIDEND INCOME	% YIELD
100	$100	$10,000	$ 450	4.5%
100	80	8,000	450	5.6%
100	60	6,000	450	7.5%
300		$24,000	$1,350	

You would now "own" 300 shares at an average cost of $80 per share. Your average yield would be around 5.6 percent.

The rule of thumb here is to tend to average *down* in conservative stocks with low P/Es and high yields. On the other hand, one should strive to average *up* with growth stocks.

The purposes of averaging down is hopefully to make it easier to break even. Here are your options for the future. If your typical conservative stock rises again to around $80 per share, you will just about be breaking even. If the stock moves up higher to approach or exceed your first purchase price of $100, you will then have a handsome paper profit. On the other hand, if your stock dropped still lower owing to a sudden drop in earnings per share, a cut in the dividend, or further deterioration of the economic environment, you could be faced with a substantial paper loss and the dismal prospects of a long siege as you waited for the company to engineer a return to its previous profit status and dividend payout rate. And there are no guarantees that such will occur. As you can see, investment involves risks.

15th Step—Spend the Time Necessary to Read, Study and Calculate

In investing, the harder you work the "luckier" and more successful you should be. It is necessary to devote time to your investments: hours for reading and research, and calculating and re-evaluating the current status of your investments. The investor should be constantly asking himself such questions as:

- Do my present positions seem sound?
- Should any changes be made?
- At what point in the future should I consider making portfolio changes?

When you first start to fill in the Profit-Estimate Sheet, you will find that you can easily spend two or more hours evaluating a single stock. Fortunately, the set-up of the Profit-Estimate Sheet lends itself to computer programming and the authors lean toward using a computer program for all stocks on the New York and American stock exchanges, to more readily identify the potentially undervalued stocks.

16th Step—Be Satisfied With a 15 Percent Annual Compounded Growth Rate

The authors believe that you should be more than satisfied to attempt to achieve a 15 percent annual compounded growth rate over a reasonable period of time (See Figures 1 and 2). Here's why. It means that you could double your money every five years. More importantly, it also means that you will be *outperforming* practically all of the major institutions such as mutual funds, bank trusts, pension plans and investment advisors based on the public record of their stock market performance for the last twenty years. In terms of actual money (taxes not considered), a 15 percent annual compounded growth rate means that—after five years—$1 billion grows to $2 billion, or $1 million grows to $2 million, or $100,000 grows to $200,000, or $10,000 grows to $20,000, or $1,000 grows to $2,000. You will be deceiving yourself if you believe that because you have less money to invest, you should risk a faster growth rate.

A Final Word

You now have in your hands a Profit-Estimate Sheet and some investment strategy, which, if wisely and carefully used, should increase your financial success in the stock market. In the slightly changed words of an old friendship toast:

May your investments always have above them
The warm, bright sun of earnings,
and,
May they always have behind them
The strong, warm winds of profit!
Good luck and GOD speed!

Appendix I

The following is a complete example of a "Record of Policy Actions of the Federal Open Market Committee" as it actually appeared in the Federal Reserve Bulletin for July 1971. Note the "tight money" decision pointed out by Arrow No. 1 page 211.

Records of policy actions taken by the Federal Open Market Committee at each meeting, in the form in which they will appear in the Board's Annual Report, are released approximately 90 days following the date of the meeting and are subsequently published in the Federal Reserve BULLETIN.

The record for each meeting includes the votes on the policy decisions made at the meeting as well as a résumé of the basis for the decisions. The summary descriptions of economic and financial conditions are based on the information that was available to the Committee at the time of the meeting, rather than on data as they may have been revised since then.

Policy directives of the Federal Open Market Committee are issued to the Federal Reserve Bank of New York—the Bank selected by the Committee to execute transactions for the System Open Market Account.

Records of policy actions have been published regularly in the BULLETIN beginning with the July 1967 issue, and such records have continued to be published in the Board's Annual Reports.

The records for the first three meetings held in 1971 were published in the BULLETINS for April, pages 320–27; May, pages 391–98; and June, pages 503–11. The record for the meeting held on April 6, 1971, follows:

MEETING HELD ON APRIL 6, 1971

Authority to effect transactions in System Account.

Information reviewed at this meeting suggested that real output of goods and services had risen substantially in the first quarter primarily because of the post-strike recovery of production in the automobile industry, but that the unemployment rate had remained high. Growth in real GNP was expected to slow in the current quarter. While wage rates were continuing to rise at a rapid pace in most sectors of the economy, the rate of advance in some major price indexes seemed to have moderated recently.

In March nonfarm payroll employment was about unchanged, and the unemployment rate moved back up to 6.0 per cent after having dipped to 5.8 per cent in February. Incomplete data suggested that retail sales had risen moderately and that industrial production had remained near the February level. Apart from fluctuations related to the auto strike, it appeared that in the first quarter as a whole retail sales were about the same as in the fourth quarter of 1970 and that industrial production had declined somewhat further. On the other hand, private housing starts continued at the high January rate in February and may have increased further in March.

Wholesale prices of industrial commodities rose further from mid-February to mid-March, but the increase in that period—and over the first quarter as a whole—was at a rate below the average pace of 1970. The rate of advance in the consumer price index slowed in February for the second successive month.

Expansion in real GNP was expected to moderate in the second quarter mainly because consumer and business spending on motor vehicles would be increasing much less rapidly than it had in the first quarter in the aftermath of the auto strike. In addition, defense spending was expected to decline further. As before, however, the staff projections suggested that residential construction expenditures and State and local government outlays would continue to rise at substantial rates, and that business inventory investment would be augmented by continued stockpiling of steel in anticipation of a possible strike in that industry at the beginning of August.

The possibility of a steel strike lent a high degree of uncertainty to the economic outlook for the second half of 1971. However, the average growth rate in real GNP over the second half was projected to be somewhat higher than the rate now anticipated for the second quarter, on the assumption that the duration of any such strike would be limited to about 60 days. It was expected that expansion in consumer spending would be sustained in part by the recently enacted increase in social security benefits, under which payments retroactive to January 1 were scheduled to be made in late June; possibly by a military pay increase around midyear; and possibly by some decline in the personal saving rate in the third and fourth quarters. In line with the results of the latest Commerce–SEC survey of business spending plans, taken in February, growth in business fixed investment outlays was projected to increase moderately over the second half. Continued sizable gains appeared to be in prospect for State and local government outlays, but it seemed likely that residential construction expenditures would expand more slowly than earlier in the year.

The U.S. foreign trade surplus was very small in January and February. With respect to the over-all balance of payments, it seemed likely that in the first quarter as a whole the deficit on the liquidity basis was at a rate higher than in the first half of 1970 and much higher than in the second half of that year. The worsening reflected principally an increase in net capital outflows.

On the official settlements basis, the first-quarter deficit in the payments balance was exceptionally large. International flows of interest-sensitive funds continued heavy in March, and major European countries experienced very substantial reserve gains. Recently, several European central banks had lowered their discount rates; in particular, the German Federal Bank and the Bank of England had made reductions of a full percentage point on April 1. These actions tended to narrow the wide differentials between short-term interest rates in Europe and the United States. Nevertheless, exchange market demands for German marks were very strong at the beginning of April, and there were indications of speculative and hedging activity. At the time of this meeting, however, the markets appeared to be quieting.

On April 1 the U.S. Treasury announced an offering of $1.5 billion of special securities to foreign branches of U.S. banks, for payment

April 9. Like similar Export-Import Bank issues earlier in the year, this offering was intended to help restrain the flows of funds to other countries.

In domestic securities markets, the Treasury announced on March 16 that it would offer $5 billion of new bills in three segments: a $2 billion addition to the outstanding tax-anticipation bills that were to mature on April 22, to be auctioned on March 24; a strip of bills maturing from July 8 to September 16, totaling $2.2 billion, to be auctioned on March 31; and $200 million increments to four consecutive weekly offerings of 6-month bills, beginning with the March 22 offering. The Treasury was expected to announce on April 28 the terms on which it would refund notes maturing in mid-May, including $5.8 billion held by the public.

Interest rates on most types of short-term securities had risen on balance in recent weeks. For example, the market rate on 3-month Treasury bills, at about 3.70 per cent on the day before this meeting of the Committee, was approximately 40 basis points above its level at the time of the March 9 meeting. The upturn in short-term yields reflected in part the additions to the outstanding supply of bills resulting from the Treasury's new offerings and the somewhat firmer money market conditions that developed during the period.

In March public offerings of new corporate bonds—which had been very large in recent months—expanded to an unprecedented volume, and offerings of State and local government issues continued heavy. Nevertheless, yields on new corporate and municipal bonds declined sharply after early March, reversing the advance of preceding weeks; and yields on Treasury notes and bonds also moved lower. The capital market rally was apparently a consequence of reports suggesting that the economy was recovering less rapidly than many market participants had anticipated and, more generally, of a modification of earlier views that long-term interest rates had already passed their cyclical lows. Although bond yields subsequently advanced somewhat, they still were well below the levels of 4 weeks earlier at the time of this meeting.

Interest rates on conventional home mortgages continued to decline in February. Yields in secondary markets for federally insured mortgages, which also had declined further in February, remained about unchanged over the course of March. At nonbank thrift institutions, inflows of savings funds had reached extraordinarily high levels in January and February, when interest rates on competitive short-term market instruments were falling markedly. These inflows continued at an extremely rapid pace in March, according to incomplete data for that month.

Although many commercial banks reduced their offering rates on consumer-type time and savings deposits during March, inflows of such deposits remained heavy at banks also. However, large-denomination CD's expanded only moderately further. The volume of business loans outstanding (including loans that had been sold to affiliates) declined during the month, and on March 11 major banks again reduced their prime lending rates—some by ½ of a percentage point, to 5¼ per cent, but most by ¼ of a point. On March 19 the 5¼ per cent prime rate became general. Banks continued to increase their holdings of securities at a substantial pace and to reduce their reliance on nondeposit sources of funds, including borrowings of Euro-dollars from their foreign branches.

Preliminary estimates indicated that there had been a substantial increase from February to March in total bank credit, as measured by the adjusted proxy series—daily-average member bank deposits adjusted to include funds from nondeposit sources. However, the increase was less than that expected at the time of the March 9 meeting of the Committee and also less than the rise recorded in the previous month. Like bank credit, both the narrow and broader measures of the money stock—M_1 and M_2—rose substantially on the average in March, although less sharply than in February. In contrast to bank credit, however, both M_1 (defined as private demand deposits plus currency in circulation) and M_2 (defined as M_1 plus commercial bank time deposits other than large-denomination CD's) increased considerably more than had been anticipated. Annual rates of growth over the first quarter as a whole [1] were estimated at about 11 per cent for the proxy series and about 8 and 17.5 per cent, respectively, for M_1 and M_2.

System open market operations since the preceding meeting of the Committee had been directed at achieving a slight firming of money market conditions, as incoming data indicated that M_1 and M_2

---

[1] Calculated on the basis of the daily-average level in the last month of the quarter relative to that in the last month of the preceding quarter.

were growing considerably faster than expected. At the same time, efforts were made during the period to counter repetitive tendencies toward undue firmness that arose from market factors affecting reserves. The Federal funds rate, which had averaged about 3½ per cent shortly before the March 9 meeting, subsequently fluctuated mostly around 3¾ per cent—although it rose to 4 per cent or above on a number of days in mid-March and again in late March and early April. As in other recent weeks, an important part of reserve needs was met by System purchases of intermediate- and long-term Treasury securities.

Staff analysis suggested that, if prevailing money market conditions were maintained, M_1 would continue to rise rapidly early in the second quarter and would grow somewhat faster over the quarter as a whole than it had in the first quarter. The analysis also suggested that expansion in time and savings deposits other than large-denomination CD's would slow substantially in coming months, in part because of the spreading practice among banks of reducing rates offered on such deposits. As a result, it was expected that growth in M_2 would moderate in the second quarter from its exceptionally rapid first-quarter pace. In addition, it appeared likely that the volume of CD's outstanding would increase relatively little further over the quarter and that this development, along with slower expansion of other time deposits, would contribute to an expected moderation in the growth of the adjusted bank credit proxy.

The Committee decided that open market operations at present should be directed at attaining temporarily some minor firming of money market conditions. Some members favored this course primarily for the purpose of achieving less rapid growth in the monetary aggregates than the staff analysis indicated might eventuate in the second quarter under unchanged money market conditions. Others placed main emphasis on the objective of contributing, at least marginally, to a narrowing of the differentials between short-term interest rates in this country and abroad, in the interest of moderating capital outflows. In the former connection, the Committee indicated that it would like to see more moderate expansion in the monetary aggregates in the second quarter than had occurred in the first. As a step in that direction it was felt that growth in M_1 in April at a slower rate than in March and more in line with the first-quarter rate would be desirable, and various members expressed a desire for further slowing in M_1 as the quarter progressed. It was recognized that the aggregates were likely to increase at faster rates in April than over the second quarter as a whole. The Committee agreed that money market conditions should be modified somewhat if the monetary and credit aggregates appeared to be deviating substantially from the growth paths desired.

The Committee also decided that needs for reserves should continue to be met to the extent feasible by purchases of long-term Treasury securities, in the interest of promoting accommodative conditions in long-term credit markets. It was noted that later in April even-keel considerations related to the forthcoming Treasury refunding would begin to place constraints on operations in coupon issues, as well as on operations directed at modifying money market conditions.

The following current economic policy directive was issued to the Federal Reserve Bank of New York:

> The information reviewed at this meeting suggests that real output of goods and services rose substantially in the first quarter primarily because of the resumption of higher automobile production, but that the unemployment rate remained high. More moderate growth in real GNP appears to be in prospect for the current quarter. Wage rates in most sectors are continuing to rise at a rapid pace. The rate of advance in consumer prices and in wholesale prices of industrial commodities appears to have moderated recently. In March bank credit and the money stock both narrowly and broadly defined again expanded substantially, although the increases were less sharp than in February. Inflows of consumer-type time and savings funds to banks and nonbank thrift institutions reached unusually high levels in the first quarter as interest rates on competitive short-term market instruments declined considerably further. In recent weeks, however, key short-term interest rates have moved up somewhat on balance. Yields on new issues of corporate and municipal bonds declined during much of March despite a continuing heavy calendar of offerings, but most recently long-term market yields have also risen somewhat. The over-all balance of payments deficit in the first quarter was exceptionally large. The trade surplus for the first two months was very small, and capital outflows have been stimulated by wide short-term interest rate differentials. Despite recent reductions

in the discount rates of several European central banks, these differentials remain wide. In light of the foregoing developments, it is the policy of the Federal Open Market Committee to foster financial conditions conducive to the resumption of sustainable economic growth, while encouraging an orderly reduction in the rate of inflation, moderation of short-term capital outflows, and attainment of reasonable equilibrium in the country's balance of payments.

To implement this policy, while taking account of the Treasury financing the terms of which are to be announced late in the month, System open market operations until the next meeting of the Committee shall be conducted with a view to attaining temporarily some minor firming in money market conditions, while continuing to meet some part of reserve needs through purchases of coupon issues in the interest of promoting accommodative conditions in long-term credit markets; provided that money market conditions shall be modified if it appears that the monetary and credit aggregates are deviating significantly from the growth paths desired.

> Votes for this action: Messrs. Burns, Brimmer, Clay, Daane, Maisel, Mayo, Morris, Robertson, and Sherrill. Votes against this action: Messrs. Hayes and Kimbrel.
> Absent and not voting: Mr. Mitchell.

In dissenting, Messrs. Hayes and Kimbrel noted that they favored more firming of money market conditions than contemplated under this directive, although not so much firming as to cause serious repercussions in bond markets. Mr. Hayes thought the directive gave inadequate recognition to the need for moving toward somewhat higher short-term interest rates in light of the international financial situation, and he also expressed concern about the risk of excessive growth in the money stock. Mr. Kimbrel believed that higher short-term interest rates would be desirable mainly to hold growth in the monetary and credit aggregates to a moderate pace in order to avoid a rekindling of inflationary expectations.

Appendix II: Selected Readings

The selected readings noted below basically cover two categories of publications. One includes various books and pamphlets which are essentially educational in nature. By reading them you will know more about the mechanics of money and stocks. The other category comprises various publications and investment services which the authors have personally found useful in their daily work of keeping up to date in the current investment climate. There are many publications and many services available to you. Some are free, others you must pay for. The authors have no axe to grind, since they pay full price for those services which they use. Hence they can maintain their objectivity.

Government Publications

The Federal Reserve System—Purposes and Functions . A difficult-to-read, 275-page book on the Federal Reserve System. Available free of charge from the Division of Administrative Services, Board of Governors of the Federal Reserve System, Washington, D.C. 20551.

Open Market Operations A general, 47-page explanation of how the Federal Open Market Committee tends to operate. Available free of charge from the Federal Reserve Bank of New York, New York, N.Y. 10005.

The three booklets below are available free from the Federal Reserve Bank of Richmond, Richmond, Virginia 23213:

Readings on Money Discusses in conventional terms the nature of money, its role in our modern economy, and the processes of its creation and circulation. 59 pages.

Keys for Business Forecasting Describes in nontechnical terms the statistical tools used by a number of economists to help forecast business conditions. 31 pages.

The Federal Reserve at Work Gives an understanding of the role the Federal Reserve System plays in the economy. Provides a digest of the Fed's actions from the 1960–61 recession to late 1968. 31 pages.

Each of the Federal Reserve Banks publishes a monthly review of credit and business conditions. More important, some of the banks issue weekly and monthly data on a number of economic indicators. The authors believe that the most useful data for investors are provided by the Federal Reserve Bank of St. Louis. The four publications below may be obtained free from the Research Department, Federal Reserve Bank of St. Louis, P.O. Box 442, St. Louis, Missouri 63166.

Quarterly Economic Trends Published every three months. Its importance to investors is that it employs a business programmed computer to estimate the Gross National Product (GNP) of the United States for eighteen to twenty-one months ahead.

Please note that the estimated GNP figures *vary* with the rate of change of money growth, which is controlled solely by the Federal Reserve Board.

U.S. Financial Data Using a graph format, this weekly publication presents data on the prevailing money supply, bank credits, 91-day Treasury bills percent yield rate, discount rate, prime rate, federal funds rate, net free reserves, etc. It is perhaps the most comprehensive and easiest to understand of any such financial summary.

Monetary Trends Issued monthly, in graph format, this publication presents the "big picture" of financial conditions over the past three or four years. It covers much of the same material as *U.S. Financial Data,* but for a longer time period.

Review (Monthly) This publication offers essays by economists on prevailing financial and business conditions in the United States. It emphasizes the hypothetical impact of changes in the money supply on these conditions. The *Review* presents much economic research data.

The next item is the house organ of the Federal Reserve Board.

The Federal Reserve Bulletin This bulletin presents articles, economic essays, research reports, and financial and business statistics. It contains the important "Record of Policy Actions of the Federal Open Market Committee." In Appendix I you will find a complete example of a "Record of Policy Actions of the FOMC" as it *actually* appeared in the *Federal Reserve Bulletin* of July 1971. Note the "tight money" decision pointed out by Arrow No. 1. The bulletin is available at a subscription price of $6.00 per year from the Division of Administrative Services, Board of Governors of the Federal Reserve System, Washington, D.C. 20551.

Books

Edwards, Robert D., and Magee, John. *Technical Analysis of Stock Trends.* Springfield, Mass.: John Magee, 1966. This "bible" of technical analysts, first published in 1948, describes most of the chart formations and offers interpretations. The authors have found two sections of the book to be particularly useful. One of these describes the Dow Theory, which attempts to forecast stock-market moves. The other is a rather complete description of a chart pattern termed "Heads and Shoulders" which tends to be associated with market tops. It is a matter of record that the majority of major stock-market sell-offs in this last decade have appeared to develop out of "Heads and Shoulders" patterns.

Engel, Louis. *How to Buy Stocks.* Boston: Little, Brown and Company, 1967; 252 pages. A good primer for the novice investor on the basic mechanics of what you should know before you buy your first stock or bond.

Friedman, Milton, and Schwartz, Anna. *A Monetary History of the United States, 1867–1960.* Princeton, N.J.: Princeton University Press, 1963. An advanced economic study for the more studiously inclined. The book that formed the basis for the renaissance of the monetarists' point of view in economics.

Keynes, John Maynard. *The General Theory of Employment, Interest and Money.* New York: Harcourt, Brace and World, 1936. The basic book out of which practically all Keynesian ideas involving economics have surfaced.

Peisner, Robert N. *How to Select Rapid Growth Stocks.* New York: E. P. Dutton & Company, Inc., 1966; 160 pages. Describes in considerable detail six practical, workable investment tools that should be helpful to you in selecting aggressive growth stocks, using the fundamental approach of earnings per share. A number of such stocks have been known to rise admirably.

Ritter, Lawrence and Silber, William. *Money.* New York: Basic Books, 1970; 212 pages. This easy-to-read account of how money works in the United States of the 1970s covers inflation, debt, devaluation, and various economic theories. It is a good economic primer for investors.

Sprinkel, Beryl W. *Money & Markets—A Monetarist View.* Hometown, Illinois: Richard D. Irwin, Inc., 1971; 295 pages. This book offers a good look at the monetarist school of economics. A completely revised and updated edition of Mr. Sprinkel's previous book, *Money and Stock Prices,* it describes the monetarist economic theory and its implications for predicting business cycles, stock prices, bond prices, inflation and economic growth.

Weil, Gordon and Davidson, Ian. *The Gold War.* New York: Holt, Rinehart and Winston, 1970; 236 pages. This book describes the actors and the behind-the-scenes events leading up to the current decline of the dollar, the various devaluations, the speculative rushes on gold, the creation of the Special Drawing Rights, and the two-tier gold system.

Newspapers, Magazines and Periodicals

The Wall Street Journal, published daily by Dow Jones & Company, Inc., is the key newspaper of the financial community. Reading it daily is a must if you possess any substantial security holdings. It contains the "Digest of Earnings Reports" and the most accurate reporting on the Federal Reserve System. Its national circulation exceeds one million. For subscription rates write to *The Wall Street Journal,* 22 Cortlandt Street, New York, N.Y. 10007.

Barron's, published by Dow Jones & Company, Inc., contains the weekly statistical tables covering stock transactions on the New York and American stock exchanges, over-the-counter markets and bond markets. *Barron's* offers a combination of news reports, commentary and pertinent stock market research data. For subscription rates write to *Barron's,* 22 Cortlandt Street, New York, N.Y. 10007.

Fortune, published monthly by Time Inc. Most articles in this magazine tend to be of a business historical nature and are apt to have a Monday-morning-quarterback overtone. Two features, however, consistently give good information to investors. The first is the "Business Roundup," a perceptively written economic review aimed at businessmen. The "Business Roundup" makes economic projections, with explanations of the reasoning behind these views, which are quite helpful for investors. Also, the "Personal Investing" column frequently presents interesting new stock market research. For subscription rates, write to *Fortune,* 541 No. Fairbanks Ct., Chicago, Illinois 60611.

Forbes magazine, published twice monthly by Forbes, Inc. Its articles also tend to be historical and are therefore of limited value to investors. The main attraction in this magazine for investors is its finance section, in which five highly competent stock market analysts present, twice monthly, their thoughtful opinions, which are easy to read. A careful reading of these five writers will usually give you an insight into the market's current emotional, technical and fundamental structure. For subscription rates write to *Forbes,* 60 Fifth Avenue, New York, N.Y. 10011.

The Financial Analysts Journal, published every other month by the Financial Analysts Federation. It contains scholarly articles on the current stock market. Articles tend to be ivory-tower oriented, though some contain pertinent stock market research. Written ponderously and often difficult to read. For subscription rates write to the journal at 219 East 42nd Street, New York, N.Y. 10017.

The Monthly Economic Letter, published monthly by the First National City Bank of New York. It possesses a superior economic research and writing team. The publication leans toward the monetarist point of view in economics, and attempts to spotlight potential economic problems. It often criticizes the Federal Reserve Board and suggests economic solutions. Well written and easy to read. Letter is mailed free. Send requests to Public Relations Department, First National City Bank, 399 Park Avenue, New York, N.Y. 10022.

Investment Advisory Services

The Earnings Forecaster, published weekly by Standard and Poor's Corporation. It gives statistical information only, tabulating Wall Street analysts' estimates of the earnings per share of well over 1,000 leading corporations. The authors feel this service is a must if you wish to research potentially undervalued stocks. For subscription rates write to Standard and Poor's Corporation, 345 Hudson St., New York, N.Y. 10014.

The Value Line Investment Survey, published weekly by Arnold Bernhard & Company, Inc. It covers over 1,400 stocks and estimates earnings-per-share for the coming year and also breaks down the yearly estimates into quarterly estimates. The information is updated every three months. The service also presents a fifteen-year historical record of each stock and makes projections for three to five years ahead. For subscription rates write *The Value Line,* 5 East 44th St., New York, N.Y. 10017.

The Stock Fundamentals Company publishes three items:
The Report on Companies Showing Very Sharp Increases in Earnings, published irregularly as growth stocks appear to fundamentally meet the specifications given in Robert Peisner's book, *How to Select Rapid Growth Stocks.*
The Undervalued Stock Report, published irregularly as the computer program divulges stocks which appear to meet the eight tests outlined in this book.
The Short-Term Market Timing Report, published twice monthly, gives general comments of a technical, fundamental and economic nature on the current stock market.
For subscription rates write the Stock Fundamentals Company, Dept. DAR, Post Office Box 838, Beverly Hills, California 90213. Darryl Peisner is affiliated with this advisory service.

Chart Services

Graphic Stocks, published every other month by F. W. Stephens Company, gives the long-term picture going back about twelve years. Each chart shows the *monthly* price range and volume. The publication covers about 1,600 stocks. The charts in Chapter Twenty of this book are from *Graphic Stocks.* For subscription rates write *Graphic Stocks,* P.O. Box A, Newfoundland, N.J. 07435.

The Mansfield Stock Chart Service, published weekly by R. W. Mansfield Company. Each chart shows the *weekly* price range and volume. The last eighteen months of price action are usually covered, along with much supporting data. Just about all stocks on the New York and American stock exchanges are reviewed. The chart used in Figure 20A is a Mansfield chart. Selected Over-the-Counter stocks (about 1,000) are also covered. For subscription rates write the service at 26 Journal Square, Jersey City, N.J. 07306.

Daily Basis Stock Charts, published weekly by Trendline, a division of Standard and Poor's. Each chart shows a stock's price action for the last six or seven months, with the *daily* price range and volume of sales. The service covers about 740 stocks actively traded on the New York and American stock exchanges (no Over-the-Counter stocks). For subscription rates write Standard and Poor's Corporation, 345 Hudson St., New York, N.Y. 10014.

Computer Services

The Trade Levels Report—Computer Calculated, published weekly by Trade Levels, Inc. It covers 5,000 stocks listed on the N.Y., Amex exchanges and D-T-C. A limitation of this computer service is that it is technical, being geared solely to price and volume. Fundamentals are not considered. For each stock the computer will signal a suggested investment posture—buy, hold, sell, sell short, hold short or cover short. Accuracy tends to be greater in the higher price stocks. The computer is programmed to respond quickly to market action. For subscription rates write Trade Levels, Inc., Mutual Savings Building, 301 East Colorado Blvd., Pasadena, California 91101.

Appendix III: A Glossary of the Language of Investing

The language spoken in America's investment world may sound like a strange tongue to the newcomer. It is often vivid, colorful, flavored with the idioms of many eras. Some expressions have filtered down from the days when brokers traded securities under a buttonwood tree at the foot of New York's Wall Street, in the open air. Others are so new that they have seldom been glossed before.

Any glossary of this special language involves certain problems. Some words and phrases cannot be defined completely without going into related background material—others have nuances of meaning that even the experts may dispute.

The following definitions have been prepared to be simple and easy, omitting subtle shades of meaning in the interest of brevity and readability.

New investors, and many seasoned ones, are often puzzled by words and phrases relating to investment. We hope they will find this glossary helpful. Investment, after all, is not the province of a few people only, but the right of men and women everywhere.

This glossary is published courtesy of the New York Stock Exchange and consists of excerpts from its publication, *The Language of Investing*.

ACCRUED INTEREST: Interest accrued on a bond since the last interest payment was made. The buyer of the bond pays the market price plus accrued interest. Exceptions include bonds that are in default and income bonds.

AMORTIZATION: A generic term; includes various specific practices such as depreciation, depletion, write-off of intangibles, prepaid expenses and deferred charges.

ANNUAL REPORT: The formal financial statement issued yearly by a corporation to its shareowners. The annual report shows assets, liabilities, earnings —how the company stood at the close of the business year and how it fared profit-wise during the year.

ARBITRAGE: A technique employed to take advantage of differences in price.

If, for example, XYZ stock can be bought in New York for $10 a share and sold in London at $10.50, an arbitrageur may simultaneously purchase XYZ stock here and sell the same amount in London, making a profit of 50¢ a share, less expenses. (*See* CONVERTIBLE; RIGHTS.)

ASSETS: Everything a corporation owns or that is due to it: cash, investments, money due it, materials and inventories, which are called "current assets"; buildings and machinery, which are known as "fixed assets"; and patents and goodwill, called "intangible assets." (*See* LIABILITIES.)

AVERAGES: Various ways of measuring the trend of securities prices, the most popular of which is the Dow-Jones average of thirty industrial stocks listed on the New York Stock Exchange. The term "average" has led to considerable confusion. A simple average for, say, fifty leading stocks would be obtained by totaling the prices of all and dividing by fifty. But if one of the stocks in the average is split, the price of each share of that stock is then automatically reduced because more shares are outstanding. Thus the average would decline even if all other issues in the average were unchanged. That average thus becomes inaccurate as an indicator of the market's trend.

Various formulas—some very elaborate—have been devised to compensate for stock splits and stock dividends and thus give continuity to the average. Averages and individual stock prices belong in separate compartments.

In the case of the Dow-Jones Industrial Average, the prices of the 30 stocks are totaled and then divided by a divisor that is intended to compensate for past stock splits and dividends and that is changed from time to time. As a result, point changes in the average have only the vaguest relationship to dollar price changes in the stocks included in the average. In November 1972 the divisor was 1.661, so that a one-point change in the industrial average at that time was actually the equivalent of 5.6¢. (*See* NYSE COMMON STOCK INDEX; POINT; SPLIT.)

AVERAGING: (*See* DOLLAR COST AVERAGING.)

BALANCE SHEET: A condensed statement showing the nature and amount of a company's assets, liabilities and capital on a given date. In dollar amounts the balance sheet shows what the company owned, what it owed, and the ownership interest in the company of its stockholders. (*See* ASSETS; EARNINGS REPORT.)

BEAR: One who believes the market will decline. (*See* BULL.)

BEAR MARKET: A declining market. (*See* BULL MARKET.)

BID AND ASKED: Often referred to as a "quotation" or "quote." The *bid* is the highest price anyone has declared that he wants to pay for a security at a given time, the *asked* is the lowest price anyone will take at the same time. (*See* QUOTATION.)

BIG BOARD: A popular term for the New York Stock Exchange.

BLUE CHIP: Common stock in a company known nationally for the quality and wide acceptance of its products or services, and for its ability to make money and pay dividends. Usually such stocks are relatively high-priced and offer relatively low yields.

BOARD ROOM: A room for customers in a broker's office where opening, high, low and last prices of leading stocks are posted on a board throughout the market day.

BOND: Basically an IOU or promissory note of a corporation, usually issued in multiples of $1,000, although $100 and $500 denominations are not uncommon. A bond is evidence of a debt on which the issuing company usually promises to pay the bondholders a specified amount of interest for a specified length of time, and to repay the loan on the expiration date. In every case a bond represents debt—its holder is a creditor of the corporation and not a part owner as is the shareholder. (*See* CONVERTIBLE.)

BOOK VALUE: An accounting term; book value of a stock is determined from a company's records, by adding all assets (generally excluding such intangibles as goodwill), then deducting all debts and other liabilities, plus the liquidation price of any preferred issues. The sum arrived at is divided by the number of common shares outstanding and the result is book value per common share. Book value of the assets of a company or a security may have little or no significant relationship to market value.

BROKER: An agent, often a member of a stock-exchange firm or an exchange member himself, who handles the public's orders to buy and sell securities or commodities. For this service a commission is charged. (*See* COMMISSION BROKER; DEALER.)

BULL: One who believes the market will rise. (*See* BEAR.)

BULL MARKET: An advancing market. (*See* BEAR MARKET.)

CALL: (*See* PUTS AND CALLS.)

CALL LOAN: A loan that may be terminated or "called" at any time by the lender or borrower; used to finance purchases of securities.

CAPITAL GAIN: Profit from the sale of a capital asset; a capital gain, under current federal income-tax laws, may be either short-term (six months or less) or long-term (more than six months). A short-term capital gain is taxed at the reporting individual's full income-tax rate.

CAPITAL STOCK: All shares representing ownership of a business, including preferred and common. (*See* COMMON STOCK; PREFERRED STOCK.)

CAPITALIZATION: Total amount of the various securities issued by a corporation; capitalization may include bonds, debentures, preferred and common stock and surplus. Bonds and debentures are usually carried on the books of the issuing company in terms of their par or face value. Preferred and common shares may be carried in terms of par or stated value. Stated value may be an arbitrary figure decided upon by the directors or may represent the amount received by the company from the sale of the securities at the time of issuance. (*See* PAR.)

CASH FLOW: Reported net income of a corporation *plus* amounts charged off for depreciation, depletion, amortization, and extraordinary charges to reserves, which are bookkeeping deductions and not paid out in actual dollars and cents. It is a yardstick used in recent years because of the larger noncash deductions appearing to offer a better indication of the ability of a company to pay dividends and finance expansion from self-generated cash than the conventional reported net-income figure. (*See* AMORTIZATION; DEPLETION; DEPRECIATION.)

CASH SALE: A transaction of the floor of the Stock Exchange that calls for delivery of the securities the same day. In "regular way" trades, the seller is to deliver on the fifth business day.

CERTIFICATE: The actual piece of paper that is evidence of ownership of stock in a corporation. Watermarked paper is finely engraved with delicate etchings to discourage forgery. Loss of a certificate may at the least cause a great deal of inconvenience; at the worst, financial loss.

CLOSED-END INVESTMENT TRUST: (*See* INVESTMENT TRUST.)

COMMISSION: The broker's fee for purchasing or selling securities or property for a client. On the New York Stock Exchange the average commission is about one percent of the market value of the stocks involved in the transaction and approximately one-quarter of one percent on bonds.

COMMISSION BROKER: An agent who executes the public's orders for the purchase or sale of securities or commodities. (*See* BROKER; DEALER.)

COMMON STOCK: Securities that represent an ownership interest in a corporation. If the company has also issued preferred stock, both the common and preferred have ownership rights, but the preferred normally has prior claim on dividends and, in the event of liquidation, assets. Claims of both common- and preferred-stock holders are junior to claims of bondholders or other creditors of the company. Common-stock holders assume the greater risk, but generally exercise the greater control and may gain the greater reward in the form of dividends and capital appreciation. The terms "common stock" and "capital stock" are often used interchangeably when the company has no preferred stock. (*See* CAPITAL STOCK; PREFERRED STOCK.)

CONGLOMERATE: A corporation which has diversified its operations by acquiring enterprises in widely varied industries.

CONVERTIBLE: A bond, debenture or preferred share that may be exchanged by the owner for common stock or another security, usually of the same company, in accordance with the terms of the issue.

COVERING: Buying a security previously sold short. (*See* SHORT SALE; SHORT COVERING.)

CUMULATIVE PREFERRED: A stock having a provision that, if one or more dividends are omitted, the omitted dividends must be paid before dividends may be paid on the company's common stock.

CURB EXCHANGE: Former name of the American Stock Exchange, second largest exchange in the country. The term comes from the market's origin on a street in downtown New York.

CURRENT ASSETS: Those assets of a company which are reasonably expected to be realized in cash, or sold, or consumed during the normal operating cycle of the business. These include cash, U.S. government bonds, receivables and money due usually within one year, and inventories.

CURRENT LIABILITIES: Money owed and payable by a company, usually within one year.

CUSTOMERS' MAN: (*See* REGISTERED REPRESENTATIVE.)

DEALER: An individual or firm in the securities business acting as a principal rather than as an agent. Typically, a dealer buys for his own account and sells to a customer from his own inventory. The dealer's profit or loss is the difference between the price he pays and the price he receives for the same security. The dealer's confirmation must disclose to his customer that he has acted as principal. The same individual or firm may function, at different times, either as broker or dealer. (*See* NASD; SPECIALIST.)

DEBENTURE: A promissory note backed by the general credit of a company and usually not secured by a mortgage or lien on any specific property. (*See* BOND.)

DEPLETION: Natural resources, such as metals, oils and gas, or timber, which conceivably can be reduced to zero over the years, present a special problem in capital management. Depletion is an accounting practice consisting of charges against earnings based upon the amount of the asset taken out of the total reserves in the period for which accounting is made. A bookkeeping entry, it does not represent any cash outlay nor are any funds earmarked for the purpose.

DEPRECIATION: Normally, charges against earnings to write off the cost, less salvage value, of an asset over its estimated useful life. It is a bookkeeping entry and does not represent any cash outlay, nor are any funds earmarked for the purpose.

DIRECTOR: Person elected by shareholders to establish company policies. The directors appoint the president, vice presidents, and all other operating officers. Directors decide, among other matters, if and when dividends shall be paid. (*See* MANAGEMENT; PROXY.)

DISCRETIONARY ORDER: An order in which the customer empowers the broker to act on his behalf with respect to the choice of security to be bought or sold, the total amount of any securities to be bought or sold, and/or whether any such transaction shall be one of purchase or sale.

DIVERSIFICATION: Spreading investments among different companies in different fields. Another type of diversification is also offered by the securities of many individual companies because of the wide range of their activities. (*See* INVESTMENT TRUST.)

DIVIDEND: The payment designated by the Board of Directors to be distributed pro rata among the shares outstanding. On preferred shares, it is generally a fixed amount. On common shares, the dividend varies with the fortunes of the company and the amount of cash on hand, and may be omitted if business is poor or the directors determine to withhold earnings to invest in plant and equipment. Sometimes a company will pay a dividend out of past earnings even if it is not currently operating at a profit.

DOLLAR COST AVERAGING: A system of buying securities at regular intervals with a fixed dollar amount. Under this system the investor buys by the dollars' worth rather than by the number of shares. If each investment is of the same number of dollars, payments buy more when the price is low and fewer when it rises. Thus temporary downswings in price benefit the investor if he continues periodic purchases in both good times and bad and the price at which the shares are sold is more than their average cost. (*See* FORMULA INVESTING.)

DOW THEORY: A theory of market analysis based upon the performance of the Dow-Jones industrial and rail stock price averages. The Theory says that the market is in a basic upward trend if one of these averages advances above a previous important high, accompanied or followed by a similar advance in the other. When the averages both dip below previous important lows, this is regarded as confirmation of a basic downward trend. The Theory does not attempt to predict how long either trend will continue, although it is widely misinterpreted as a method of forecasting future action. Whatever the merits of the Theory, it is sometimes a strong factor in the market because many people believe in the Theory—or believe that a great many others do. (*See* TECHNICAL POSITION.)

EARNINGS REPORT: A statement—also called an income statement—issued by a company showing its earnings or losses over a given period. The earnings report lists the income earned, expenses and the net result. (*See* BALANCE SHEET.)

EQUITY: The ownership interest of common and preferred stockholders in a company. Also refers to excess of value of securities over the debit balance in a margin account.

EX-DIVIDEND: A synonym for "without dividend." The buyer of a stock selling ex-dividend does not receive the recently declared dividend. Open buy and sell stop orders, and sell stop limit orders in a stock on the ex-dividend date are ordinarily reduced by the value of that dividend. In the case of open stop limit orders to sell, both the stop price and the limit price are reduced. Every dividend is payable on a fixed date to all shareholders recorded on the books of the company as of a previous date of record. For example, a dividend may be declared as payable to holders of record on the books of the company on a given Friday. Since five business days are allowed for delivery of stock in a "regular way" transaction on the New York Stock Exchange, the Exchange would declare the stock "ex-dividend" as of the opening of the market on the preceding Monday. That means anyone who bought it on and after Monday would not be entitled to that dividend. (*See* CASH SALE; NET CHANGE; TRANSFER.)

EXTRA: The short form of "extra dividend." A dividend in the form of stock or cash in addition to the regular or usual dividend the company has been paying.

FISCAL YEAR: A corporation's accounting year. Due to the nature of their particular business, some companies do not use the calendar year for their bookkeeping. A typical example is the department store which finds December 31 too early a date to close its books after the Christmas rush. For that reason many stores wind up their accounting year January 31. Their fiscal year, therefore, runs from February 1 of one year through January 31 of the next. The fiscal year of other companies may run from July 1 through the following June 30. Most companies, though, operate on a calendar year basis.

FIXED CHARGES: A company's fixed expenses, such as bond interest, which it has agreed to pay whether or not earned, and which are deducted from income before earnings on equity capital are computed.

FLOOR: The huge trading area—about two-thirds the size of a football field —where stocks and bonds are bought and sold on the New York Stock Exchange.

FLOOR BROKER: A member of the Stock Exchange who executes orders on the floor of the Exchange to buy or sell any listed securities. (*See* BROKER.)

FORMULA INVESTING: An investment technique. One formula calls for the shifting of funds from common shares to preferred shares or bonds as the market, on average, rises above a certain predetermined point—and the return of funds to common share investments as the market average declines. (*See* DOLLAR COST AVERAGING.)

FREE AND OPEN MARKET: A market in which supply and demand are expressed in terms of price. Contrasts with a controlled market in which supply, demand and price may all be regulated.

GOVERNMENT BONDS: Obligations of the U.S. Government, regarded as the highest grade issues in existence.

GROWTH STOCK: Stock of a company with prospects for future growth—a company whose earnings are expected to increase at a relatively rapid rate.

INACTIVE STOCK: An issue traded on an exchange or in the over-the-counter market in which there is a relatively low volume of transactions. Volume may be no more than a few hundred shares a week or even less. On the New York Stock Exchange many inactive stocks are traded in 10-share units rather than the customary 100. (*See* ROUND LOT.)

IN-AND-OUT: Purchase and sale of the same security within a short period— a day, week, even a month. An in-and-out trader is generally more interested in day-to-day price fluctuations than in dividends or long-term growth.

INDEX: A statistical yardstick expressed in terms of percentages of a base year or years. For instance, the Federal Reserve Board's index of industrial production is based on 1957–59 as 100. In October, 1968 the index stood at 165.7, which meant that industrial production that month was about 66 percent higher than in the base period. An index is not an average. (*See* AVERAGES: NYSE COMMON STOCK INDEX.)

INTEREST: Payments a borrower pays a lender for the use of his money. A corporation pays interest on its bonds to its bondholders. (*See* BOND; DIVIDEND.)

INVESTMENT: The use of money for the purpose of making more money, to gain income or increase capital, or both. Safety of principal is an important consideration. (*See* SPECULATION.)

INVESTMENT BANKER: Also known as an underwriter. He is the middleman between the corporation issuing new securities and the public. The usual practice is for one or more investment bankers to buy outright from a corporation a new issue of stocks or bonds. The group forms a syndicate to sell the securities to individuals and institutions. Investment bankers also distribute very large blocks of stocks or bonds—perhaps held by an estate.

Thereafter the market in the security may be over-the-counter, on a regional stock exchange, the American Exchange or the New York Stock Exchange. (*See* OVER-THE-COUNTER.)

INVESTMENT COUNSEL: One whose principal business consists of acting as investment adviser and a substantial part of his business consists of rendering investment supervisory services.

INVESTMENT TRUST: A company or trust which uses its capital to invest in other companies. There are two principal types: the closed-end and the open-end, or mutual fund. Shares in closed-end investment trusts, some of which are listed on the New York Stock Exchange, are readily transferable in the open market and are bought and sold like other shares. Capitalization of these companies remains the same unless action is taken to change, which is seldom. Open-end funds sell their own new shares to investors, stand ready to buy back their old shares, and are not listed. Open-end funds are so called because their capitalization is not fixed; they issue more shares as people want them.

INVESTOR: An individual whose principal concerns in the purchase of a security are regular dividend income, safety of the original investment, and, if possible, capital appreciation. (*See* SPECULATOR.)

ISSUE: Any of a company's securities, or the act of distributing such securities.

LEGAL LIST: A list of investments selected by various states in which certain institutions and fiduciaries, such as insurance companies and banks, may invest. Legal lists are often restricted to high quality securities meeting certain specifications.

LEVERAGE: The effect on the per-share earnings of the common stock of a company when large sums must be paid for bond interest or preferred stock dividends, or both, before the common stock is entitled to share in earnings. Leverage may be advantageous for the common when earnings are good but may work against the common stock when earnings decline. Example: Company A has 1,000,000 shares of common stock outstanding, no other securities. Earnings drop from $1,000,000 to $800,000 or from $1 to 80 cents a share, a decline of 20 percent. Company B also has 1,000,000 shares of common but must pay $500,000 annually in bond interest. If earnings amount to $1,000,000, there is $500,000 available for the common or 50 cents a share. But earnings drop to $800,000 so there is only $300,000 available for the common, or 30 cents a share—a drop of 40 percent. Or suppose earnings of the company with only common stock increased from $1,000,000 to $1,500,000—earnings per share would go from $1 to $1.50, or an increase of 50 percent. But if earnings of the company which had to pay $500,000 in bond interest increased that much—earnings per common share would jump from 50 cents to $1 a share, or 100 percent. When a company has common stock only, no leverage exists because all earnings are available for the common, although relatively large fixed charges payable for lease of substantial plant assets may have an effect similar to that of a bond issue.

LIABILITIES: All the claims against a corporation. Liabilities include accounts and wages and salaries payable, dividends declared payable, accrued taxes payable, fixed or long-term liabilities such as mortgage bonds, debentures and bank loans. (*See* ASSETS; BALANCE SHEET.)

LIQUIDITY: The ability of the market in a particular security to absorb a reasonable amount of buying or selling at reasonable price changes. Liquidity is one of the most important characteristics of a good market.

LISTED STOCK: The stock of a company which is traded on a securities exchange, and for which a listing application and a registration statement, giving detailed information about the company and its operations, have been filed with the Securities & Exchange Commission, unless otherwise exempted, and the exchange itself. The various stock exchanges have different standards for listing. Some of the guides used by the New York Stock Exchange for an original listing are national interest in the company, a minimum of 1-million shares outstanding with at least 800-thousand shares publicly held among not less than 2,000 shareholders including at least 1,800 round-lot stockholders. The publicly held common shares should have a minimum aggregate market value of $16-million. The company should have net income in the latest year of over $2.5-million before federal income tax and $2-million in each of the preceding two years (1972 requirements).

LONG: Signifies ownership of securities: "I am long 100 U.S. Steel" means the speaker owns 100 shares. (*See* SHORT POSITION; SHORT SALE.)

MANAGEMENT: The Board of Directors, elected by the stockholders, and the officers of the corporation, appointed by the Board of Directors.

MARGIN: The amount paid by the customer when he uses his broker's credit to buy a security. Under Federal Reserve regulations, the initial margin required in the past 20 years has ranged from 40 percent of the purchase price all the way to 100 percent. (*See* EQUITY; MARGIN CALL.)

MARGIN CALL: A demand upon a customer to put up money or securities with the broker. The call is made when a purchase is made; also if a customer's equity in a margin account declines below a minimum standard set by the Exchange or by the firm. (*See* MARGIN.)

MARKET ORDER: An order to buy or sell a stated amount of a security at the most advantageous price obtainable after the order is represented in the Trading Crowd. (*See* STOP ORDER.)

MARKET PRICE: In the case of a security, market price is usually considered the last reported price at which the stock or bond sold.

MEMBER CORPORATION: A securities brokerage firm, organized as a corporation, with at least one member of the New York Stock Exchange who is a director and a holder of voting stock in the corporation. (*See* MEMBER FIRM.)

MEMBER FIRM: A securities brokerage firm organized as a partnership and having at least one general partner who is a member of the New York Stock Exchange. (*See* MEMBER CORPORATION.)

MORTGAGE BOND: A bond secured by a mortgage on a property. The value of the property may or may not equal the value of the so-called mortgage bonds issued against it. (*See* BOND, DEBENTURE.)

MUNICIPAL BOND: A bond issued by a state or a political subdivision, such as county, city, town or village. The term also designates bonds issued by state agencies and authorities. In general, interest paid on municipal bonds is exempt from federal income taxes.

MUTUAL FUND: (*See* INVESTMENT TRUST.)

NASD: The National Association of Securities Dealers, Inc. An association of brokers and dealers in the over-the-counter securities business. The Association has the power to expel members who have been declared guilty of unethical practices. NASD is dedicated to—among other objectives—"adopt, administer and enforce rules of fair practice and rules to prevent fraudulent and manipulative acts and practices, and in general to promote just and equitable principles of trade for the protection of investors."

NET ASSET VALUE: A term usually used in connection with investment trusts, meaning net asset value per share. It is common practice for an investment trust to compute its assets daily, or even twice daily, by totaling the market value of all securities owned. All liabilities are deducted, and the balance divided by the number of shares outstanding. The resulting figure is the net asset value per share. (*See* ASSETS; INVESTMENT TRUST.)

NET CHANGE: The change in the price of a security from the closing price on one day and the closing price on the following day on which the stock is traded. In the case of a stock which is entitled to a dividend one day, but is traded "ex-dividend" the next, the dividend is considered in computing the change. For example, if the closing market price of a stock on Monday—the last day it was entitled to receive a 50-cent dividend—was $45 a share, and $44.50 at the close of the next day, when it was "ex-dividend," the price would be considered unchanged. The same applies to a split-up of shares. A stock selling at $100 the day before a 2-for-1 split and trading the next day at $50 would be considered unchanged. If it sold at $51, it would be considered up $1. The net change is ordinarily the last figure in the stock price list. The mark +1⅛ means up $1.125 a share from the last sale on the previous day the stock traded. (*See* EX-DIVIDEND; POINT; SPLIT.)

NEW ISSUE: A stock or bond sold by a corporation for the first time. Proceeds may be issued to retire outstanding securities of the company, for new plant or equipment or for additional working capital.

NONCUMULATIVE: A preferred stock on which unpaid dividends do not accrue. Omitted dividends are, as a rule, gone forever. (*See* CUMULATIVE PREFERRED.)

NYSE COMMON STOCK INDEX: A composite index covering price movements of all common stocks listed on the "Big Board." It is based on the close of the market December 31, 1965 as 50.00 and is weighted according to the number of shares listed for each issue. The index is computed continuously by the Exchange's Market Data System and printed on the ticker tape each half hour. Point changes in the index are converted to dollars and cents so as to provide a meaningful measure of changes in the average price of listed stocks. The composite index is supplemented by separate indexes for four industry groups: industrials, transportation, utilities and finances. (*See* AVERAGES.)

ODD-LOT: An amount of stock less than the established 100-share unit of 10-share unit of trading: from 1 to 99 shares for the great majority of issues, 1 to 9 for so-called inactive stocks. (*See* ROUND LOT; INACTIVE STOCK.)

OFFER: The price at which a person is ready to sell. Opposed to bid, the price at which one is ready to buy. (*See* BID AND ASKED.)

OPEN-END INVESTMENT TRUST: (*See* INVESTMENT TRUST.)

OPTION: A right to buy or sell specific securities or properties at a specified price within a specified time. (*See* PUTS AND CALLS.)

OVERBOUGHT: An opinion as to price levels. May refer to a security which has had a sharp rise or to the market as a whole after a period of vigorous buying, which it may be argued, has left prices "too high." (*See* TECHNICAL POSITION.)

OVERSOLD: An opinion—the reverse of overbought. A single security or a market which, it is believed, has declined to an unreasonable level. (*See* TECHNICAL POSITION.)

OVER-THE-COUNTER: A market for securities made up of securities dealers who may or may not be members of a securities exchange. Over-the-counter is mainly a market made over the telephone. Thousands of companies have insufficient shares outstanding, stockholders, or earnings to warrant application for listing on the N.Y. Stock Exchange. Securities of these companies are traded in the over-the-counter market between dealers who act either as principals or as brokers for customers. The over-the-counter market is the principal market for U.S. Government bonds and municipals and stocks of banks and insurance companies. (*See* NASD.)

PAPER PROFIT: An unrealized profit on a security still held. Paper profits become realized profits only when the security is sold.

PAR: In the case of a common share, par means a dollar amount assigned to the share by the company's charter. Par value may also be used to compute the dollar amount of the common shares on the balance sheet. Par value has little significance so far as market value of common stock is concerned. Many companies today issue no-par stock but give a stated per share value on the balance sheet. Par at one time was supposed to represent the value of the original investment behind each share in cash, goods or services. In the case of preferred shares and bonds, however, par is important. It often signifies the dollar value upon which dividends on preferred stocks, and interest on bonds, are figured. The issuer of a 3 percent bond promises to pay that percentage of the bond's par value annually. (*See* CAPITALIZATION; TRANSFER TAX.)

PASSED DIVIDEND: When a regular or scheduled dividend is not paid, it is said to have been "passed."

PENNY STOCKS: Low-priced issues, often highly speculative, selling at less than $1 a share. Frequently used as a term of disparagement, although a few penny stocks have developed into investment-caliber issues.

PERCENTAGE ORDER: A market or limited price order to buy (or sell) a stated amount of a specified stock after a fixed number of shares of such stock have traded.

POINT: In the case of shares of stock, a point means $1. If General Motors shares rise 3 points, each share has risen $3. In the case of bonds a point means $10, since a bond is quoted as a percentage of $1,000. A bond which rises 3 points gains 3 percent of $1,000, or $30 in value. An advance from 87 to 90 would mean an advance in dollar value from $870 to $900 for each $1,000 bond. In the case of market averages, the word point means merely that and no more. If, for example, the Dow-Jones industrial average rises from 470.25 to 471.25, it has risen a point. A point in this average, however, is not equivalent to $1. (*See* AVERAGES.)

PORTFOLIO: Holdings of securities by an individual or institution. A portfolio may contain bonds, preferred stocks and common stocks of various types of enterprises.

PREFERRED STOCK: A class of stock with a claim on the company's earnings before payment may be made on the common stock and usually entitled to priority over common stock if company liquidates. Usually entitled to dividends at a specified rate—when declared by the Board of Directors and before payment of a dividend on the common stock—depending upon the terms of the issue. (*See* CUMULATIVE PREFERRED; PARTICIPATING PREFERRED.)

PRICE-EARNINGS RATIO. The current market price of a share of stock divided by earnings per share for a twelve-month period. For example, a stock selling for $100 a share and earning $5 a share is said to be selling at a price-earnings ratio of 20 to 1.

PRINCIPAL: The person for whom a broker executes an order, or a dealer buying or selling for his own account. The term "principal" may also refer to a person's capital or to the face amount of a bond.

PROXY: Written authorization given by a shareholder to someone else to represent him and vote his shares at a shareholders' meeting.

PROXY STATEMENT: Information required by SEC to be given stockholders as a prerequisite to solicitation of proxies for a security subject to the requirements of Securities Exchange Act.

PUTS AND CALLS: Options which give the right to buy or sell a fixed amount of a certain stock at a specified price within a specified time. A put gives the holder the right to sell the stock; a call the right to buy the stock. Puts are purchased by those who think a stock may go down. A put obligates the seller of the contract to take delivery of the stock and pay the specified price to the owner of the option within the time limit of the contract. The price specified in a put or call is usually close to the market price of the stock at the time the contract is made. Calls are purchased by those who think a stock may rise. A call gives the holder the right to buy the stock from the seller of the contract at the specified price within a fixed period of time. Put and call contracts are written for 30, 60 or 90 days, or longer. If the purchaser of a put or call does not wish to exercise the option, the price he paid for the option becomes a loss.

QUOTATION: Often shortened to "quote." The highest bid to buy and the lowest offer to sell a security in a given market at a given time. If you ask your broker for a "quote" on a stock, he may come back with something like

"45¼ to 45½." This means that $45.25 is the highest price any buyer wanted to pay at the time the quote was given on the floor of the Exchange and that $45.50 was the lowest price which any seller would take at the same time. (*See* BID AND ASKED.)

RALLY: A brisk rise following a decline in the general price level of the market, or in an individual stock.

RECORD DATE: The date on which you must be registered as a shareholder on the stock book of a company in order to receive a declared dividend or, among other things, to vote on company affairs. (*See* DELIVERY; EX-DIVIDEND; TRANSFER.)

REGISTERED REPRESENTATIVE: Present name for the older term "customers' man." In a New York Stock Exchange Member Firm, a Registered Representative is a full time employee who has met the requirements of the Exchange as to background and knowledge of the securities business. Also known as an Account Executive or Customer's Broker.

REGISTRATION: Before a public offering may be made of new securities by a company, or of outstanding securities by controlling stockholders—through the mails or in interstate commerce—the securities must be registered under the Securities Act of 1933. Registration statement is filed with the SEC by the issuer. It must disclose pertinent information relating to the company's operations, securities, management and purpose of the public offering. Securities of railroads under jurisdiction of the Interstate Commerce Commission, and certain other types of securities, are exempted. On security offerings involving less than $300,000, less information is required.

Before a security may be admitted to dealings on a national securities exchange, it must be registered under the Securities Exchange Act of 1934. The application for registration must be filed with the exchange and the SEC by the company issuing the securities. It must disclose pertinent information relating to the company's operations, securities and management. Registration may become effective 30 days after receipt by the SEC of the certification by the exchange of approval of listing and registration, or sooner by special order of the Commission.

REGULATION T: The federal regulation governing the amount of credit which may be advanced by brokers and dealers to customers for the purchase of securities. (*See* MARGIN.)

REGULATION U: The federal regulation governing the amount of credit which may be advanced by a bank to its customers for the purchase of listed stocks. (*See* MARGIN.)

RETURN: (*See* YIELD.)

RIGHTS: When a company wants to raise more funds by issuing additional securities, it may give its stockholders the opportunity, ahead of others, to buy the new securities in proportion to the number of shares each owns. The piece of paper evidencing this privilege is called a right. Because the additional stock is usually offered to stockholders below the current market price, rights ordinarily have a market value of their own and are actively traded. In most cases they must be exercised within a relatively short period. Failure to exercise or sell rights may result in actual loss to the holder. (*See* WARRANT.)

ROUND LOT: A unit of trading or a multiple thereof. On the NYSE the unit of trading is generally 100 shares in stocks and $1,000 par value in the case of bonds. In some inactive stocks, the unit of trading is 10 shares.

SEAT: A traditional figure-of-speech for a membership on an exchange. Price and admission requirements vary.

SEC: The Securities and Exchange Commission, established by Congress to help protect investors. The SEC administers the Securities Act of 1933, the Securities Exchange Act of 1934, the Trust Indenture Act, the Investment Company Act, the Investment Advisers Act, and the Public Utility Holding Company Act.

SELLING AGAINST THE BOX: A method of protecting a paper profit. Let's say you own 100 shares of XYZ which has advanced in price, and you think the price may decline. So you sell 100 shares short, borrowing 100 shares to make delivery. You retain in your security box the 100 shares which you own. If XYZ declines, the profit on your short sale is exactly offset by the loss in the market value of the stock you own. If XYZ advances, the loss on your short sale is exactly offset by the profit in the market value of the stock you have retained. You can close out your short sale by buying 100 shares to return to the person from whom you borrowed, or you can send them the 100 shares which you own. (*See* SHORT SALE.)

SHORT COVERING: Buying stock to return stock previously borrowed to make delivery on a short sale.

SHORT POSITION: Stocks sold short and not covered as of a particular date. On the NYSE, a tabulation is issued a few days after the middle of the month listing all issues on the Exchange in which there was a short position at the mid-month settlement date of 5,000 or more shares, and issues in which the short position had changed by 2,000 or more shares in the preceding month. This tabulation is based on reports of positions on member firms' books. Short position also means the total amount of stock an individual has sold short and has not covered, as of a particular date. Initial margin requirements for a short position are the same as for a long position. Proceeds from short sales are excluded entirely from this report. The initial margin required of the short seller, however, and profits and losses on short sales are reflected in stock margin debt. (*See* MARGIN; SHORT SALE.)

SHORT SALE: A person who believes a stock will decline and sells it though he does not own any has made a short sale. For instance: You instruct your broker to sell short 100 shares of ABC. Your broker borrows the stock so he can deliver the 100 shares to the buyer. The money value of the shares borrowed is deposited by your broker with the lender. Sooner or later you must cover your short sale by buying the same amount of stock you borrowed for return to the lender. If you are able to buy ABC at a lower price than you sold it for, your profit is the difference between the two prices— not counting commissions and taxes. But if you have to pay more for the stock than the price you received, that is the amount of your loss. Stock exchange and federal regulations govern and limit the conditions under which a short sale may be made on a national securities exchange. (*See* MARGIN.)

SPECIALIST: A member of the New York Stock Exchange who has two functions: First, to maintain an orderly market, insofar as reasonably practicable, in the stocks in which he is registered as a specialist. In order to maintain an orderly market, the Exchange expects the specialist to buy or sell for his own account, to a reasonable degree, when there is a temporary disparity between supply and demand. Second, the specialist acts as a broker's broker. When a commission broker on the Exchange floor receives a limit order, say, to buy at $50 a stock then selling at $60—he cannot wait at the post where the stock is traded until the price reaches the specified level. So he leaves the order with the specialist, who will try to execute it in the market if and when the stock declines to the specified price. At all times the specialist must put his customers' interests above his own. There are about 350 specialists on the NYSE. (*See* BOOK; LIMITED ORDER.)

SPECULATION: The employment of funds by a speculator. Safety of principal is a secondary factor. (*See* INVESTMENT.)

SPECULATOR: One who is willing to assume a relatively large risk in the hope of gain. His principal concern is to increase his capital rather than his dividend income. The speculator may buy and sell the same day or speculate in an enterprise which he does not expect to be profitable for years. (*See* INVESTOR.)

SPLIT: The division of the outstanding shares of a corporation into a larger number of shares. A 3-for-1 split by a company with 1 million shares outstanding results in 3 million shares outstanding. Each holder of 100 shares before the 3-for-1 split would have 300 shares, although his proportionate equity in the company would remain the same; 100 parts of 1 million are the equivalent of 300 parts of 3 million. Ordinarily splits must be voted by directors and approved by shareholders. (*See* STOCK DIVIDENDS.)

STOCK DIVIDEND: A dividend paid in securities rather than cash. The dividend may be additional shares of the issuing company, or in shares of another company (usually a subsidiary) held by the company. (*See* EX-DIVIDEND; SPLIT.)

STOP ORDER: A stop order to buy becomes a market order when a transaction in the security occurs at or above the stop price after the order is represented in the Trading Crowd. A stop order to sell becomes a market order when a transaction in the security occurs at or below the stop price after the order is represented in the Trading Crowd. A stop order may be used in an effort to protect a paper profit, or to try to limit a possible loss to a certain amount. Since it becomes a market order when the stop price is reached, there is no certainty that it will be executed at that price. (*See* MARKET ORDER.)

STREET: The New York financial community in the Wall Street area.

STREET NAME: Securities held in the name of a broker instead of his customer's name are said to be carried in a "street name." This occurs when the securities have been bought on margin or when the customer wishes the security to be held by the broker.

SWITCHING: Selling one security and buying another.

TAX-EXEMPT BONDS: The securities of state, cities and other public authorities specified under federal law, the interest on which is either wholly or partly exempt from federal income taxes.

TECHNICAL POSITION: A term applied to the various internal factors affecting the market; opposed to external forces such as earnings, dividends, political considerations and general economic conditions. Some internal factors considered in appraising the market's technical position include the size of the short interest, whether the market has had a sustained advance or decline without interruption, a sharp advance or decline on small volume and the amount of credit in use in the market. (*See* OVERBOUGHT; OVERSOLD.)

THIN MARKET: A market in which there are comparatively few bids to buy or offers to sell or both. The phrase may apply to a single security or to the entire stock market. In a thin market, price fluctuations between transactions are usually larger than when the market is liquid. A thin market in a particular stock may reflect lack of interest in that issue or a limited supply of or demand for stock in the market. (*See* BID AND ASKED; LIQUIDITY; OFFER.)

TICKER: The instrument which prints prices and volume of security transactions in cities and towns throughout the U.S. and Canada within minutes after each trade on the floor.

TIPS: Supposedly "inside" information on corporation affairs.

TRADER: One who buys and sells for his own account for short-term profit. (*See* INVESTOR; SPECULATOR.)

TRADING CROWD: The group of brokers congregated around a Trading Post willing to buy or sell stocks traded there.

TRADING FLOOR: (*See* FLOOR.)

TRANSFER: This term may refer to two different operations. For one, the delivery of a stock certificate from the seller's broker to the buyer's broker and legal change of ownership, normally accomplished within a few days. For another, to record the change of ownership on the books of the corporation by the transfer agent. When the purchaser's name is recorded on the books of the company, dividends, notices of meetings, proxies, financial reports and all pertinent literature sent by the issuer to its securities holders are mailed direct to the new owner.

TRANSFER TAX: A tax imposed by New York State when a security is sold or transferred from one person to another. The tax is paid by the seller. On sales by New York State residents, it ranges from 1.25 cents a share to 5 cents a share sold for $20 or more. Sales by out-of-state residents not employed in New York are taxed at reduced rates. There is no tax on transfers of bonds.

TURNOVER: The volume of business in a security or the entire market. If turnover on the NYSE is reported at 15 million shares on a particular day, 15,000,000 shares changed hands. Odd-lot turnover is tabulated separately and ordinarily is not included in reported volume.

UNLISTED: A security not listed on a stock exchange. (*See* OVER-THE-COUNTER.)

VOTING RIGHT: The stockholder's right to vote his stock in the affairs of his company. Most common shares have one vote each. Preferred stock usually has the right to vote when preferred dividends are in default for a specified period. The right to vote may be delegated by the stockholder to another person. (*See* PROXY.)

WARRANT: A certificate giving the holder the right to purchase securities at a stipulated price within a specified time limit or perpetually. Sometimes a warrant is offered with securities as an inducement to buy. (*See* RIGHTS.)

WHEN ISSUED: A short form of "when, as and if issued." The term indicates a conditional transaction in a security authorized for issuance but not as yet actually issued. All "when issued" transactions are on an "if" basis, to be settled if and when the actual security is issued and the Exchange or National Association of Securities Dealers rules the transactions are to be settled.

WIRE HOUSE: A member firm of an exchange maintaining a communications network linking either its own branch offices, offices of correspondent firms, or a combination of such offices.

WORKING CONTROL: Theoretically ownership of 51 percent of a company's voting stock is necessary to exercise control. In practice—and this is particularly true in the case of a large corporation—effective control sometimes can be exerted through ownership, individually or by a group acting in concert, of less than 50 percent.

YIELD: Also known as return. The dividends or interest paid by a company expressed as a percentage of the current price—or, if you own the security, of the price you originally paid. The return on a stock is figured by dividing the total of dividends paid in the preceding 12-months by the current market price—or, if you are the owner, the price you originally paid. A stock with a current market value of $40 a share which has paid $2 in dividends in the preceding 12 months is said to return 5 percent ($2.00 ÷ $40.00). If you paid $20 for the stock five years earlier, the stock would be returning you 10 percent on your original investment. The current return on a bond is figured the same way. A 3 percent $1,000 bond selling at $600 offers a return of 5 percent ($30 ÷ $600). Figuring the yield of a bond to maturity calls for a bond yield table. (*See* DIVIDEND; INTEREST.)

Appendix IV: Profit-Estimate Sheet

Designed by Robert N. Peisner

CONSERVATIVE GROWTH – LOW PRICE/EARNINGS RATIO – HIGH DIVIDEND % YIELD

SECTION ONE – BASIC DATA

1) Date of Analysis . . . . _____

2) Company: _____

3) Exchange & Symbol . . . . Exchange:_____ ; Symbol:_____

4) Primary Industry: _____

5) Continuous cash dividends paid since:. . . . . _____

6) Number shares of stock outstanding: . . . . _____

7) Number of institutions holding:. . . . . _____

8) Number of shares institutions hold: . . . . _____

9) % shares institution hold (line 8_____ divided by
line 6_____) . . . . _____ %

10) Source of historical investment data:_____

SECTION TWO – HISTORICAL EARNINGS AND STOCK DATA

	(A) FISCAL YEAR ENDING – MONTH	(B) 1st QTR ENDING	(C) 2nd QTR ENDING	(D) 3rd QTR ENDING	(E) 4th QTR ENDING	(F) FISCAL YEARLY EARN	(G) $ DIV	(H) STOCK PRICE HI LO	(J) PRICE/ EARN RATIO P/E HI LO	(K) $ ANNUAL SALES
11)										
12)	,19									
13)	,19									
14)	,19									
15)	,19	E	E	E	E	E	E	E	E	E

SECTION THREE – CURRENT DATA

16) Today's stock price: . . . . $_____

17) Indicated current cash dividend per share: . . . . $_____

(18) Current Yield: (line 17 $_____ divided by line 16 $_____ ; [____]OK
Caution if under 4.5%): . . . . %_CAUTION

19) Most recent quarterly earnings report: Qtr_____ Month_____
Fiscal Year_____

20) Latest 12 months earnings (Addition of 4 most recent quarters) . . . . . $_____

(21) Current dividend protection ratio (line 20 $_____ divided by [____]OK
line 17 $_____ ; Caution if protection ratio less than 1.4): . . . . CAUTION

(22) Current (P/E) Price/Earnings Ratio (line 16 $_____ divided by [____]OK
line 20 $_____ ; Caution if P/E is more than 15 to 1): . . . . . . P/E CAUTION

SECTION FOUR - CRITERIA FOR FUTURE ESTIMATES

23) (A): Average LOW Price/Earnings Ratio (P/E) last 2 years
     (13J LO_____ plus 14J LO_____ divided by 2 equals_____);
     (B): <u>JUDGMENT</u> - use LOW P/E of: . . . . _____ P/E

24) (A): Average HIGH Price/Earnings Ratio (P/E) last 2 years
     (13J HI_____ plus 14J HI_____divided by 2 equals _____);
     (B): <u>JUDGMENT</u> - use HIGH P/E of (but not more than 1-1/2 times
     P/E of 23B): . . . . _____ P/E

25) Enter estimated HIGH (HI) and LOW (LO) Price/Earnings Ratio in box 15J

26) Estimated earnings per share for fiscal year ending 19_____;   ┌──────┐ OK
     (Caution if less than line 20; Enter in box 15F) . . . . │$ │ CAUTION
                                                                              └──────┘

27) Source of estimate _____

28) Estimated quarterly earnings (fill in boxes 15B, 15C, 15D and 15E)

29) Estimated dividends per share for fiscal 19_____; (Enter in box 15G) . $_____

30) Estimated dividend protection ratio (line 26 $_____ divided by   ┌──────┐ OK
     line 29 $_____; Caution if less than 1.4): . . . . │   │ CAUTION
                                                                             └──────┘

SECTION FIVE - ESTIMATED LOSS VERSUS GAIN

31) Estimated 19_____ LOW stock price
     (line 23B _____ LOW P/E x line 26 $_____) . . . .ˊ . . . .$_____ LOW

32) Estimated 19_____ HIGH stock price
     (line 24B _____ HIGH P/E x line 26 $_____) . . . .$_____ HIGH

33) Enter estimated HIGH (HI) and LOW (LO) stock prices in box 15H

34) Estimated loss per share (line 16 $_____ minus line 31 $_____) . $_____

35) % Potential Downside Risk (line 34 $_____ divided by   ┌──────┐ OK
     line 16 $_____; Caution if more than 20%) . . . . │   % │ CAUTION
                                                                            └──────┘

36) Estimated profit per share (line 32 $_____ minus line 16 $_____) $_____

37) % Potential Upside Gain (line 36 $_____ divided by line 16 $_____) _____ %

38) Gain to Loss Ratio (line 36 $_____ divided by line 34 $_____;   ┌──────┐ OK
     Caution if less than 2 to 1) . . . . │   │ CAUTION
                                                                            └──────┘

SECTION SIX - PROFIT ESTIMATE FOR STOCK (100% CASH)

39) Assume a cash investment of . . . . $_____

40) Number of shares purchaseable (line 39 $_____ divided by
line 16 $_____): . . . . _____ SH.

41) Estimated gross profit (line 36 $_____ x line 40 _____ SH) . . . . $_____

42) Commissions: a) Buy $_____ b) Sell $_____ c) SUM of a + b . . $_____

43) Estimated net CAPITAL GAINS profit (line 41 $_____ minus
line 42c $_____) . . . . $_____

44) Dividends received per year (line 29 $_____ x line 40_____ SH) . . $_____

45) Total dividends received (line 44 $_____ x _____ years) . . . . . $_____

46) Total estimated return from capital gains and dividends
(line 43 $_____ + line 45 $_____) . . . . $_____

47) ESTIMATED ANNUAL % NET GAIN (line 46 $_____ divided by
line 39 $_____; Caution if less than 25%). . . . . [_____] OK
[_____] % CAUTION

SECTION SEVEN - MARGIN PROFIT ESTIMATE

48) Current Stock Margin requirements set by FRB or Exchange . . . . . . _____ %

49) Assume same number of shares as line 40 . . . . _____ SH.

50) Cash required to purchase shares per line 49 (line 39 $_____ x
line 48 _____%) . . . . $_____

51) Amount of margin loan (line 39 $_____ minus line 50 $_____) . . . $_____

52) Margin call when stock price is (1ine 16 $_____ x _____%) . . . . $_____

53) Approx. cash required for one margin call (line 51 $_____ x
_____%) . . . . $_____

54) Maximum $ amount of margin calls (same as line 51; amount of loan) . . . $_____

55) Margin interest costs for one year (line 51 $_____ x _____%) . . . $_____

56) Total estimated return from capital gains and dividends
(line 46 $_____ minus line 55 $_____) . . . . $_____

57) ESTIMATED ANNUAL % NET GAIN USING MARGIN (line 56 $_____
divided by line 50 $_____) . . . . _____ %

IT IS ADVISED THAT A PERSON UNABLE TO KEEP AN ADEQUATE CASH RESERVE, OR UNABLE
TO HONOR ONE OR MORE MARGIN CALLS, NOT PARTICIPATE IN ANY MARGIN PURCHASES.

Index